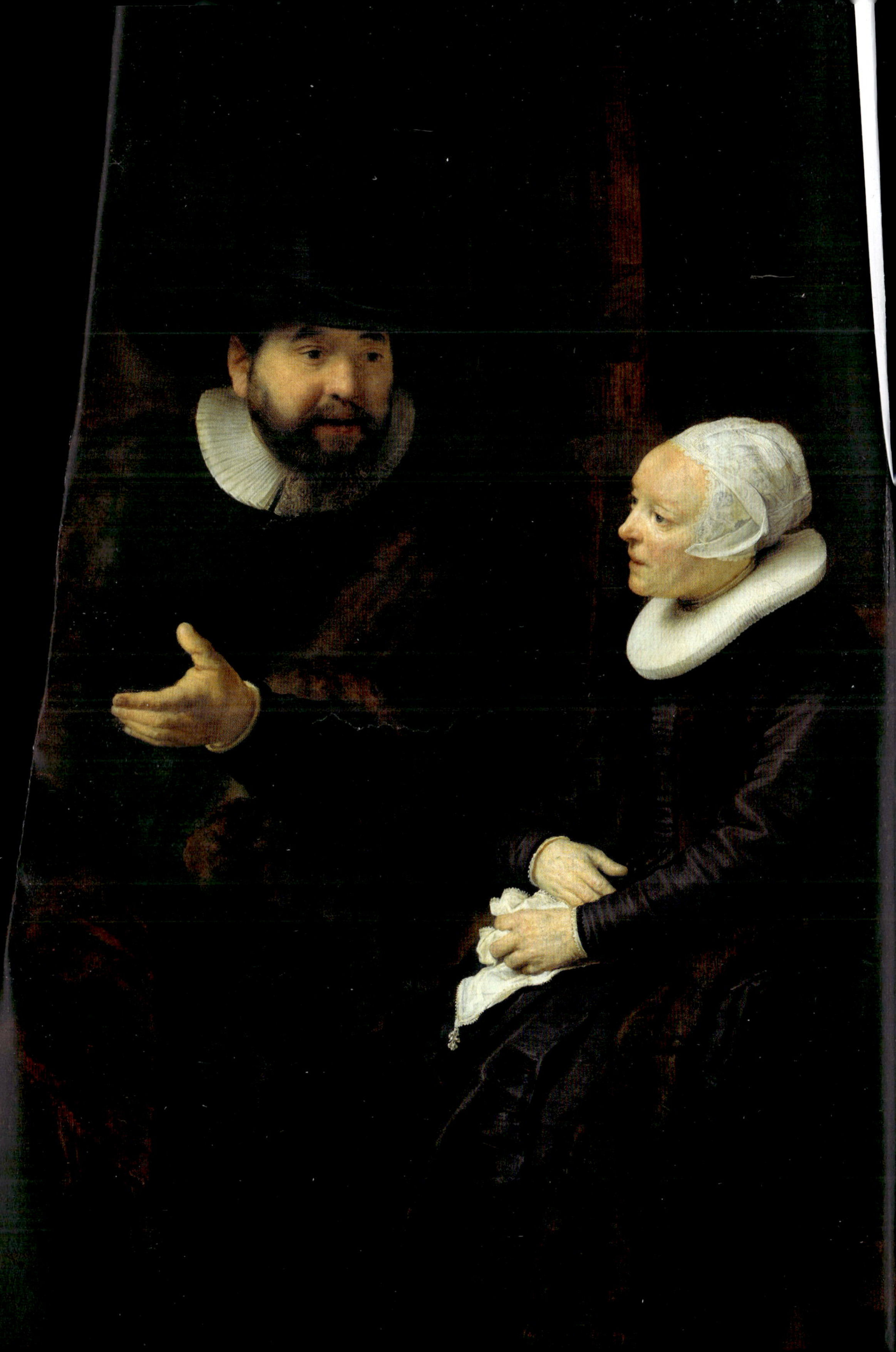

The Intimate Rembrandt

The Intimate Rembrandt

CHRISTOPHER WHITE

Unicorn Press

First published in Great Britain in 2022 by Unicorn Press
60 Bracondale
Norwich
NR1 2BE

tradfordhugh@gmail.com
www.unicornpublishing.org

A CIP record of this book can be obtained from the British Library

ISBN 978 1 83839 532 2

Design by newtonworks.uk
Printed in the UK by Swallowtail Print, Norwich

FRONTISPIECE: Detail of *Cornelis Claesz. Anslo and his Wife, Aeltje Schouten*. 1641. (See Fig. 39)

PAGE VI: Detail of *Bathsheba with King David's Letter*. 1654. (See Fig. 150)

PAGE VIII: Detail of *Jan Six*. 1654. (See Fig. 45)

PAGE X: Detail of *Isaac and Rebecca ('The Jewish Bride')*. *c.*1665. (See Fig. 161)

PAGE XIV: *Self-portrait Etching at a Window*. 1648. (See Fig. 20)

CONTENTS

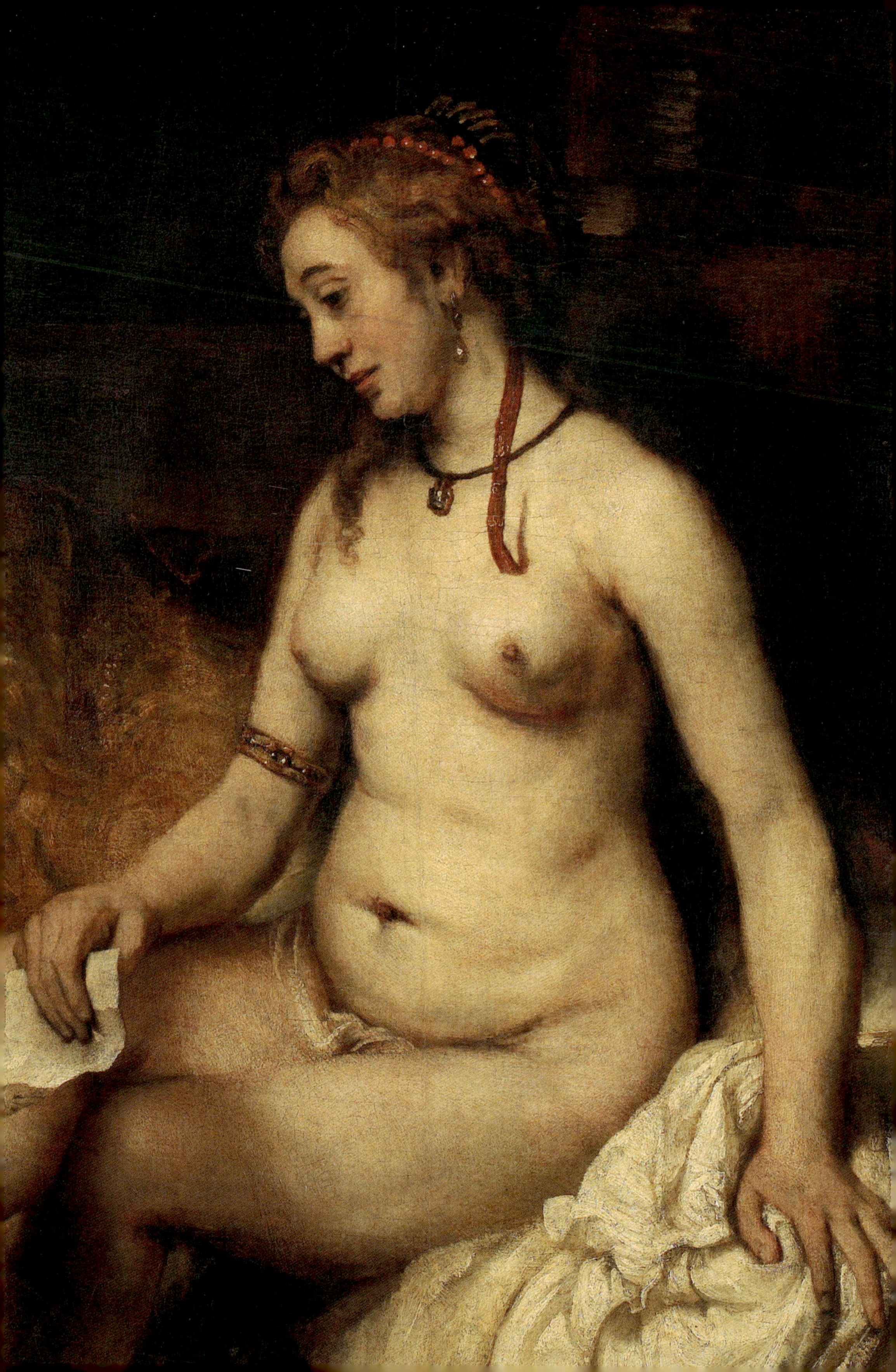

PREFACE

As a student at the Courtauld Institute of Art I wrote an essay on the subject of Rembrandt's drawings, which served to ignite my involvement in the artist which has continued over the following seventy years. Now, having reached an advanced age, I find myself in the position of having to prepare to say farewell to the artist, and much else besides. Aspiring to write a slightly different general book on the artist, I have concentrated on one aspect which has particularly attracted me, namely the often intimate, reflective and personal side to Rembrandt's work; these are qualities which are somewhat elusive concepts, so I must stress that my selection, perhaps on the liberal side, should be taken *cum grano salis*. Throughout his life Rembrandt showed a predilection for the intimate often smaller aspects of the world around him, either in scale or treatment, a feature, of course, found in much of contemporary art in Holland. At the same time in treating subjects from history or the Bible, he increasingly showed a more introspective interpretation than many of his contemporaries. It can be said to be an intimacy of a different kind. Overall my selection offers a very partial view of Rembrandt. It also allows me to discuss a number of lesser known works. It leaves out much of the more formal (e.g. most of his portraits) and large scale (e.g. many of the narrative subjects) that make up his *œuvre*, in fact many of his most renowned works, but with an artist of such a wide range one may be allowed to concentrate on one aspect of his work. One underlying theme has been Rembrandt's technique, studied from an aesthetic rather than a scientific point of view; his willingness to experiment, whether painting, drawing or etching, is a notable feature of his work, and by discussing examples of the three different media side-by-side I hope to demonstrate their interdependence. I should conclude by saying that no thesis is being promulgated apart from establishing the validity of the title. Given what is omitted, I venture to suggest that it should not be the first book on Rembrandt to be read, but it could well be the second.

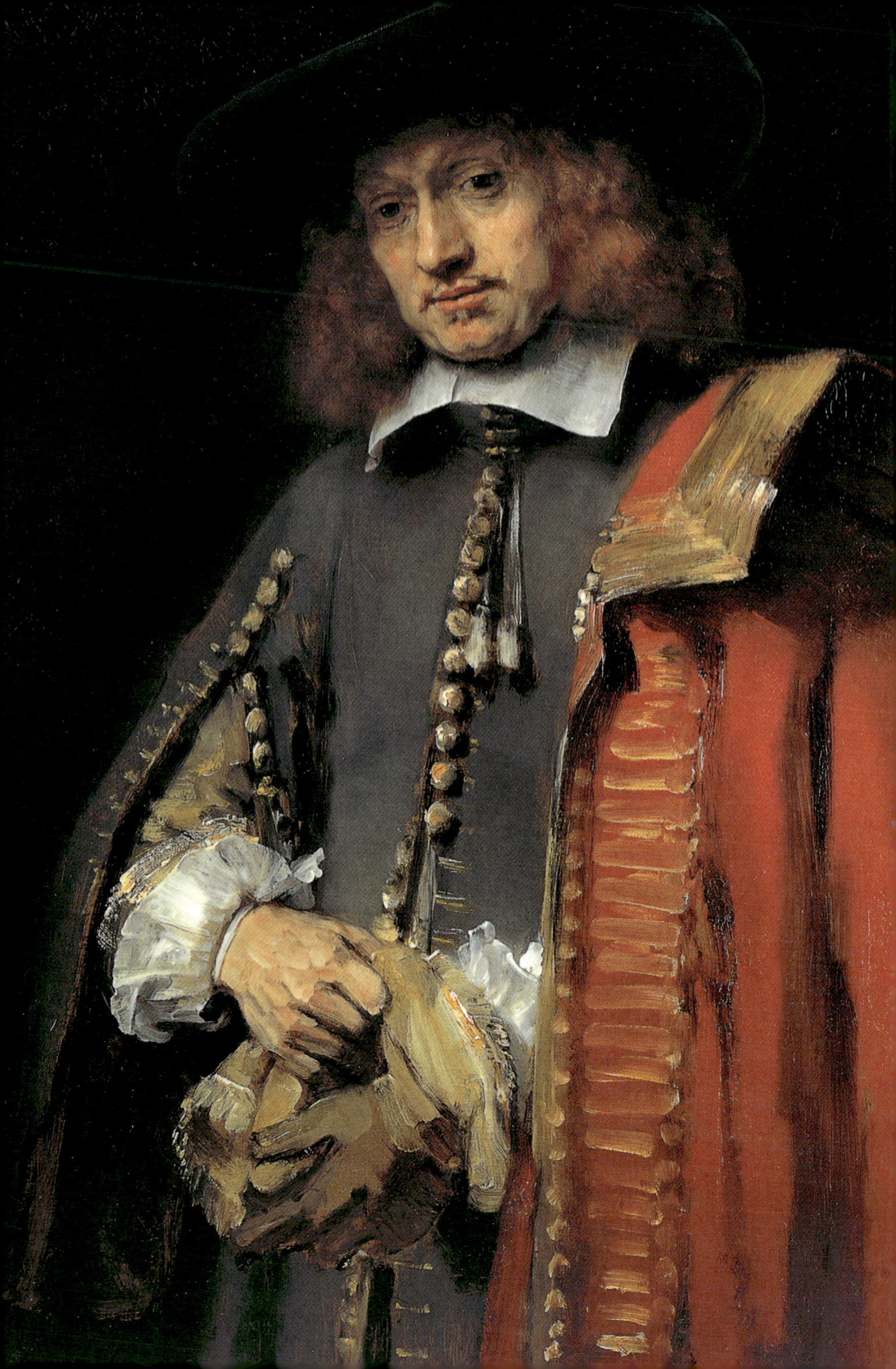

I am greatly indebted to the writings of other Rembrandt scholars, a selection of whose works will be found at the end. Since the book is intended for a general audience, I have not made detailed reference to them. I am very grateful to both Gillian Malpass and Brian Allen, both of whom kindly read the MS as it progressed and offered me encouragement. Martin Royalton-Kisch kindly answered a number of detailed questions. I would like to thank Maria Ranauro for her efficient collecting of the images and George and Nick Newton for their excellent design.

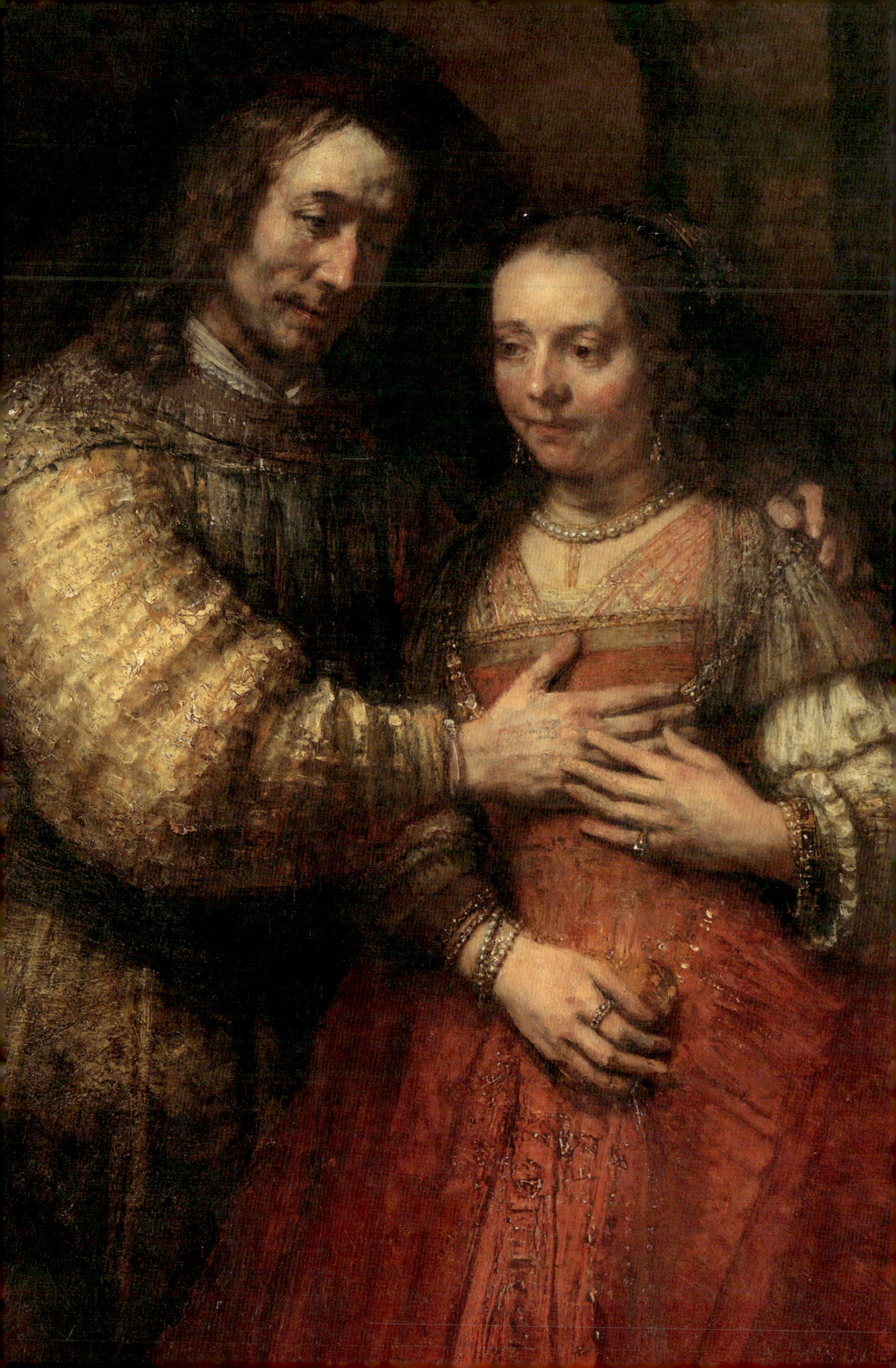

LIFE

1606 15 July. Rembrandt is born in Leiden, the ninth child of the miller, Harmen Gerritsz. van Rijn (1569–1630) and his wife, Neeltgen Willemsdr. van Zuytbrouck (1568–1640).

c. 1613–5 He attends the Latin School in Leiden.

1620 May. He enrols at Leiden Univsersity, still living with his parents.

1622 He begins a three-year apprenticeship with the Leiden painter, Jacob Isaacsz. van Swanenburg (1571–1638).

1625–6 He spends six months studying with the history painter, Pieter Lastman (1583–1633), in Amsterdam.

c. 1626 He sets up as an independent artist in Leiden.

1628 He is now regularly mentioned as an artist in Leiden, and, on 14 February, he accepts his first pupil, the fourteen-year old, Gerrit Dou (1613–1675).

1631 20 June. Probably at end of the year he partly moves to Amsterdam where he lives in the St Anthonis-Breestraat with the Amsterdam art dealer, Hendrick van Uylenburgh (1587–1661), who also runs an 'academy', in which Rembrandt teaches.

1632 Paints *The Anatomy Lesson of Dr Nicolaes Tulp* (Mauritshuis, The Hague).

1633 He is betrothed to Saskia van Uylenburgh (1612–1642), a burgomaster's daughter from Leeuwarden and cousin of Hendrick van Uylenburgh.

1634 22 June. He is married in the church of St Anne in Friesland.

1635 22 February. He is still living with Van Uylenburgh. His first child, Rumbartus, is born but dies two months later.

1636 He moves to Nieuwe Doelenstraat with a view across the river Amstel.

1637 May. He moves to a house called 'The Confectionary' (De Suijkerbackerei) on the Binnen Amstel (now Zwanenburgerstraat).

1638 16 July. In a document drawn up in Leeuwaarden, members of Saskia's family complain that she is squandering her inheritance, but to no avail.

22 July. Cornelia is born but lives only a few weeks.

1639 5 January. With the help of substantial loans, he buys a grand merchant's house for 13,000 guilders in the Sint-Anthonisbreestraat (now the Jodenbreestraat, and called the Rembrandthuis), and next door to where he lived with Van Uylenburgh.

1640 12 August. His second daughter, also called Cornelia, is born and dies within a few weeks.

His mother is buried in St Peter's Church, Leiden, leaving Rembrandt 10,000 guilders.

1641 22 September. His only surviving child, Titus, is baptized in the Zuiderkerk.

1642 5 June. Saskia 'lying sick abed' makes her second will, in which she stipulates that Rembrandt is to have the *usufrucht* of her estate provided that he does not remarry. She dies on 14 June and is buried in the Ouide Kerk.

The widow Geertje Dircx (1610/15– after 1656) moves in as Titus's dry nurse. Embarking on an intimate relationship, she tries to persuade Rembrandt to marry her.

Paints *The Night Watch* (Rijksmuseum, Amsterdam).

1647 His estate, including inheritance from Saskia amounts to 40,750 guilders.

Hendrickje Stoffels (*c.*1625–1663) probably begins work as housekeeper in this year.

1648 Geertje Dircx, 'infirm but able to walk and stand, and in possession and full capacity of her mind'. makes a will leaving all her possessions to Titus van Rijn.

1649 1 October. Hendrickje 'spinster aged 23' testifies in a court case brought against Rembrandt by Geertje Dircx for breaking his troth and says an agreement has been reached with Geeertje.

14 November. In court case re. Geertje, Rembrandt is described as 'the honourable and widely celebrated painter'.

23 October. At the Town Hall, Commissioners for Marital Affairs hear that Rembrandt has slept with Geertje but made no promise of marriage. She is awarded 200 guiders in alimony.

1650 4 July. A successful scheme is carried out to have Geertje Dircx committed to the house of correction in Gouda.

*c.*1652 His brother Adriaen (*c.*1597), a miller, dies in Leiden.

1653 Receives very large bill for his house in the Jodenbreestraat and borrows money from Jan Six and two others.

1654 Hendrickje summoned before the council of the Reformed Congregation for 'practising whoredome with the painter Rembrandt' and admits to her relationship.

20 October. Cornelia, illegitimate daughter, is baptized.

1655 Geertje Dircx is released from the house of correction in Gouda.

1656 14 July. Rembrandt applies for a '*cessio bonorum*' (voluntary surrender of effects to his creditors). He faces financial problems due to 'losses suffered in business as well as damages and losses at sea'.

Inventory made of his possessions, including a large number of works of art, following which sales take place.

1658 Further sale of possessions; his house is distrained and sold.

May. Rembrandt, Titus, Hendrickje and Cormelia move into a rented house in the Rozengracht in the Jordaan, opposite the Nieuwe Doolhof (the maze).

1659 Rembrandt gives Titus power of attorney to act for him in 'petty matters'.

1660 15 December. Hendrickje and Titus transfer the 'company and trade in paintings, graphic art, engravings and woodcuts' to their names. Rembrandt ceases to have financial control, but he is allowed to continue painting.

In her will Hendrickje makes Titus her universal heir but Rembrandt is allowed the *usufrucht*.

1662 He sells Saskia's grave.

He paints *The Syndics of the Amsterdam Drapers' Guild* (Rijksmuseum, Amsterdam).

1663 24 July. Hendrickje dies, probably a victim of the plague, and is buried in a rented grave in the Westerkek.

1664 The painter Christiaen Dusart (1618–1682) appointed guardian of Cornelia. In the document Rembrandt is described as 'hale and hearty, in full use of his mind, memory and speech'.

1665 Titus is granted *veniam aetatis* (legal maturity).

1666 18 November. Titus becomes Rembrandt's legal agent.

1667 Cosimo de' Medici (1642–1723) calls on Rembrandt, who is described as 'pittore famoso'.

1668 28 February. Titus marries Magdalena van Loo (1642–1669). In 1659 her father, the silversmith, Jacob van Loo, deposed that he and his wife had been very close friends of Rembrandt and his late wife Saskia.

Titus dies and on 7 September, shortly before his twenty-seventh birthday, is buried in the Westerkerk.

1669 4 October. Rembrandt dies and, on 8 October, is buried in an anonymous rented grave in the Westerkerk.

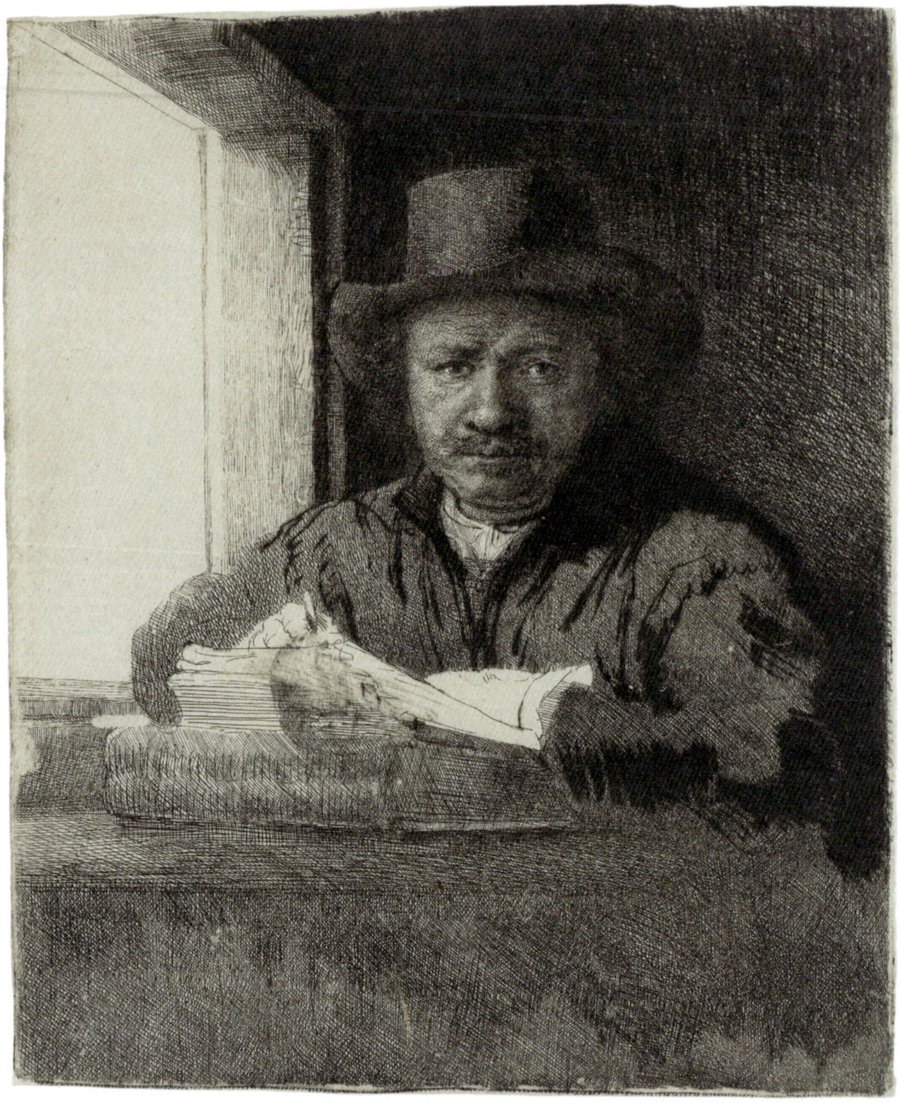

CHAPTER 1

The artist and his family

IN SEVENTEENTH-CENTURY Holland a number of artists have left some record of themselves and often of their families, but none more so than Rembrandt. In the latter's case his use of his family was extensive and varied. He almost certainly produced portraits for posterity. At the same time he employed family members as convenient models with no personal identity intended, but often he leaves us in a state of uncertainty as to which category the work belongs. This is particularly so with the case of the two women in his life, Saskia and Hendrickje, a distillation of whose appearances can often be detected but without any certainty.

From his earliest years Rembrandt used his own image, probably as well as that of his mother and possibly of his father, Harmen Gerritsz. van Rijn. The latter came from a family of millers in Leiden, who owned their own windmill, and, in the case of Harmen, other property in the town, indicating that he was reasonably prosperous. In the year of his death, 1630, Rembrandt then or shortly before, made a drawing of an old man [Fig. 1], inscribed with the father's name, which was very probably written by the artist himself. If so it would establish it as the only certain image of the father.

The drawing is a bust-length study of an elderly bearded man, wearing a cap, who is portrayed from the front. In a state of self-absorption, he is clearly detached from the world, suggesting someone who was near the end of his life. The eyes appear to be closed, which might, as has been proposed, indicate that he was blind. If so, it would explain the artist's predilection for themes connected with blindness, particular incidents from the Book of Tobit, which became, as will be seen, a favourite source for illustration. The soft modelling of the head, and in particular the details of the flowing beard, were achieved by a delicate use of black and red chalk, a medium favoured in equal measure to pen and ink in the artist's early years. Over this basis Rembrandt added a liberal amount

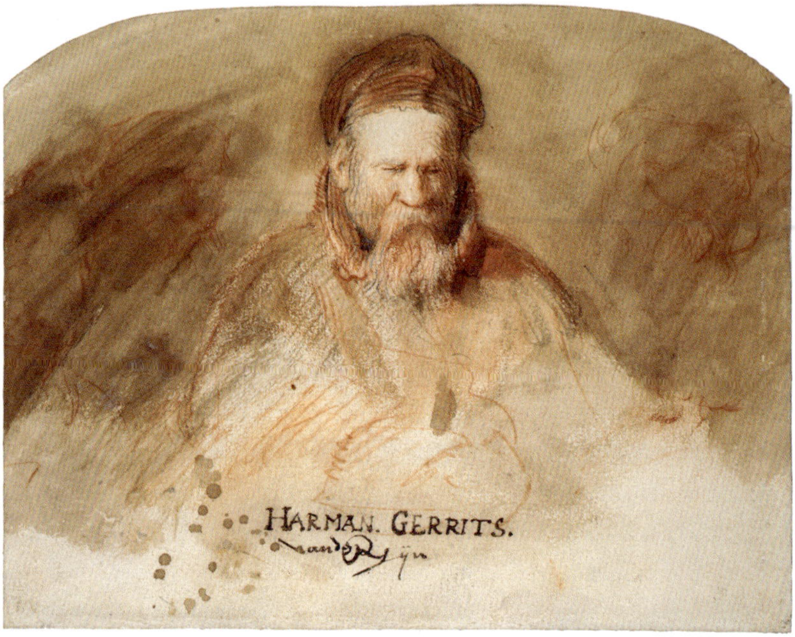

1. *Artist's Father*. *c.*1630. Red and black chalk, with brown wash. 19 × 24 cm. Ashmolean Museum, Oxford.

of brown wash, which set the figure in a pattern of light and shade and established a background from which the figure is projected. For a relatively simple drawing it is a powerful image.

From the beginning of his career Rembrandt drew either in red or black chalk or pen and brown ink, sometimes with wash. In this drawing we have an unusual combination of the four media. After one or two examples of combined red and black chalk done at the very beginning of his career, Rembrandt opted for one or the other up to the mid-1630s, after which he worked almost exclusively in pen, often with wash, and on a very few occasions solely with the brush.

Rembrandt's mother, Neeltgen Willemsdr. van Zuytbrouck was born into a relatively wealthy Leiden family in 1568. She outlived her husband by four years. Although there is a record of an etched portrait of her in a later seventeenth-century inventory, there is no certainty that she is the very recognisable model who appears as an image of benign old age in a number of early paintings and etchings. Against the identification is the fact that at the time of these works she would only have been in her early sixties and the model looks considerably older. But since the old woman disappears from his work about the time of his mother's death, we may be prepared to give the identification the benefit of doubt, all the more so because she would have served as a model rather than the sitter for a portrait.

The woman we assume to have been Rembrandt's mother appears unmistakeably in the painting of an *Old Woman in Prayer* [Fig. 2] executed about 1630. Clearly not a portrait, it is a *tronie* (a study of a head not usually to be identified, very popular at the time) or possibly a Biblical figure such as, as has been suggested, the Prophetess Anna. It has the technical distinction of being one of three paintings by Rembrandt painted about this time on copper and prepared with a gold ground. The use of the latter may have been intended to added a basic radiance to the picture, and can be seen showing through in the old woman's face and scarf and in the background. It unquestionably adds a glow

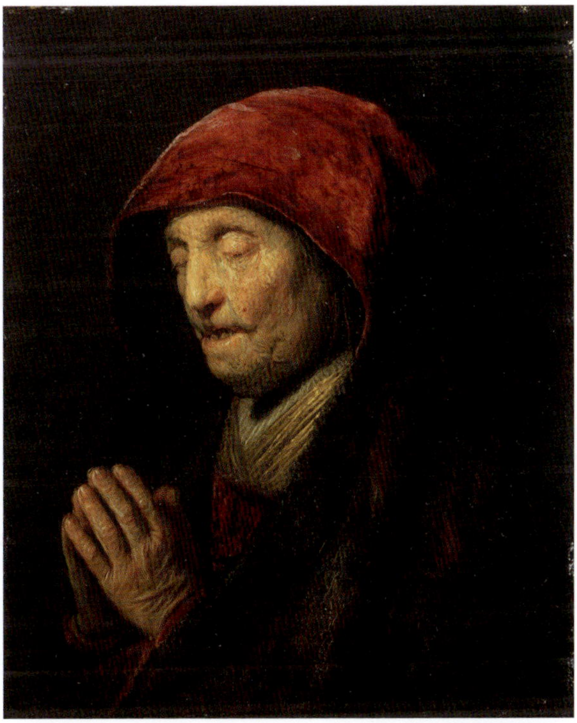

2. *Old Woman in Prayer*. *c.*1630. Gilded copper.
15.5 × 12.2 cm. Residenzgalerie, Salzburg.

to her face as, with eyes closed and hands clasped together, she concentrates on her prayers. She appears totally detached from the world, living in an intermediate existence between life and death. Her mouth is slightly open, suggesting that she might be mumbling her prayers to herself. What is unusual is that her teeth are showing, a detail found in one or two self-portraits (e.g. Fig. 4) and a portrait of Saskia (see Fig. 9). Presumably because of the poor dental care, seventeenth-century artists rarely showed teeth in portraits. (Van Dyck, for example only included them in one portrait.) Rembrandt revels in the wrinkled skin on her face and hands, so different from the smoother and less interesting skin of a younger woman. Enabled by the use of a copper support, this is achieved by brushwork which makes use of small flecks of paint, quite thickly applied. Her red hat provides the one accent of colour in the sombre picture. For all its precision of execution this image of gnarled old age does not exactly gladden the heart.

Born on 15 July 1606 in Leiden, Rembrandt Harmensz. van Rijn was still living with his parents in the Weddesteg in 1622, together with several brothers and sisters. Although attempts have been made to identify Adriaen and Lisbeth among early models or sitters, none is convincing. On the other hand what are clearly identifiable are the numerous images of himself, dating from his earliest years until the year of his death. Although the exact number of his self-portraits is disputed, we know of some forty-one paintings, thirty-one etchings and seven drawings. Self-portraits are by their very nature intimate, but in Rembrandt's case some are more intimate than others. Moreover, for the most part they were not straightforward self-portraits but had a purpose which varied over the years. Sometimes interpreted as an act of self-analysis, they are more prosaically likely to be answering the demand by art lovers for self-portraits by the famous man Rembrandt was very quickly recognised to be. Despite popular myth of his supposed later neglect, he maintained an increasingly international reputation until the end of his life. Already in one of his earliest paintings, *The Stoning of Stephen* (Musée des Beaux-Arts, Lyon), dated 1625, Rembrandt gives the spectator just above the martyred saint his own features. The same phenomenon occurs in several other early history paintings, as if the artist was intent on making an identifying mark on his own creations.

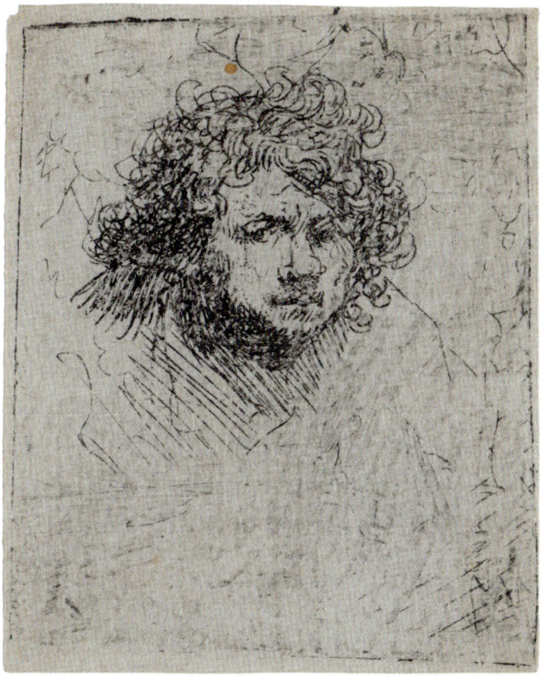

3. *Self-portrait Leaning Forward: Bust. c.*1629. Etching. 4.3 × 4 cm. Rijksmuseum, Amsterdam.

Rembrandt was probably twenty-six years old when he made his first stand-alone paintings and etchings with his own image. The earliest example in etching may well be the *Self-portrait Leaning Forward: Bust* [Fig. 3]. No more than just under 50 mm high in its final state, it was etched on a piece of copper used for the original state of *The Flight into Egypt* (NHD 4), which he had cut down to concentrate on the figure of St Joseph. The staring expression is one of serious intent as the artist leans forward from the page in an attempt to engage the spectator, who feels himself or herself almost forced to stand back. The drawing with the etching needle is wonderfully free in the execution of details, notably the hair, partially overlaid with cross-hatching and stippling to create a pattern of light and shadow. For such a lightly-worked plate on a small scale it is a marvellously complete work.

On a slightly larger scale, but small in size for a painting, the *Self-portrait Laughing* [Fig. 4], executed about 1628 and only recently discovered, is another of the few works executed on copper, but without the gold

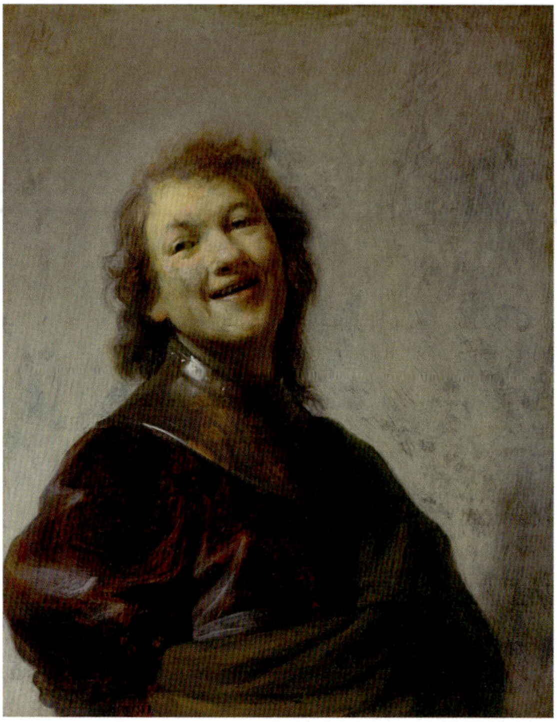

4. *Self-portrait Laughing. c.*1628. Copper.
22.2 × 17.1 cm. J. Paul Getty Museum, Los Angeles.

ground seen, for example, in the *Old Woman in Prayer* (see Fig. 2), at the beginning of the artist's career. Rather than a straight portrait of himself, the work is likely to have been intended as a study in expression, using himself as the nearest model to hand. It also would have answered the taste of the time for *tronies* or heads. Rembrandt, posing as a soldier, wears an iron gorget around his neck, a feature found in other early self-portraits, and he is swathed in a dark cloak. He is seen leaning back from the spectator, eyes shining and mouth open in a laugh, with teeth showing. A lovelock may be hanging down beside his face. A strong light coming from the upper left illumines the highlights on the hair and face, casting the right side of the head into shadow. Already he shows a masterly handling of the paintbrush as, for example, he freely adds touches of pink and yellow in short strokes to the face. Rembrandt almost invariably started work on the background, which served to give the whole picture a tonal unity. Unlike other artists who used one colour unvaried in tone, he designed his backgrounds with a varied surface, created here by visible brushstrokes which serve to enhance the subject in the foreground, subtly creating an all encompassing play of light and shadow. Later works by the artist were to become more sophisticated, but already one can see the pattern of transparent blue painted over brownish yellow, varied in tone from the darker area at the top to the brighter area on either side of the figure. This brilliant little sketch offers an image of infectious *joie de vivre*. Its confidence in execution justifies the remark of a certain Arnout van Buchell, a visiting jurist from Utrecht in 1628, who reported that Rembrandt was already 'esteemed highly' in Leiden, although he thought, 'but before his time'.[1]

Other artists who illustrated the subject of the artist at work in his studio usually cluttered the space with paraphernalia related to the practice of painting or including objects with symbolic meaning. Probably executed in 1628, Rembrandt [Fig. 5] offers a fairly bleak image of a largely empty room with bare walls in a condition which had seen better days. It has the

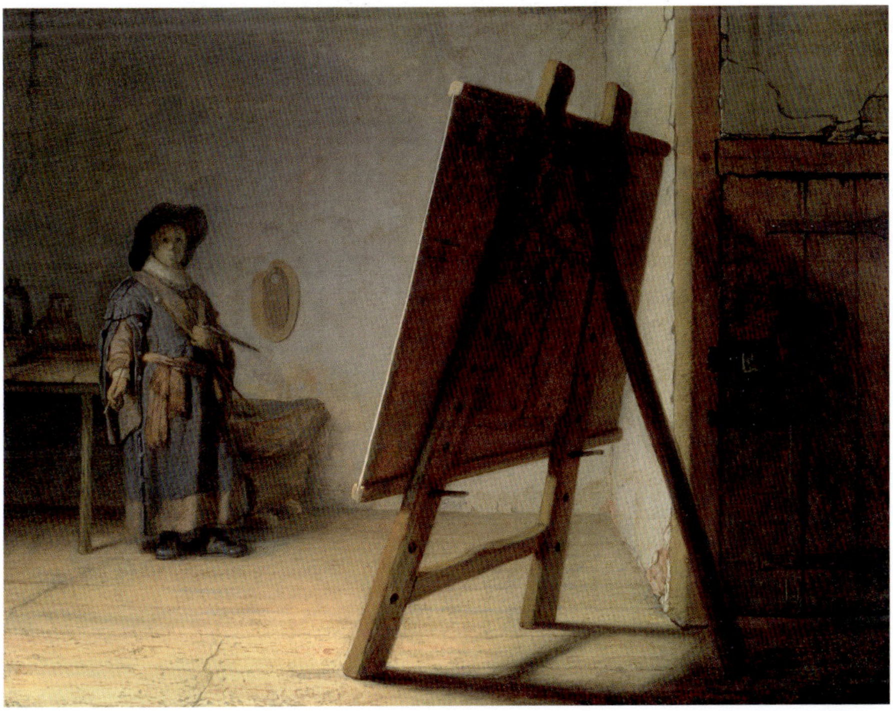

5. *Self-portrait in his Studio*. *c.*1628. Panel. 24.8 × 31.7 cm. Museum of Fine Arts, Boston.

appearance of an actual room, possibly Rembrandt's studio, rather than a space created out of the imagination. Crumbling plasterwork can be seen on the right at the bottom of the wall and above the door. And as an instance of further wear and tear, two cavities in the floorboards beneath the front of the easel can be made out, caused by the shuffling feet of the artist, who at that time usually sat rather than stood at his work. An easel bearing a large panel, tantalisingly seen from the back, fills the whole height of the right foreground. We are given no idea whether the panel is blank or has been worked on. Diagonally placed at the back of the room, the artist, on this occasion on his feet rather than seated, stands back to ponder the progress of his work. Seemingly of small stature, in fact when the distance across the room is taken into account, his height is perfectly normal. Wearing a wide-brimmed black hat, he is warmly dressed in his working clothes, namely a *tabbaard*, or gown, tied at the waist, to protect him against the cold in a seemingly unheated room. In his left hand, he holds the tools of his trade – maulstick, brushes and palette – and in his other hand, the paintbrush which he is clearly using. Behind him, on a table, can be seen some bottles and earthenware pots. At his side is a tree trunk bearing a grinding stone to prepare pigments, above which are two clean palettes ready for use. It includes everything the artist needs to get to work with no unnecessary adornments to the room.

The panel can be interpreted as a straightforward record of the artist at work in his studio. The dominance of the easel in this closed space suggests art rather than the artist was the primary focus. But a deeper more specific meaning has been suggested, as was described by Rembrandt's pupil, Samuel van Hoogstraten writing about another artist: 'he was first forming in his imagination the whole conception of his work; he was first making the painting in his mind before he put his brush into the paint'.[2] In other words the artist is portrayed at the crucial moment of seeking inspiration through contemplation. It would fit in with contemporary art theory which demanded that the artist formulated the subject in his mind before he actually started execution.

What we see in this picture may be a scene which would have greeted Constantijn Huygens (1596–1687), Secretary to the Stadholder, Prince Frederick Henry, when he paid a visit to Leiden about the time the picture was painted. As he wrote in his autobiography, Huygens took the opportunity to call on Rembrandt and his nearly exact contemporary, Jan Lievens (1607–1674), who may have shared a studio at the time. Huygens was first of all struck that two men from such humble backgrounds could produce such noble art, thereby disproving the superiority of noble blood, a theory frequently aired in the aristocratic circles of the writer. Huygens was greatly impressed by their industry, but regretted that they were too self-absorbed in their own narrow worlds, refusing, as was the custom of the time, to visit Italy to study the great art of the past. Yet he prophesied a great future for them, excelling their contemporaries.

Such praise, were Rembrandt to have heard it, would have encouraged his growing awareness that Leiden was too small a town to satisfy his ambition and the lure of Amsterdam beckoned. He had already, in 1624 or 1625, had experience of that increasingly vibrant commercial city when he spent six months in the studio of the Amsterdam artist Pieter Lastman (*c.*1583–1633), one of the most influential Dutch artists of the time. In 1631 Rembrandt started to make a move there, and in the following year made his mark in the city with his renowned *The Anatomy Lesson of Dr Nicolaes Tulp* (Mauritshuis, The Hague), finally becoming a permanent resident two years later.

In the first year of his migration he made a small self-portrait etching of his head and shoulders [Fig. 6], which has the distinction of having been subjected to a major change in the course of execution. As close inspection reveals, Rembrandt first drew in the top of his head and hair and only subsequently added the fur cap. The latter is a feature of a number of earlier self-portraits and other studies of male figures. Here in a bust-length portrait, Rembrandt wears a dark cloak with a fur-trimmed collar. The expression is stern and searching as he examines himself in the mirror. He has an almost grim look of determination, which is appropriate for his move onto a larger stage.

Having previously made studies of himself bareheaded or sometimes covering his head with a cap or beret, Rembrandt now adopts fashionable dress in the *Self-portrait* [Fig. 7], dated 1632, in which he wears a stylish wide-brimmed hat. For all its austerity in the overall effect, the artist pays particular attention to those small details which create an impression of tasteful opulence; such as his golden hatband, a wide falling ruff and a doublet with gold buttons. In formal attire, Rembrandt assumes the

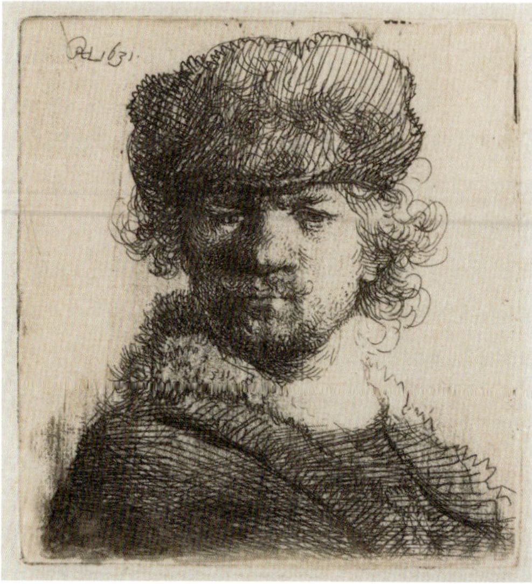

6. *Self-portrait in a Heavy Fur Cap: Bust*. 1631. Etching. 6.3 × 5.7 cm. Rijksmuseum, Amsterdam.

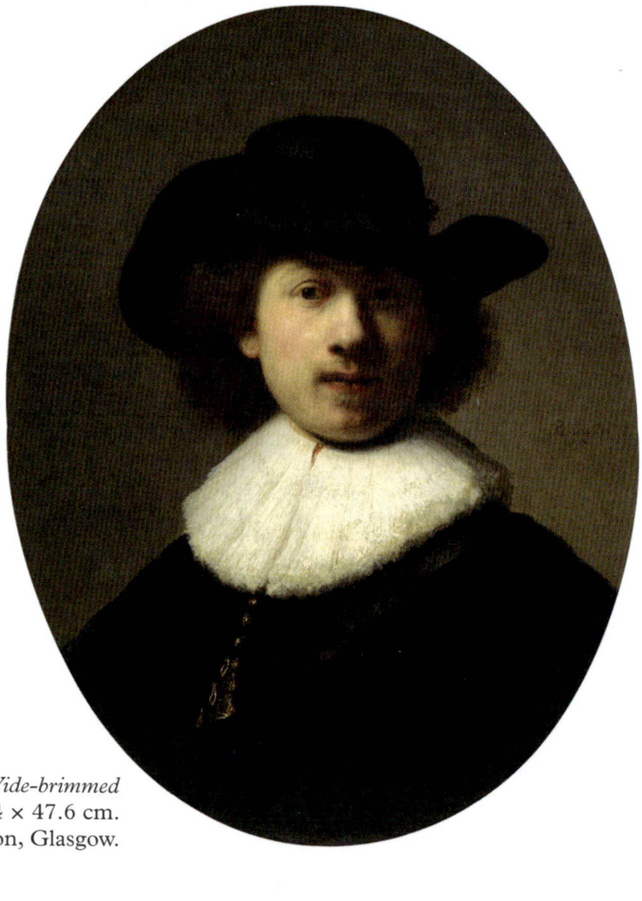

7. *Self-portrait with a Wide-brimmed Hat*. 1632. Panel. 64.4 × 47.6 cm. Burrell Collection, Glasgow.

role of a well-heeled citizen of Amsterdam, firmly burying the image of a provincial youth from Leiden. It was clearly a work intended for public consumption and only included here to illustrate his change of life-style.

A document of 1632 establishes that Rembrandt was living in Amsterdam in a house in the St Anthonis-Breestraat, which belonged to the art dealer, Hendrick van Uylenburgh, who was twenty years older than the artist. He ran a flourishing business with many contacts, which must have proved useful for the newly-arrived young artist from Leiden. He clearly played an important part in establishing Rembrandt's quickly burgeoning career. It was probably in his house that Rembrandt met the dealer's cousin, Saskia van Uylenburgh, who was born in Leeuwaarden on 2 August 1612, the daughter of a wealthy and successful government attorney. What happened next is touchingly told in a drawing [Fig. 8], which Rembrandt inscribed with the words: 'This is drawn after my wife, when she was twenty-one years old, the third day after we were betrothed

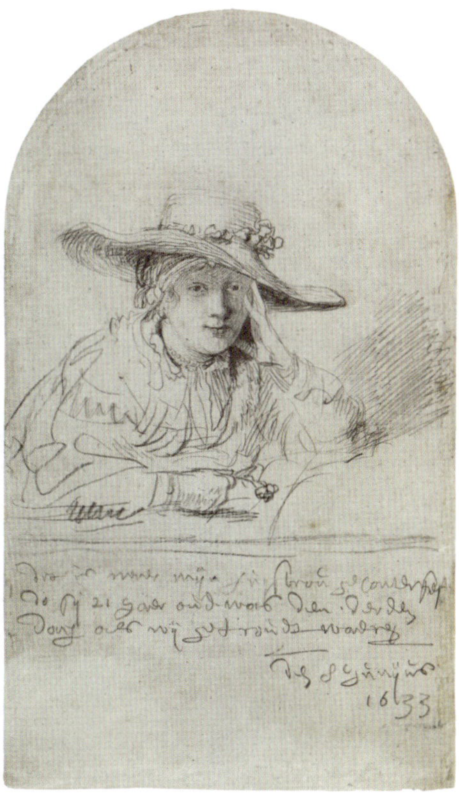

8. *Saskia*. 1633. Silverpoint on white prepared parchment. 18.5 × 10.6 cm. Kupferstichkabinett, Staatliche Museen zu Berlin.

(i.e. exchanged betrothal vows) – 8 June 1633'. It was executed in silverpoint on prepared parchment, a medium which Rembrandt only used on three other occasions, and surely acknowledges its personal importance to the artist. It was not, however, unique since similar portraits in silverpoint had been produced earlier by such artists as Hendrick Goltzius (1558– 1615) and Jacques de Gheyn (1565–1629).

Saskia, seen half-length leaning on a wall, has a tender expression as she gazes very directly at her fiancé drawing her. She is clothed in an informal costume of the kind she might wear around the home. Giving the portrait a country air, she has a wide-brimmed straw hat, decorated with a flowers, which was only worn outdoors. In her right hand, she holds a flower, probably a rose, the symbol of love. It has been suggested that the drawing was made in Saskia's sister's garden or on a walk in a village in rural Friesland, where she was living when Rembrandt came to propose. The fine modelling of the face and underside of the hat brim contrasts with the freely executed delineation of her body. Her unshaded left hand with its elegant tapering fingers, is held up against her cheek, and stands out as a highlight. The inscription, which is an essential part of the drawing, takes up the lower half of the sheet and documents the image for posterity. The portrait stands as one of the most personal works the artist ever made; it is not too fanciful to describe it as a lover's drawing.

With the same happy mood prevailing, Rembrandt painted a bust-length portrait of Saskia [Fig. 9] in the same year. The details of her face are fleshed out so that one becomes aware of her chubby cheeks and double chin. Softened by a mysterious shadow cast by her hat, her narrowly open eyes, set between full eyelids, are sparkling and her small mouth is slightly open, wreathed in a smile, and with her teeth just showing. The picture has a powerful sense of immediacy as if the artist had just come across his fiancée by chance, to be greeted with spontaneous pleasure. It illustrates the precept set out by Karel van Mander in *Het Schilder-Boeck* that a laughing mouth is a sign of love, and, elsewhere he wrote, that happiness should be conveyed by half-closed eyes.[3] What is particularly striking about the picture is the richness of colour of what she is wearing. Rembrandt never dressed his wife in contemporary clothing, but always presented her in fancy or historical costume. Her wide-brimmed hat, adorned with a red feather, which fills nearly a third

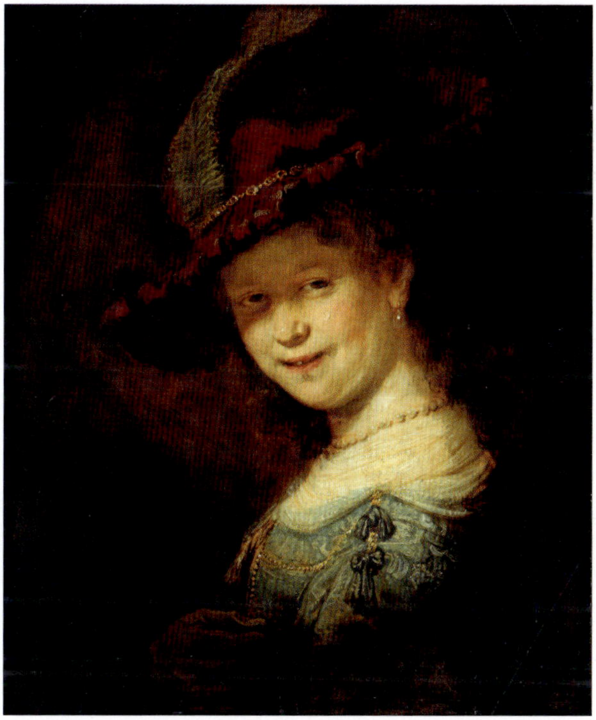

9. *Saskia Smiling*. 1633. Panel. 52.5 × 44.5 cm.
Gemäldegalerie, Dresden.

of the height of the panel, is a rich red. What is an old-fashioned dress for the times is pale blue, with the buttons and braiding on the dress picked out in bright yellow blobs of paint, creating a trio of colours which gives an unusual element of gaiety to the picture. Allied with this colouristic effect is the remarkable freedom of the brushwork, varying between thick and thinly applied paint, with transparent glazes to suggest an underlying glow to the panel. Given the decorative qualities of the picture it is not impossible that, rather than a portrait of his fiancée, it was intended as a *tronie*, or an unidentified image of a pretty woman, which would look attractive on a collector's walls, in the same way that some of his self-portraits appear to have fulfilled the same purpose.

For the first two years the couple lived in Van Uylenburgh's house, and then moved to two further houses before, in 1639, purchasing, at a high price, a grand merchant's house in the Sint-Anthonisbreestraat, next door to Van Uylenburgh's house, which remained the artist's residence for the next nineteen years. Although producing numerous studies of his wife and himself individually, he only portrayed them together in two works, very different in presentation from one another. Neither appear to be straightforward portraits, the one a *portrait historié* and the other bearing an underlying meaning. In a large painting, executed *c.*1635, their images are used in a flamboyant representation of *The Prodigal Son in the Tavern* (Gemäldegalerie, Dresden), in which she is seated demurely on his lap, while he, grinning widely, teeth flashing, raises a glass of wine in a triumphant gesture. If the subject is intended to bear any relation to the sitters' lives, it suggests an extravagant existence, about which Saskia's relatives complained, when they accused her of squandering her inheritance a few years later.

The etching of the couple together [Fig. 10] with its quiet sober portrayal could not offer a greater contrast. Rembrandt is seated in the foreground, at work holding what is more likely to be chalk in a holder than an etching needle. On the sheet in front of him he appears to have drawn

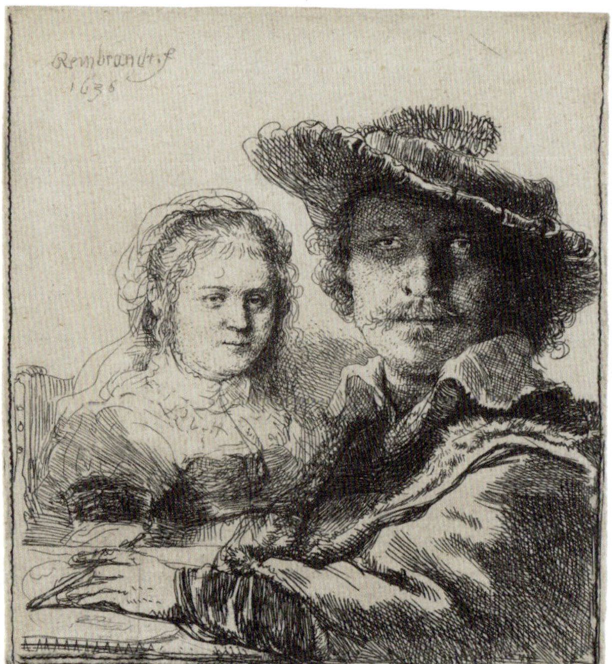

10. *Self-portrait with Saskia*. 1636. Etching. 10.4 × 9.5 cm. Rijksmuseum, Amsterdam.

a circle; whether that has any meaning, such as a reference to the circles supposedly drawn by Giotto and signifying artistic genius, remains an open question. Saskia is placed behind him, seated relaxedly in a chair. Both look at the spectator tight-lipped and serious. At first glance it might be taken as an image of the pair quietly at home in harmony with one another; no mutual glances at one another were required to suggest their intimacy. The first unusual aspect of the print is their placement, she immediately behind him with no space between their bodies, so that the image becomes uncomfortably two-dimensional. One might suspect that the etching began with her figure alone, on top of which he subsequently etched his own figure bitten more deeply, to suggest their relative placing. That her dress continues beneath his garment can be seen as an argument in favour. Unfortunately no intermediate state exists to document this supposition.

The second unusual feature in the print is that the artist wears historical rather than contempory costume; his high white collar is worn under a fur-trimmed cloak and a sixteenth-century hat, with a large feather, on his head. This penchant for dress of a past age, which can be seen in a number of self-portraits, reflects the artist's undoubted wish to measure himself against the great artists of the past, such as Leonardo da Vinci and Titian. For her part Saskia is dressed in old-fashioned clothes with a veil on her head. Rather than recording a straightforward domestic scene, the etching would seem more likely intended to illustrate the beneficial effects of marriage on the artist, following the theme of an old Dutch motto; '*Liefde baart kunst*' (Love brings forth art). Though found in contemporary Dutch paintings of family and double portraits, this appears to be the only occasion in seventeenth-century printmaking, illustrating once again Rembrandt's originality.

In their life together, Saskia served as the ever-present and presumably willing model. But so wholehearted is Rembrandt's recording of every aspect of her daily life in affectionate detail that it is fair to assume that his interest in her was inspired by love. Often it is difficult to be certain, particularly in his more freely executed drawings, that she is the model. Nevertheless a general template of her facial appearance based on her betrothal drawing can be established. This uxorious devotion echoes Rubens's passion for his second wife, Helena Fourment, which infused

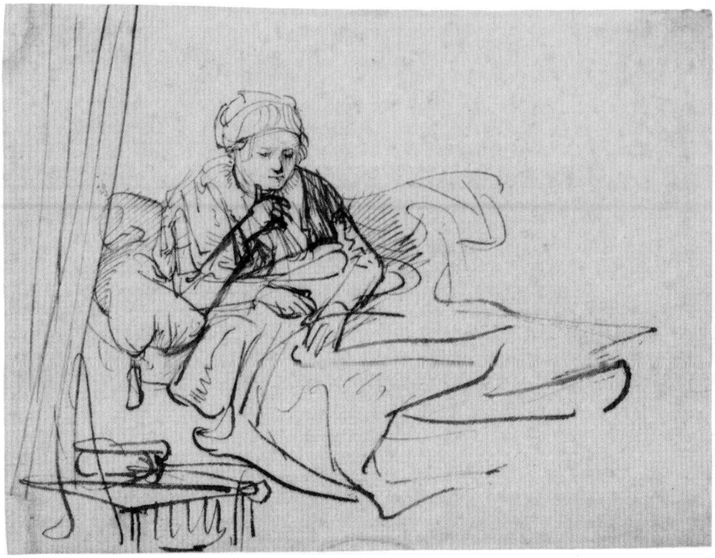

11. *Saskia Sitting Up in Bed. c.*1636. Pen and brown ink.
14.8 × 19.1 cm. Groninger Museum, Groningen.

so much of his later painting and drawing, often with a similar ambiguity as to whether or not she is the model.

Saskia was constantly under the observation of the artist's eye, with the bedroom playing a frequent role as a setting. Whether these studies catch her during one of her periods of pregnancy, as often supposed, or whether they represent general daily life is hard to tell. In one pen drawing [Fig. 11] she is sitting up in bed very much awake. Supported by pillows she looks down in contemplation, seemingly unaware that she is under scrutiny. This gives her an air of complete detachment from the artist studying her. Originally both hands were resting on the coverlet in front, but the artist made a very noticeable change by moving her right hand to rest on her chin, giving her a more pensive pose. A curtain is drawn to one side, with a chamber pot on a bedside table visible in the immediate foreground. The diagonally placed bed suggests depth and although no background is indicated one senses the space surrounding her. With maximum economy of line – free and suggestive rather than precise in execution – it is a very complete image. More would be less.

No less masterly in execution is the drawing of Saskia asleep [Fig. 12], in which he takes the pictorial conception a stage further. The setting is

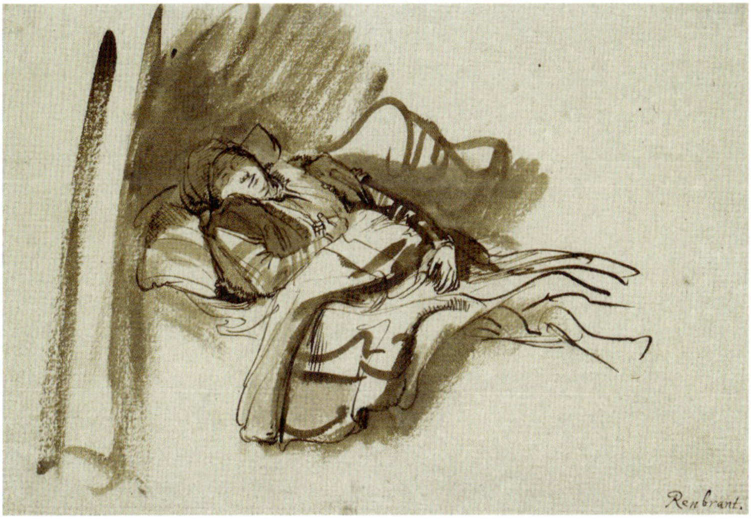

12. *Saskia Asleep in Bed. c.*1636. Pen and brown ink with brown wash. 13.7 × 20.3 cm. Ashmolean Museum, Oxford.

similar with a diagonally placed bed and a drawn curtain to one side. With one hand placed across her body and the other resting on the coverlet, she lies serene in peaceful slumber, unaware of the artist imposing his presence. It is a voyeur's dream. On this occasion Rembrandt started work with the pen, loosely defining the figure stretched out on the bed. Then he worked over the drawing with the brush, suggesting the curtain at the side with two freely-executed vertical strokes, creating a penumbra within the bed-head, and strongly redefining the outlines of the figure and the bedclothes. For such a peaceful intimate scene, it is an incredibly bold, self-sufficient statement.

In one of his last uses of red chalk, Rembrandt produced one of his most touching portrayals of motherhood [Fig. 13]. From the loosely indicated features Saskia can be presumed to be the subject. In view of the likely date of the drawing, Rumbartus, the first born, who lived only two months at the end of 1635, is probably the infant represented. (Of her four children, only the last, Titus, survived into adulthood.) She lovingly swathes her infant in her arms, who looks like a little old man as male babies often do. She stares out with a look of infinite sadness, a surprising emotion for a new mother. Perhaps she was suffering from delivery, or was already aware that the child's life was likely to be short. For such

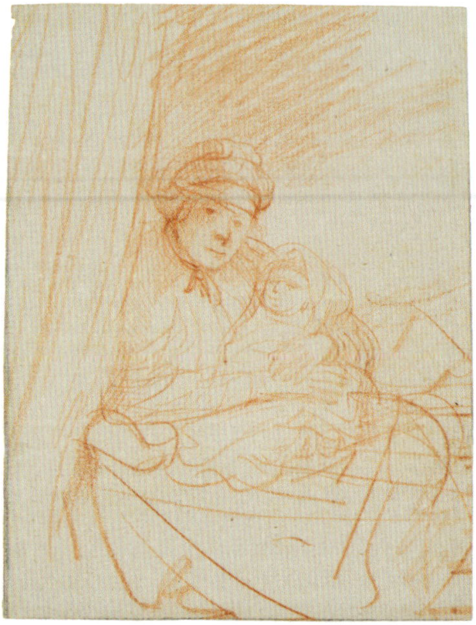

13. *Saskia Sitting Up in Bed with Rumbartus*. *c.*1636. Red chalk. 14 × 10.5 cm. Courtauld Gallery, London.

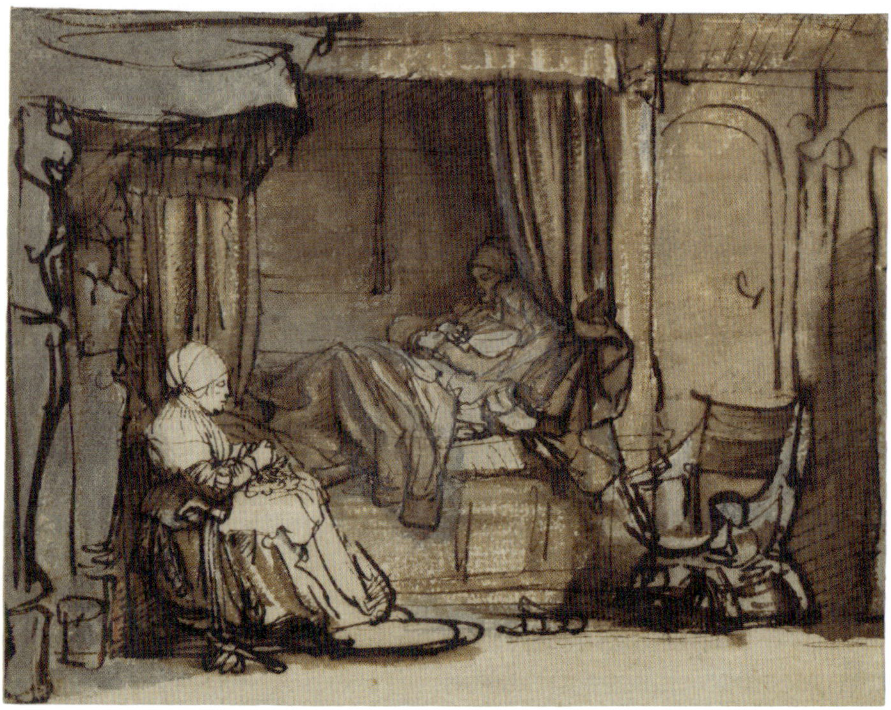

14. *Saskia's Lying-in Room*. *c.*1641. Pen and brown ink with brown and grey wash, some red and black chalk. 14.2 × 17.7 cm. Fondation Custodia, Paris.

an informal study, it is perfectly composed and complete in itself. One feels that not another line is needed. The figures emerging from an area of shadow are framed on the left by the ubiquitous curtain in bedroom scenes and by the horizontal of the bed below. Apart from the definition of the faces, the remainder of the study depends on free suggestive rather carefully descriptive lines. Given the delicacy and expressiveness that Rembrandt was able to conjure out of red chalk, it is to be regretted that he virtually abandoned its use from now on.

Another bedroom drawing [Fig. 14], executed a few years later, finds a further study of Saskia at home. The mantlepiece supported by two sculpted herms seen on the left identifies the setting as the 'back room or hall' in the house in the Breestraat, into which Rembrandt and Saskia had moved in 1639. Saskia, perhaps undergoing a pregnancy or possibly an illness, is lying, seemingly asleep, in an upright position, with knees raised and her hands folded on the coverlet in front of her. On the left a woman, engaged in needlework, is seated on a chair between the bed and the fireplace; her feet rest on a cushion. She serves as a silent companion to keep Saskia company and to attend to her needs. On the right an empty chair, perhaps waiting for the master, is placed in front of a door. The two women are absorbed in their own worlds so that the drawing, unlike the previous studies of Saskia thus becomes more a detached snapshot of daily life in the Breestraat. The medium is unusually rich, consisting principally of pen and brown wash, but with some grey wash, and a few touches of red and black chalk. The lighting has been very carefully calculated throughout. Coming from the left, presumably from a window, the light falls fully on the figure of the companion and on Saskia's body while her head remains in shadow. The underlying white of the paper is hardly to be seen. Otherwise the room is submerged in a subtly varying range of half-lights, with individual objects casting their own self-contained shadows. The overall effect is created by the extensive application of brown wash with the addition of grey wash, rarely used by Rembrandt, to extend the impression of depth within the room. The result has the appearance of a finished work of art with the qualities of a monochrome painting.

One of the occupants of the bedside seat was at certain times surely an elder sister of Saskia's, Titia van Uylenburgh [Fig. 15], who was born

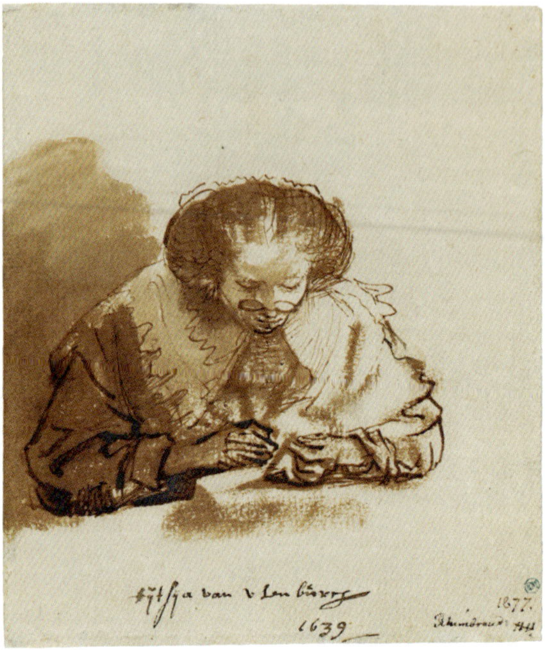

15. *Titia van Uylenburgh*. 1639. Pen and brown ink with brown wash. 14 × 14.6 cm. Nationalmuseum, Stockholm.

in 1605 and died a year before the latter. She lived with her husband in Vlissingen but was on two occasions recorded in Amsterdam, acting as a witness for two of Rembrandt's and Saskia's children in 1638 and 1640. The inscription with the sitter's name and the date 1639 makes it clear that the sheet was intended as a portrait. Titia, her pince-nez perched perilously on the end of her nose, is shown bent forward totally given up to her needlework, seemingly unaware that she is the subject of her brother-in-law's attention. At the angle at which her face is depicted, not much of her appearance can be made out but the artist is nevertheless able to suggest the air of concentration of a woman hard at work. The drawing is made up of loosely drawn penlines, over which the artist has used a brush to define the outlines of the arms and apply an area of shadow on the left, indicating the strong source of light coming from the right. Within the limited means at his disposal, the portrait has considerable depth. The figure is set in the middleground, with an area of uncovered white paper below the figure to denote the foreground and a loosely applied wash on the left to suggest the dark background. With a minimum of work it is a perfectly finished work of art.

By 1642 Saskia was in poor health, described as being 'ailing in bed'[4] in the will she made only nine days before her death on 14 June. The cause of her illness is unknown, but suggests that her confinement in bed, the location of so many studies of her, was as much to do with sickness as child-birth. Probably in this year, Rembrandt, apart from painting the monumental canvas of *The Night Watch* (Rijksmusem, Amsterdam), made by contrast a very small etching of a *Sick Woman in a Large White Headdress* [Fig. 16], which there is good reason to believe was made of Saskia in her last days. Only a few centimetres in size, one suspects that the artist may have used an unwanted piece of copper, cut off from a larger plate. It is most moving document. Gone are her plump cheeks and ample chin; the cheeks are now sunken, the face is thin and haggard, and she wears an infinitely weary expression. Her wide-open staring eyes have the glazed look of someone who is becoming detached from life. Although lightly and very freely etched in outline and some cross-hatching to

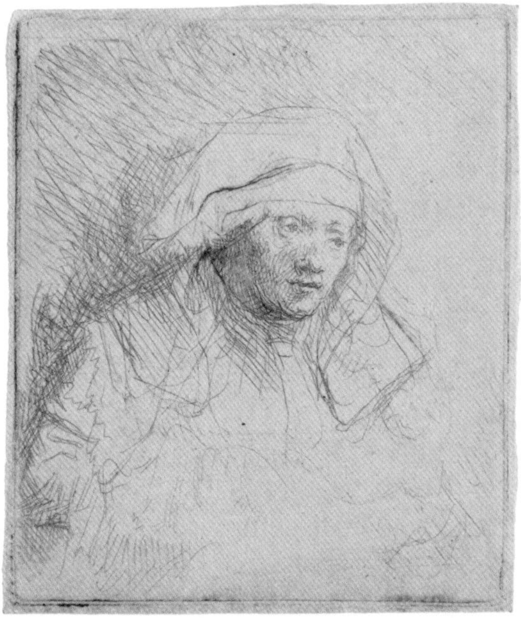

16. *Sick Woman in a Large White Headdress.*
*c.*1642. Etching and drypoint. 6.1 × 5.1 cm.
Rijksmuseum, Amsterdam.

create a pattern of light and shadow, the artist seems to have achieved his purpose, since he did no more than touch up the plate with a little work in drypoint, a tool which allowed the artist to draw directly into the plate creating ridges of copper which printed in a rich velvety black.

The death of Saskia coincided with a fundamental change in Rembrandt's art. He turned away from the flamboyant Baroque of his work in the later 1630s to a quieter more introspective style. He moved out of the orbit of the fashionable art world and became increasingly his own person. In this change of direction, self-portraiture did not play much of a part, since he has left only relatively few examples from this period. What can be regarded as his official painted image in this period is the *Self-portrait Leaning on a Stone Sill* (National Gallery, London), dated 1640, with its very obvious debt to two of the great artists of the Italian High-Renaissance, Raphael and Titian. A less formal study from this time can be found in the etching of a *Self-portrait in a Flat Cap and Embroidered Dress* [Fig. 17], probably executed in the year of Saskia's death. His knitted brow gives him an earnest quizzical look, suggestintg that he is

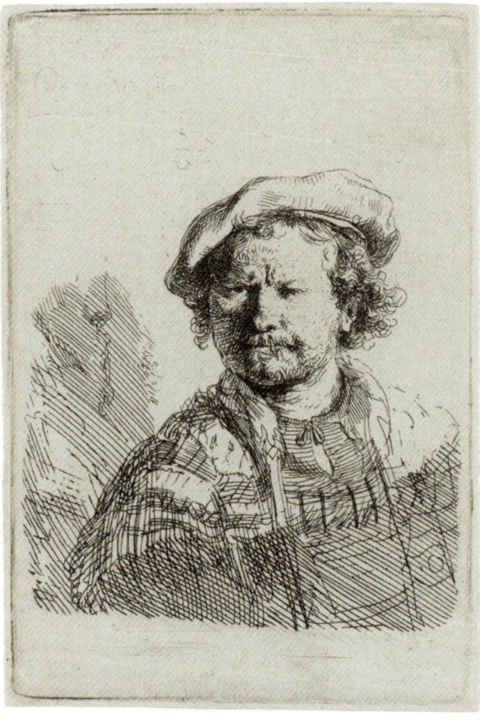

17. *Self-portrait in a Flat Cap and Embroidered Dress. c.*1642. Etching. 9.3 × 6.2 cm. Rijksmuseum, Amsterdam.

undergoing a state of reflection about his personal circumstances and his art at this moment of great change in his life. It is a curious work, since although the head is largely frontal, the body is seemingly placed at an angle, giving the impression that the right shoulder, only partially represented, is higher than the left. Once again he is dressed in old-fashioned style, a jerkin, decorated with panes or strips of cloth, with a beret on his head. The detail of the face and hair is worked up with small strokes, whereas the body is largely defined by loose cross hatching over summary outline. It is almost as if Rembrandt had worked in two separate stages. One is very much aware that the light falls strongly from the right on one side of the head and casts an area of shadow in the left background.

To help look after the newly-born Titus and presumably care for the increasingly ailing Saskia, Rembrandt employed a trumpeter's widow by the name of Geertje Dircx, who came from north Holland. She is traditionally identified with two studies, both in the same standing pose beside a table, of a youngish woman in north Holland costume, in one drawing seen from the front [Fig. 18] and the other from the back [Fig.

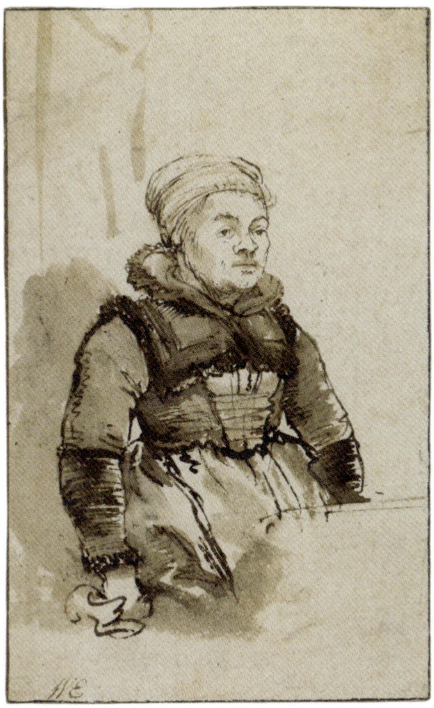

18. *A Woman in North Holland Costume (Geertje Dircx ?)*. *c.*1641. Pen and brown ink with brown wash. 13 × 7.8 cm. British Museum, London.

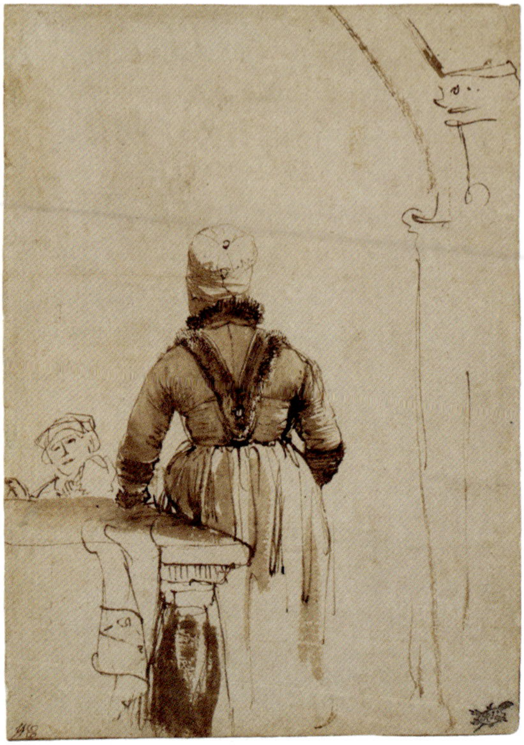

19. *A Woman in North Holland Costume, Seen from the Back (Geertje Dircx ?)*. *c.*1641. Pen and brown ink with brown wash. 22.2 × 15.4 cm. Teylers Museum, Haarlem.

19]; the latter is inscribed on the back: 'the wet nurse of Titus'. Houbraken, in his early eighteenth-century lives of the painters, describes her, on what evidence is unclear, as 'a little farm woman … rather small of person but well made in appearance and plump of body'.[5] It is, however, probably wishful thinking to identify her as the model for the two drawings for two reasons. She is here called a 'wet nurse', whereas Geertje was described as Titus's 'dry nurse' in a document of 1649. And there is the question of the date, and whether the two drawings might have been executed before Geertje's documented arrival in the Rembrandt home. But, nevertheless, they are worth discussing as a different type of drawing. Neatly executed with the pen and brush with carefully applied shading in wash, they can be classified as costume studies, calling for precise detail and presumably to be kept for reference. The face on the recto is without expression and does not suggest that the artist was at all interested in the model's personality. The costume, so lovingly described, is notable for the extensive attachment of fur to the bodice and the collar, and the 'V' shaped marking on the woman's back.

During the 1640s, Rembrandt, for whatever reason, made very few self-portraits. After the *Self-portait in a Flat Cap*, discussed above, the next example was the *Self-portrait Etching at a Window* [Fig. 20], signed and dated 1648. We are to infer we are seeing the artist in his own setting. Unlike the freely- and lightly-executed earlier work, this plate is worked in a combination of etching, drypoint and engraving, continuing the rich technique developed in the previous year in the portrait of *Jan Six* (see Fig. 44), to be discussed in a later chapter. Over a basis of finely executed cross-hatching in etching, filling both foreground and background in shades of grey, the figure emerges from the penumbra; fine flecks of the etching-needle define the face and the use of drypoint strengthens the outlines of the tunic. It took four stages, or states, to complete the work

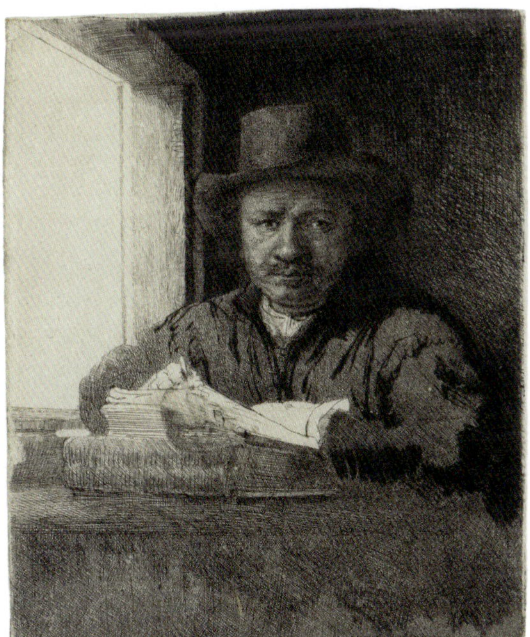

20. *Self-portrait Etching at a Window*. 1648.
Etching and drypoint. 16 × 13 cm.
Rijksmuseum, Amsterdam.

to the artist's satisfaction; here, in the second state, Rembrandt has completed the image with the play of light and shadow over the face rendered still at its most subtle. Compared with earlier etched self-portraits, it is altogether a more pictorial print, leaning towards the effect of a monochrome painting.

In the corner of a bare room, the artist is seated at a table, carefully placed right up close to the window to provide the maximum light for his minutely executed work on the plate. (In the fourth state he adds a lightly-drawn landscape.) With a cylinder-shaped hat with a narrow brim on his head, he wears a shirt over working clothes, presenting himself as a down-to-earth artist, unlike the figure dressed in fancy or ancient costumes seen in earlier self-portraits. The eyes are particularly powerful as they gaze intently at the spectator, but in fact recording what he saw in the mirror. In order to counter the effect of the image on the plate being reversed when printed, the artist had to draw himself left-handed. The overall pattern of varying tones is only broken by the highlight (in a later state of the print dulled with shading), which falls on the hand holding the etching needle, emphasising that the subject shows the artist in the act of creation.

A short time later in a drawing Rembrandt portrays himself standing. [Fig. 21], the authorship of which is often doubted. A late seventeenth-century inscription describing the subject has been pasted on the sheet: 'Drawn by Rembrandt van Rijn after his own image / as he was attired in his studio'. In contrast to the previous self-portrait, he shows himself, as it were, in a momentary break from work. Wearing the same narrow-brimmed conical hat as in the previous self-portrait, he is dressed in a long working coat with a sash tied around his waist, with slippers on his feet. It is a masterly study for which he uses his increasingly preferred method of drawing with a reed pen. (The reed pen gave a softer, broader line, compared to the previously preferred quill pen with its capacity for sharper lines. It can be seen as an equivalent to the broader brushstrokes which the artist increasingly came to favour in his paintings from the 1650s onwards.) Basically the figure is defined in outline with emphasis placed on the head and hands, plus some parallel shading added below to set the figure in space. Some corrections were made to the placing of the right hand and left foot, suggesting the immediacy with

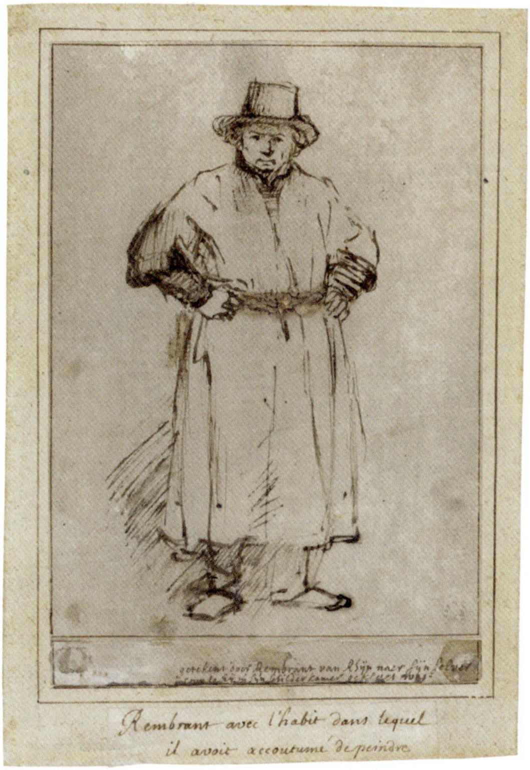

21. *Self-portrait Standing*. *c.*1650. Pen and brown ink. 20.3 × 13.4 cm. The Rembrandt House Museum, Amsterdam.

which he studied himself. The face frowning, the stance, with hands very firmly placed on his hips, is confrontational, if not outrightly aggressive. Filippo Baldinucci (1686), dependent on the testimony of a pupil, who left Amsterdam about the time of this drawing, gave a colourful snapshot of the artist: 'When he worked he would not have granted an audience to the first monarch in the world, who would have had to return again and again until he found him no longer engaged on that work'.[6] This drawing gives a hint of the reception an unexpected visitor might have received attempting to gain access to his studio.

What the large studio ('groote Schilderkamer') on the second floor in the front of the house looked like can be seen in a drawing of the *Artist's Studio with a Model* [Fig. 22]. The sheet is framed by a large easel supporting a painting on the left and the beginnings of an elaborate fireplace

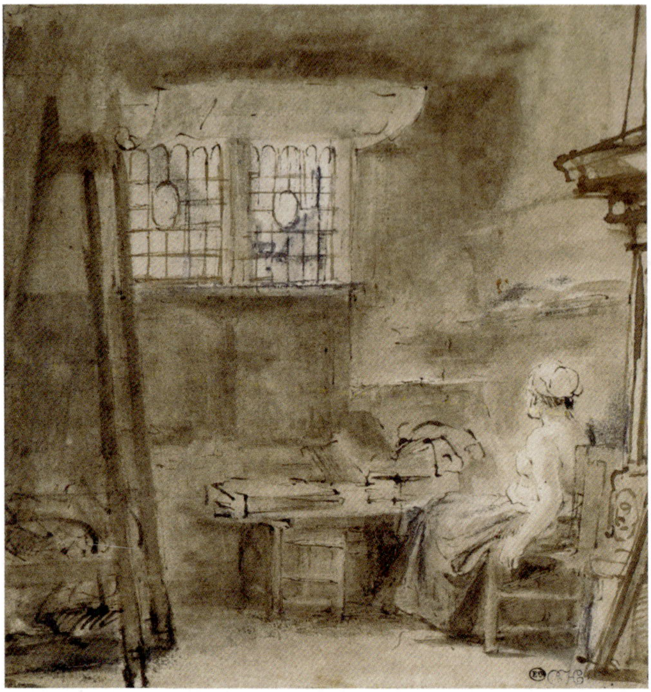

22. *Artist's Studio with a Model. c.*1654. Pen and brown ink with brown wash, heightened with white. 20.5 × 19 cm. Ashmolean Museum, Oxford.

on the right, beside which a half-naked female model, seen from the side, is seated. (It has been suggested that the model is Hendrickje Stoffels, to be discussed below, with their baby Cornelia in a cradle. But the woman's features cannot be made out and it is by no means certain that the object beside her is a cradle.) The studio is otherwise furnished with a low table, bearing books, and a stool below. The source of light emanates from the two upper windows, above which a blind has been suspended in order to control the illumination of the room; the shutters on the lower windows are firmly closed. The extensive use of varying shades of brown wash depicts the fluctuating half-lights and shadows which fill the room and create a veiled atmosphere. Only the upper windows and the upper half of the model's body remain untouched by wash, establishing the limited highlights to be seen in the drawing. This sensitive control of the amount of light introduced is consistent with Rembrandt's chiaroscuro, or play of light and shadow, which is such a predominant aspect of his art.

After Saskia's death, Geertje, while looking after the infant Titus, became Rembrandt's mistress and presumably brought some comfort to the widower. But by 1649 at the latest harmony in the home was disrupted by the arrival of Hendrickje Stoffels, a sergeant's daughter from Bredevoort. Her presence created a painful *menage à trois*, which led to the ousting of Geertje from the home. There is no question but that Rembrandt behaved very badly to the latter, playing a malign role in getting her locked up in a house of correction. But the newcomer became the essential person in Rembrandt's life, assuming the role of Saskia in all but name. Although there are no documented likenesses of Hendrickje, there are a number of paintings and drawings, but curiously no etchings, which show a model, who, it is generally agreed, must represent her. One of the first – the spurious signature and date can be ignored – must be the painting [Fig. 23], which shows the model seated three-quarter length, following a format which Rembrandt had employed for a number

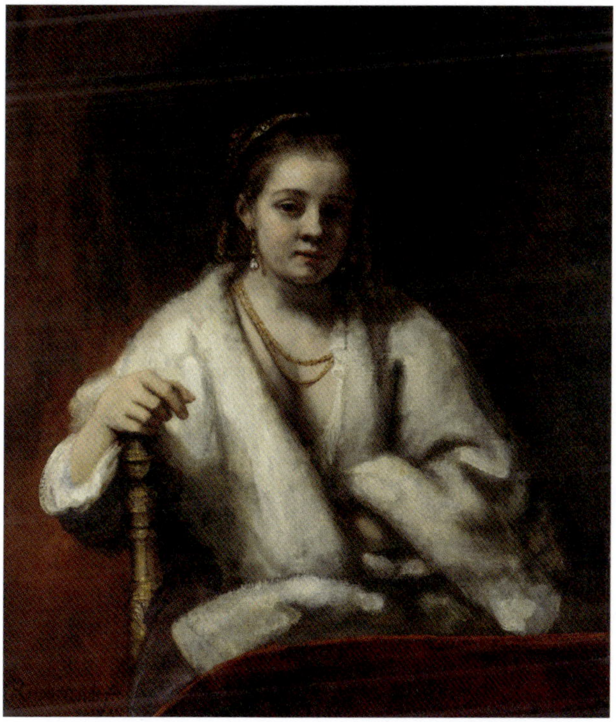

23. *Hendrickje Stoffels with a Fur Wrap. c.*1652. Canvas. 103.3 × 86.5 cm. National Gallery, London.

of etched portraits dating from the later 1640s. The picture's status is uncertain. Was it intended as a likeness of Hendrickje or solely as an exercise in painting? If the former, it can probably, with its relaxed atmosphere and such details as her striking decolletage, be regarded as an informal portrait, whether to be kept for sentimental reasons or offered for sale remains unknown. X-rays demonstrate that during the course of execution Rembrandt made a fundamental change to the pose. To begin with he painted Hendrickje with her arms folded and her hands clasped together on her lap. He then scrubbed out this area with vigorous brush strokes in lead-white and introduced, on the left, the arm of the chair on the top of which her right arm now rests, while her left hand is tucked into her wrap. With the marked triangular outline of her body, given substance by the blocked-in folds of her wrap, the change had the effect of spreading out the figure across the canvas. She now sits, behind a table with its red cloth creating depth, harmoniously fitting into the space allotted to her.

At first glance it might seem that the connoisseur of wrinkled skin found the face of his new mistress too smooth for interest, but on closer inspection one can see how softly he has modelled the cheeks, touched with pink. The slightly open mouth with its full lips is on the edge of a smile; the brown eyes are warm and engaging. She has a gold band in her golden hair and wears pearl-drop earrings and double-chain gold necklace. Her white fur wrap adds to the overall decorativeness of her quietly opulent appearance. It is not too subjective to say that a palpable bond exists between model and painter. It is a good example of what Rembrandt's contemporaries called painting in a rough manner, in which the brushstrokes are clearly visible and outlines are blurred, and became an important feature of Rembrandt later technique.

With its loosely brushed in background and summary modelling of her wrap, the canvas might be regarded as unfinished but before deciding whether that is the case, one should bear in mind Arnold Houbraken's comment that, according to Rembrandt, 'a work is finished when a master has achieved his intention in it'.[7] He might have felt that he had achieved all he wanted to in this intensely intimate picture as it stands.

Inspiration for this manner of painting undoubtedly came from Titian, the great sixteenth-century Venetian artist, whose technique cast a spell not only over Rembrandt but also over such major figures as Rubens, Van

Dyck and Velazquez in the seventeenth century. Giorgio Vasari, in his *Lives of the Painters*, paraphrased by Karel van Mander, said that Titian painted 'in patches of colour, with the result that they cannot be viewed from nearby, but appear perfect from a distance'.[8] Yet with the application of a wide variety of glazes, Titian's technique was much more complex than this simple description would have one believe. Rembrandt, obliquely referring in his own idiosyncratic way to the similar effects he learnt to obtain in his own paintings, is supposed to have told a would-be admirer not to go too close to the picture because the smell of the colours might bother him.

In 1654, in one of the marvels of Rembrandt's painting technique, he produced another work, for which, it is generally recognised, Hendrickje served as the model [Fig. 24]. In a wild woodland setting, it depicts her with a smile on her face looking down as she wades in a pool. Much of her

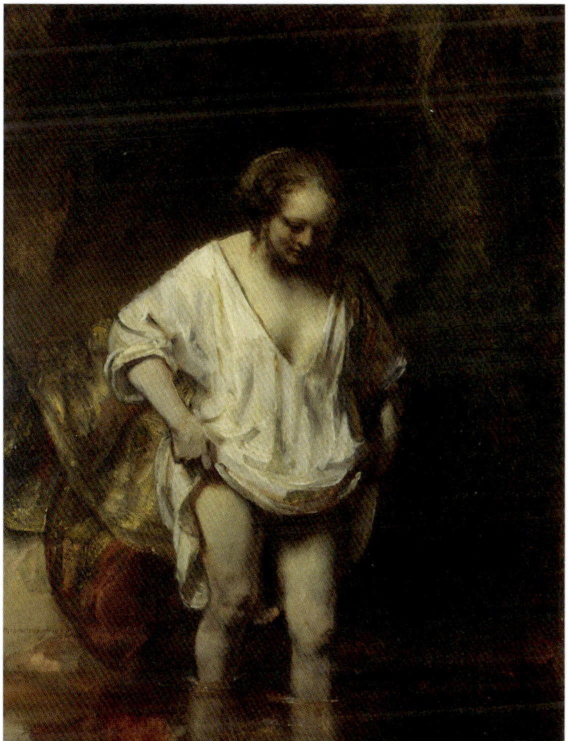

24. *Hendrickje Stoffels Wading in a Pool.* 1654. Panel. 61.8 × 47 cm. National Gallery, London.

body is exposed both above and below, as she lifts up her white shift. She might or might not be pregnant. During much of that year Hendrickje was pregnant with their illegitimate daughter Cornelia and, shortly before the birth, she was condemned by her church as living with the painter 'like a whore'.[9] Once again it is an enigmatic work. The subject, if it had one, is elusive, although it has been suggested that a Biblical heroine, such as Susanna or Bathsheba. or a classical figure such as the nymph Callisto, might have been intended. The presence of a rich red robe lying on the rocky bank, which presumably she has just discarded before entering the water, gives support to such an identification, but there is no clinching evidence. Otherwise one has to conclude it is a genre subject, offering an excuse for a brilliant display of painting, paying a personal tribute to his beloved companion.

Painted on panel, it is unusually small for Rembrandt's standard picture size, and might be thought to have been a preparatory sketch for a now lost or never executed canvas. But, with a very few exceptions in the earlier part of his career, it was not part of Rembrandt's practice to make preparatory sketches for paintings; work was carried out directly on the panel or canvas. Moreover, it is signed and dated, which would suggest that he regarded it as a finished work in own right. Yet what the panel unquestionably does is to display Rembrandt's mastery with the paintbrush, at work here over the often visible ground, and at the same time creating a world of half-lights and shadows. It gives the impression of being executed at speed, but technical evidence exists that he painted it by stages, allowing one area of paint to dry before adding another. Immediately catching the eye is the brilliantly free execution of the white shift with a virtuoso display of bold, open strokes, for all their seeming spontaneity carefully calculated in their placing one beside another. They serve to set up a contrast with the soft modelling of her body. The reflection of her legs and the rock bank in the water below gives an added luminosity to the scene, while the red and gold garments on the bank glow as they catch the light. Vegetation can vaguely be made out beyond. Although the background, painted warm brown, is not completed, there is a suggestion of a mysterious atmosphere enveloping the whole figure. If the panel is unfinished by conventional standards, one can understand why the painter left it so. A work of infinite subtlety, both of subject and

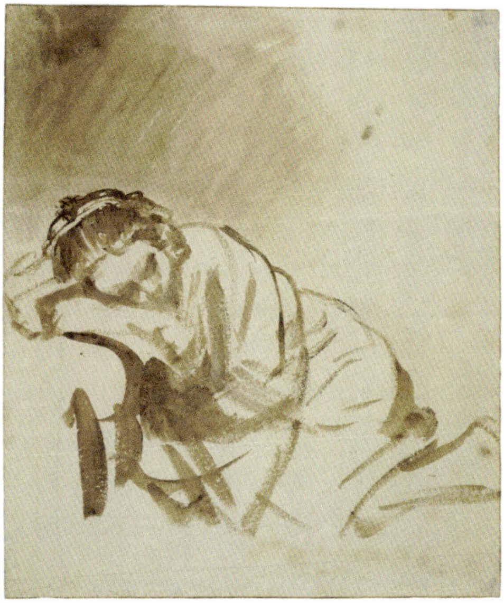

25. *Young Woman Sleeping. c.*1654.
Brush in brown ink, heightened with white.
British Museum, London.

technique, it is the painting by Rembrandt I would, were I so fortunate, most like to have hanging over my mantelpiece.

If Hendrickje Stoffels can be identified as the model for the drawing of a *Young Woman Sleeping* [Fig. 25], which seems highly probable – her appearance is very similar to the young woman in the previous painting – then she can be said to have inspired some of his most memorable works as far as technique is concerned. Here the virtuosity lies in the exercise of drawing with wash without any pen lines. Apart from two landscapes, the study is unique in Rembrandt's *œuvre*. Such is its freedom of execution, it is a commonplace to compare it with Japanese scroll painting. A young woman is lying asleep, resting her head on her right arm; the head with its braided hair is relatively carefully drawn. Otherwise the outline of her body is laid in with broad strokes, suggesting rather than carefully defining her form. Some of the brushstrokes seem quite arbitrary, unrelated to any particular detail, but nevertheless overall intensely meaningful. Despite the impressionistic effect of the work, it is a thoughtfully conceived study, with a section of blank paper establishing the foreground and an area of wash the background, so that the figure sits harmoniously in space. Knowing how calculating the artist could be in the placing of brushstrokes, as seen in the painting of the woman's shift in the previously discussed work, the apparent speed of execution may be deceptive and it is not a work which was hurriedly dashed off in a moment of creativity. Every stroke was carefully considered.

The care of Saskia's and Rembrandt's son Titus fell after her death to at first, Geertje Dircx and then, after her departure from the household, to Hendrickje Stoffels. It would seem that Titus had a happy upbringing with both women. Geertje Dircx made him the beneficiary of her will, and Hendrickje Stoffels later joined with him to form a company to trade in Rembrandt's art. As with Hendrickje, there are no documented portraits, and his likeness can only be inferred from the fairly frequent appearance in painting, drawing and etching of the same model in Rembrandt's later work.

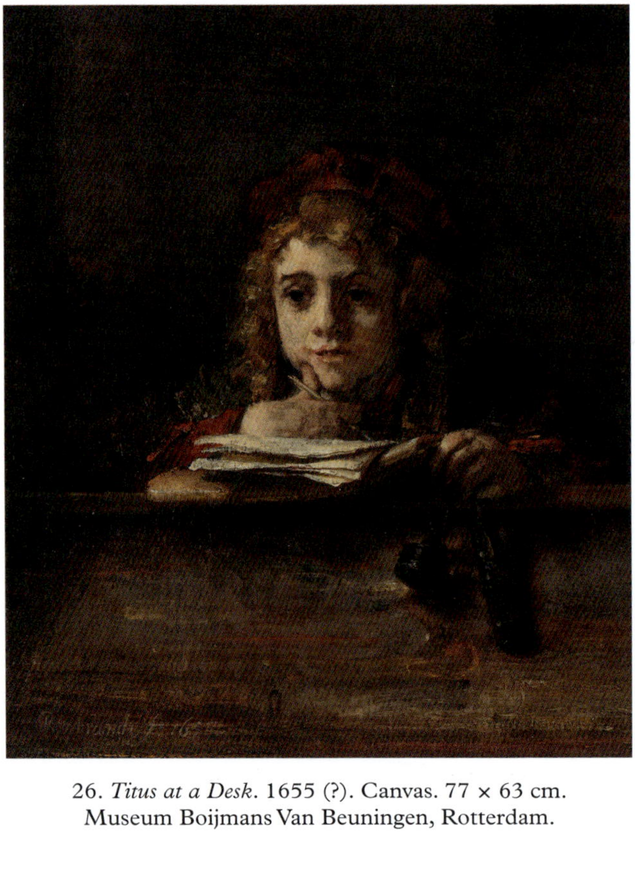

26. *Titus at a Desk*. 1655 (?). Canvas. 77 × 63 cm.
Museum Boijmans Van Beuningen, Rotterdam.

In a painting [Fig. 26], either signed or inscribed with the date 1655, Titus is seen sitting at his desk. The beret he is wearing not only became a distinguishing mark of the artist but was adopted by his pupils who portrayed themselves in similar headgear. Although it has been suggested that Titus is painting, it is usually accepted that he is in fact writing. Both his flowing curls, the wide-open eyes and the warm flesh tones of the face are a particular feature of this touching image of a fourteen-year-old. With his pen held between his forefinger and his thumb, the latter supporting his cheek, he has stopped writing in a moment of introspection as he looks up and out into space. It is to be noted that he is not looking directly at the spectator but over his or her shoulder, which gives an air of detachment to the study. Brought up close to the figure, the spectator has the sense that he or she is a voyeur at this intimate moment of a small boy engaged in his daily scholastic activities. Papers are loosely laid out in front of him – we are left to guess what was written on them – and from his left hand a portable pen and ink case dangles down the right side of the desk.

The viewpoint in the picture is low, the effect of which is enhanced by the height of the front of the desk, which takes up over a third the height of the canvas. On top of the desk, which fills the whole width of the canvas, the figure sits in a simple triangular shape in the centre of the canvas, emerging in a strong raking top light from the shadows of the indeterminate background. Colour basically consists of various shades of brown but enriched with small areas of crimson used for his cap and part of his sleeve. Paint is applied richly and freely, and we can see an early use of the palette knife in addition to the brush. In depicting the different tones of the rough, varied surface of the front of the desk, a purely decorative feature in the composition, Rembrandt offers a virtuoso display of brushwork.

A drawing [Fig. 27], generally regarded as a study of Titus and executed a few years later, shows him as a young man, probably twenty years in age. Unlike the deflected gaze in the previous work, the sitter looks very directly at the spectator. Seen three-quarter length standing in half-profile, he wears a large cap with ear-flaps, a long cloak or coat with wide turned-back sleeves, and holds a flower in his right hand. What if any the significance of the last item is remains unclear. If an allusion

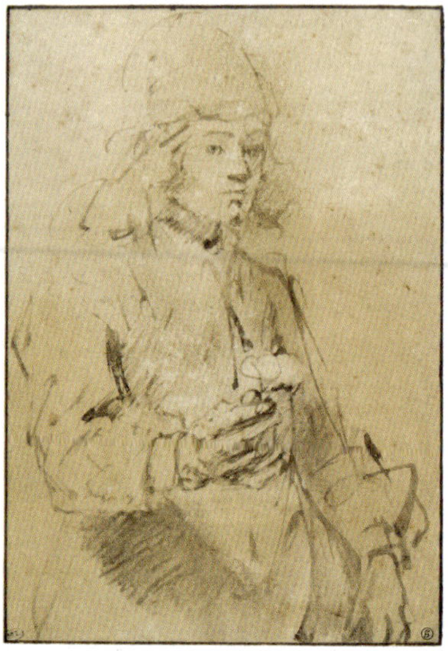

27. *Titus Standing Holding a Flower.*
*c.*1658. Pen and brown ink with
brown wash. 17.5 × 11.8 cm.
Musée du Louvre, Paris.

to marriage, as has been suggested, the drawing would, unconvincingly, have to be dated nearly ten years later, when in 1668 Titus wed Magdalena van Loo. Executed with the soft touch of the reed pen, the drawing is mainly confined to simple, bold outlines, occasionally embellished with hatching and wash to create areas of transparent shadows. For such a summarily executed drawing, it is remarkable how much sense of personality is conveyed.

As a result of Rembrandt's near bankruptcy in 1656, he moved two years later from his grand house near the centre of Amsterdam to the more impoverished district of the Jordaan in the north-west of the city. There with Titus, Hendrickje and their daughter, Cornelia he lived in a rented house, where he remained for the last eleven years of his life. To protect Rembrandt financial interests, Titus and Hendrickje formed a company, overseeing the sale of his paintings and etchings. In effect the artist became their employee. Although he continued to receive important commissions, money was in short supply and times were hard. But whereas Rembrandt had the nirvana of his work, Hendrickje was faced with the realities of daily life. Nowhere does one feel her cares more

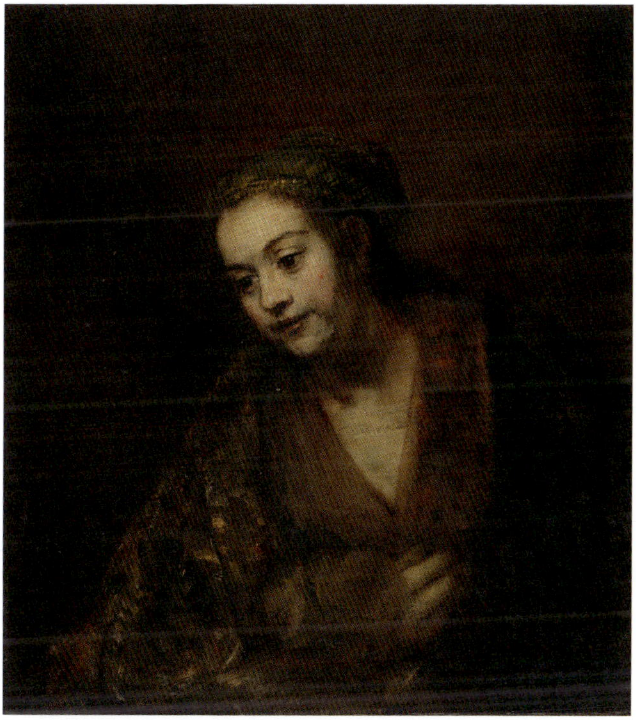

28. *Hendrickje Stoffels*. *c.*1660. Canvas. 78.4 × 68.9 cm.
Metropolitan Museum of Art, New York.

vividly than in the moving but unfortunately poorly-preserved portrait he made of her around 1660 [Fig. 28]. (The genuineness of the signature and date of 1660 have been disputed) Her wide-open lustrous eyes create an effect of pathos, as she leans forward looking down with her right hand held across her body, seemingly in a gesture of modesty. The gentle bending-forward of the body suggests devotion and submission. She is informally but richly dressed in a fur-trimmed mantle over a thin undergarment. Painted with great freedom – the picture is probably unfinished – the red and yellow touches on her warm brown-coloured garments create a glow throughout the canvas, which highlights the pallor of her softly modelled face. Seen against an indeterminate dark background, it is a work of great formal simplicity.

Although it has been wrongly paired with a self-portrait of the artist, there is no evidence that it was intended to be more than a work standing on its own. More open to question is whether it was intended as an image of his common-law wife, or a *tronie*, or whether she was serving as the model for a specific subject, such as the *Penitent Magdalen*. (The possible influence of pictures of courtesans painted by such Venetian artists as Titian and Palma Vecchio, can surely be no more than in the way it is presented.) As so often, Rembrandt in his late work, omitting symbols or identifying objects or actions, leaves us guessing as to his precise intention. Whatever the answer, it is probably the last painting he made of Hendrickje, who died shortly afterwards in 1663, probably a victim of the plague.

Ten years after is his last etched *Self-portrait* (see Fig. 20), Rembrandt made another print, once again showing himself at work on an etching plate [Fig. 29]. Smaller in size and in a narrow upright format, it is a more modest affair. Since only two impressions are known, one can assume that the artist found it unsatisfactory and quickly abandoned it, and yet it is a record of what he was concerned with at the time. In this later work he concentrates on the large head, leaving the bust and hands, smaller in proportion to the head, only lightly indicated. By cutting the sides of the body, the dominance of the head is all the greater. Wearing a flat cap

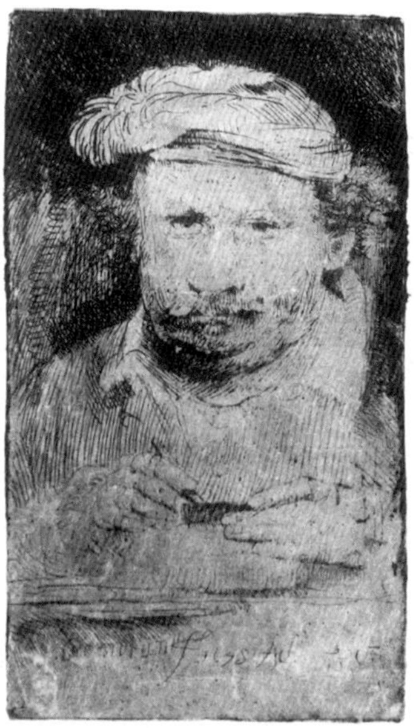

29. *Self-portrait*. 1658.
Etching. 11.4 × 6.8 cm.
Albertina, Vienna.

on his head, Rembrandt looks directly out, with black piercing eyes. The print lacks an architectural background and depends on the plain dark shading to act as a foil to the head. Drawn with loose strokes, with some parallel hatching, the artist may well have intended to complete it in drypoint and engraving, as he was accustomed to do in his later etchings. Although left unfinished, it makes in its untidy state a forceful impression. The perfectionist in Rembrandt may have felt it was beyond repair.

Self-portraiture must rank as one of the most intimate acts of painting, yet the results can be anything but, as some of Rembrandt's late self-portraits demonstrate. The *Self-portrait with Two Circles* [Fig. 30] was one of the grandest and largest he ever produced, but may be included here since he shows himself in his studio engaged in painting. In essence

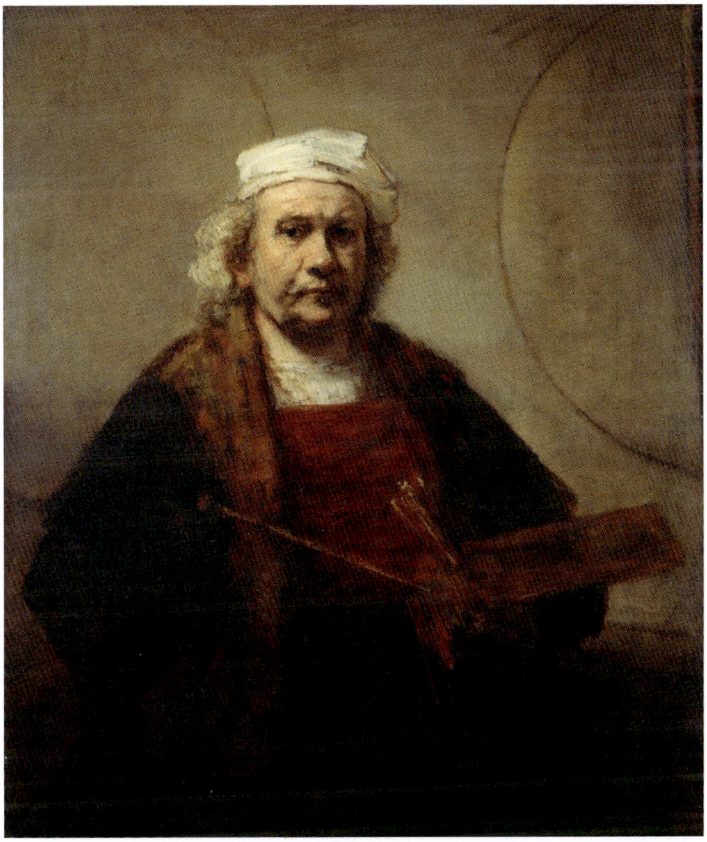

30. *Self-portrait with Two Circles*. *c.*1665/9. Canvas. 114.3 × 94 cm. Kenwood House, London.

it is a reprise of the early *Self-portrait in his Studio* (see Fig. 5] painted over forty years earlier. The contrast between the two works is startling. In the earlier diminutive picture by comparison Rembrandt was a small figure placed at the back of the room; here, seen full frontal with his body forming a triangular design, he stands assertively in the foreground, with only a short space between him and the background, which unusually is lit outlining the silhouette of his body. The wall itself is decorated with two mysterious circles. In his left hand he holds his brushes, palette and maulstick, all painted very summarily, nowhere more so than in the case of the hand holding the palette, which is suggested but not described. A small section of his easel can just be made out on the right. He portrays himself in a black gown with brown facings over a red *borstlap*, or placket, with a pleated white shirt next to the skin, both of which are common to the sixteenth rather than the seventeenth century. They reveal once again the artist's taste for archaizing costume. In decorating the edge of the shirt, Rembrandt uses the end of the brush or some sharp object to incise the pattern into the wet paint, a feature found in other late works. The cap or beret seen in earlier works is here exchanged for a white linen cap, which catches the light and gives prominence to the head, which is further framed by the white shirt below. A gold chain around his neck is tucked into his shirt front, probably suggesting some honour he had received. Even by the standards of Rembrandt's late works, the brush-strokes, with their rich impasto, are quite masterly in their freedom and power to suggest, as can be seen, for example, in the white linen cap on his head. Above all the face, framed by a rich display of curly grey hair, is modelled with broad open strokes which contribute to that sense of overpowering personality, which must have put fear into any unwanted visitor. But at the same time as painting in the rough manner, he used small flecks of the brush to build up his portrayal of the skin. It was a subtle combination of two manners of painting. Although we should probably regard the painting as unfinished – as we have seen before, what is finished or unfinished in late Rembrandt is an unanswerable question – both the impact it makes on the spectator and the manner of presentation are unlike any other self-portrait he produced.

But the final result as we know it was not achieved without substantial modification. An X-radiograph reveals that he originally showed himself in the act of painting, with his left hand holding a brush and raised to the canvas, while his right hand held his other brushes and maulstick. Rembrandt may have been prompted to make this fundamental change from a portrait of the artist in the act of painting to a less specific one of the artist in the studio by the fact, reflecting what he saw in the mirror, he had showed himself, a right-handed person, painting with his left hand. With his experience of self-portraiture, it is curious that he should have made this mistake, that is if he regarded it as such. At the same time he altered the original pose turned slightly to the right to a more frontal position, which served to emphasise the triangular shape of his body.

One unusual feature of the painting is the introduction of two large circles in the background which has led to extensive interpretation of their meaning. Despite such suggestions that they reflect the circles appearing on world maps which were often hung on domestic walls, they have never been convincingly explained. If they have some theoretical meaning as has been proposed, it would be unusual for Rembrandt. Whatever the answer, they undoubtedly serve an aesthetic function by stressing the width of the composition, thereby giving a more pronounced structure to this monumental image of the artist in his studio.

Rembrandt made several more self-portraits, including two in the year of his death, but none match the majesty of the painting just discussed.

His last years were increasingly solitary. As has been said, Hendrickje died in 1663, to be followed by Titus in 1668, just six months after his marriage, leaving Rembrandt alone with his young daughter, Cornelia for the last year of his life. Finally on 4 October he dies from unknown causes and is buried four days later in a rented grave in the Westerkerk.

CHAPTER 2

Portraits *in situ*

PORTRAITS PLAYED a major part in Rembrandt's career, establishing him as a leading artist in Amsterdam in the early 1630s. Apart from a gap of about ten years following, either specifically or coincidentally, Saskia's death in 1642, they continued to play a role in his work up to his last days. How far he regarded them primarily as a source of income or a fount of artistic satisfaction, or a combination of both, is an open question, and probably varied during the course of time. Most of his portraits are straightforward and needless to say penetrating images set against a plain background, sometimes with a generalised gesture with one or more hands. But there are a number, particularly amongst his etchings, to which he gave a more personal and intimate touch, either by portraying them in a setting or depicting them engaged in some meaningful action. It is these more unusual portraits to which this chapter is devoted.

In 1633, very early after his move to Amsterdam, Rembrandt was commissioned to paint an unusually large double portrait of *Jan Rijksen and his Wife, Griet Jans* [Fig. 31], a work popularly known as 'The Shipbuilder and his Wife'. Rijksen, shown here at the age of seventy-two, was the master shipbuilder of the East India Company, in which he was also a shareholder. His wealth is revealed by the fact that he was the highest rated tax-payer on the Rapenburg, where he lived in Amsterdam. His wife, date of birth unknown, also came from a family of shipbuilders. The old-fashioned dress worn by the couple reflects the custom of the elderly in the seventeenth century to continue to dress in the fashion of their youth. He wears a doublet with a multi-layered plain linen ruff; she wears a black gown trimmed with brown fur with padded coils at the shoulder, a black skirt and a black apron with a brown leather purse. In the dark enclosed interior of his panelled study he is at work at his desk, on which are littered various papers with MS technical notes and drawings alluding to his profession. Holding a pair of compasses in his right hand, he

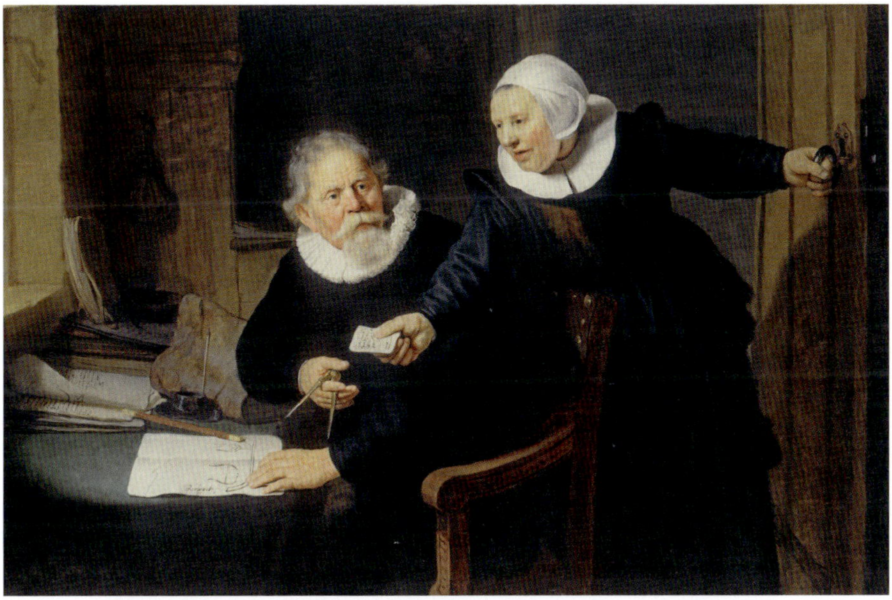

31. *Jan Rijksen and his Wife, Griet Jans*. 1633. Canvas. 111 × 166 cm.
H.M. The Queen, London.

has just drawn the keel of a ship and two profiles of a hull on the sheet of paper immediately in front of him. She, mouth partly open suggesting she is speaking, bursts into the room with her left hand still clutching the door handle, and delivers a letter addressed to him. She holds a bunch of keys, signifying her role as mistress of the household, which is suspended from her belt.

Instead of adopting the conventional arrangement of placing the sitters side-by-side. Rembrandt came up with the nearly novel solution of portraying his sitters in the act of daily life, set in a fully-described domestic interior. It is, in fact, the most dramatic representation of a couple in his painted *œuvre*. One moment his wife is there, the next moment, if the vexed look on his face at being interrupted is anything to go by, she will soon be gone. The motif of handing over a letter to a recipient had been used earlier when, in 1627, the fashionable Amsterdam portrait painter, Thomas de Keyser (1596/7–1667), had employed it for the small *Portrait of Constantijn Huygens (1596–1687) and his (?) Clerk* [Fig. 32]. If Rembrandt ever went to The Hague, he could well have seen it hanging in the house of his admirer and patron, already mentioned in the first chapter.

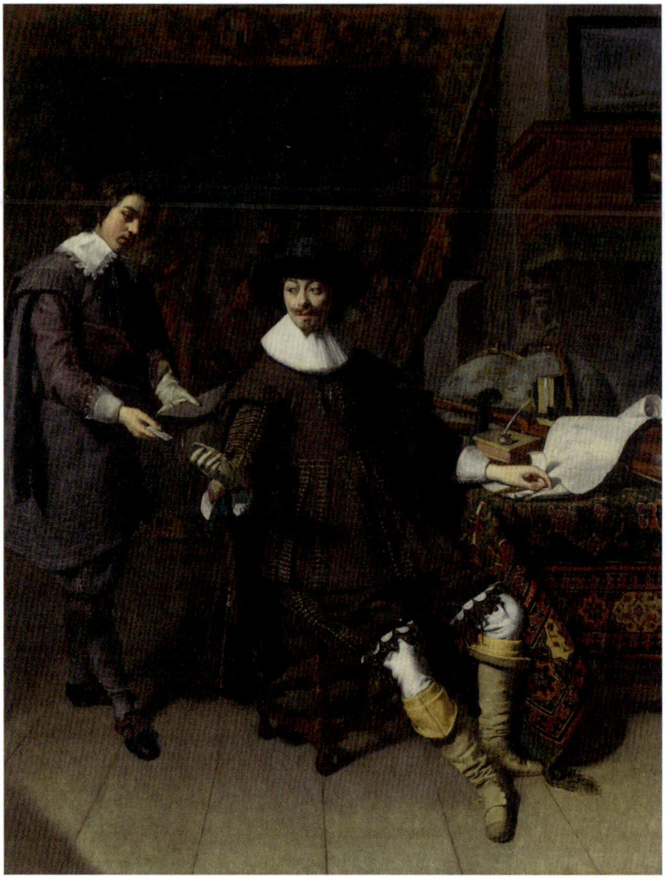

32. Thomas de Keyser, *Constantijn Huygens and his (?) Clerk*. 1627. Panel. 92.4 × 69.3 cm. National Gallery, London.

Apart from the marked difference in scale between the two portraits, a comparison with De Keyser's static image, clearly reveals how Rembrandt introduced a sense of vitality. In one picture the sitters are caught in a frozen pose set up for the painter, in the other the artist is, as it were, looking through the keyhole and catching the sitters, unaware of being observed, in a moment of fleeting action.

Rembrandt's portrait is very skilfully composed to suggest both setting and action, although one should remember it has been cut down a little at the top. Light floods in from the window on the left, throwing just enough illumination to make out the clearly defined space of the panelled interior bathed in mysterious shadow, and casting Rijksen's head half in full light and half in shadow while falling full on his wife's face. The artist subtly draws our attention to the sheet of drawings on the desk by virtue of an imaginary diagonal line starting on the right with her hand holding the latch and continuing with her right hand holding the letter, his raised right hand ready to receive it, and finally his left hand resting on the highlighted MS. In this simple arrangement, the whole of the story of this mini-drama is encompassed. Much of the painting is broadly executed, appropriate for viewing at a distance, but when it comes to the heads and hands, they are beautifully modelled with clearly visible finely applied brushstrokes. X-rays demonstrate how he made small changes, such as to the widths of his ruff and her collars, reducing one and increasing the other, as he worked on the canvas. Both heads, with their heightened colouring and vivid expressions, are masterpieces of portraiture and explain why Rembrandt's career as a portrait painter took off so quickly. It can be described as a 'one-off' in his *œuvre*, and when he repeated the exercise of a double portrait (see below) nearly a decade later, he came up with a different method of uniting the couple.

In 1635 Rembrandt etched the portrait of Jan Uytenbogaert (1557–1644) [Fig. 33], the preacher, who had been a greatly influential figure in Dutch history both as a leading light in the Armenian Remonstrant church and as a tutor to young Prince Frederick Henry, as well as filling other significant roles. As a result of religious wars between his church and the Calvinists, he was, as a strong advocate of religious tolerance, exiled for a number of years. On his return he whiled away his final years as a preacher in his church, eventually able to live in his old house in The Hague. It was at this period of his life that Rembrandt portrayed him at the age of seventy-eight. Two years earlier he had painted a three-quarter length portrait (Rijksmuseum, Amsterdam), in which it can be observed that the head is similar to that in the etching, even down to such details as the wisps of hair escaping from under his cap. Apart from a few small details, the main difference is that the sad look on Uytenbogaert's face in the painting has been replaced with a more abstracted expression, suggesting that the sitter, his left hand holding the volume in front of him, has been interrupted in the course of reading. This is a subtle way of suggesting a living portrait. It was surely intended as an official image with a panegyric in Latin celebrating the sitter's return from exile by the famous lawyer, Hugo Grotius, to be inscribed later in the development of the print at the bottom of the plate. The portrait, as opposed to the plate, is set in an oval, a popular shape in Dutch portraits at the time. To provide a suitable environment, Rembrandt chose to display him in his study, the traditional setting for the learned.

Wearing an old fashioned ruff and a fur-trimmed gown, Uytenbogaert is shown seated in scholarly calm at his desk, covered with open volumes, and looking out at the spectator. A skull-cap associated with a divine or scholar is on his head. Rembrandt took considerable trouble to suggest the different textures of the beard, the collar and the fur edging to the gown, producing a finely-worked print. It is a work in which we can watch the artist developing his thoughts as he proceeded through no less than five working states before he reached his goal. Apart from introducing a curtain on the left and some books resting on a shelf on the right, he at first (see Fig. 33) left the background empty apart from

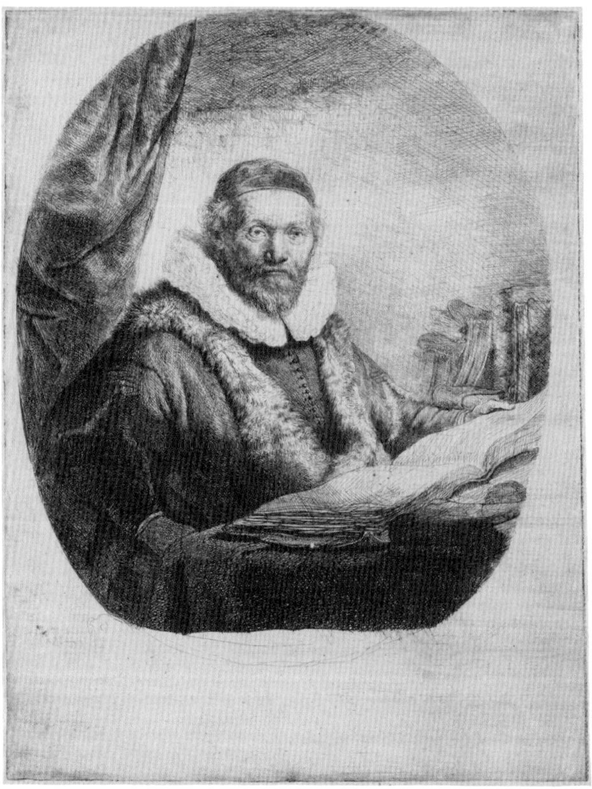

33. *The Remonstrant Preacher, Jan Uytenbogaert.* 1635. Etching. 24.9 × 18.5 cm. Rijksmuseum, Amsterdam.

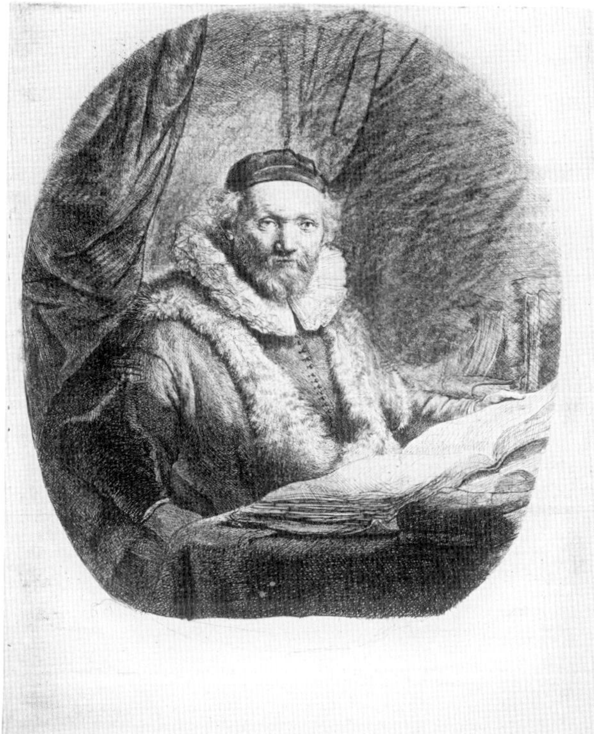

34. *The Remonstrant Preacher, Jan Uytenbogaert.* 1635. Etching and black chalk. 25 × 18.7 cm. British Museum, London.

some light shading. In the second state he only made a small change to the collar. But on one impression, illustrated here, [Fig. 34], he showed where his thoughts were leading him, by shading the background with black chalk. Whereas previously the sitter was silhouetted against a lightly shaded wall, he now emerges from the darker ground. When he came to finish the plate [Fig. 35], he filled the background with a large column on the left and another curtain on the right, divided by a dark archway. (It has been suggested that the inclusion of the first item may refer to the praise traditionally accorded to the theologian as a 'pillar of the church'.) The books sitting on the shelf, obvious references to learning, are rendered much more prominently. And, as a finishing touch, he added, in an amateurish script, the panegyric by Grotius in the space left empty for it at the bottom, trimming the actual copper plate to an octagonal shape. By considerable reworking with the combination of drypoint and the engraver's burin as well as etching, he finally attained the high finish of a monochrome painting.

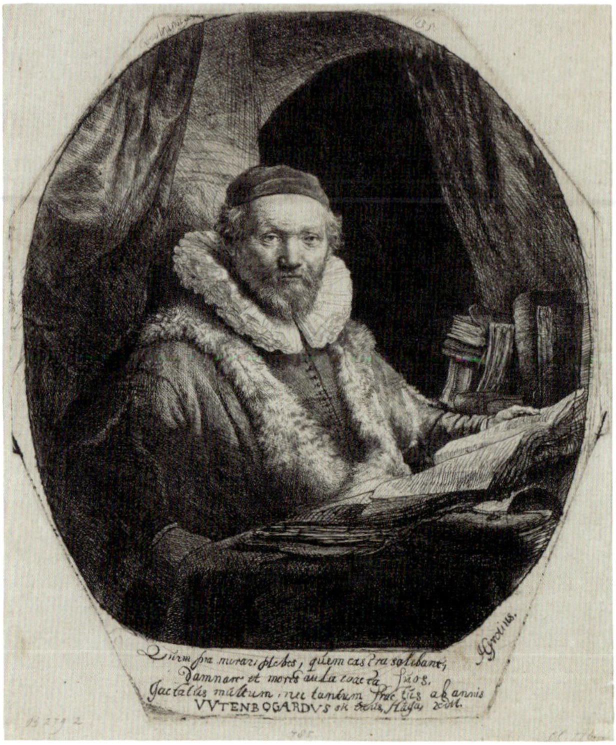

35. *The Remonstrant Preacher, Jan Uytenbogaert*. 1635. Etching. 22.4 × 18.6 cm. Rijksmuseum, Amsterdam.

Whereas the previous work was a conventional image of a divine in his study, the etching of his cousin, also called Jan Uytenbogaert (1608–1680), the Receiver-General, often known as *The Goldweigher* [Fig. 36], dated 1639, was unique in Rembrandt's etched *œuvre* by treating a portrait as a genre scene. In this instance one can adduce a personal reason for the existence of the portrait. In the 1630s Rembrandt had been engaged in painting a Passion series for the Stadholder, Frederick Henry, two of which had been finished and, as had happened to many artists working for a princely collector, he was endlessly waiting for payment. In Rembrandt's case, the need was pressing since he had just made a down payment on his new house in the St Anthonis-Breestraat. It is at this point that Jan Uytenbogaert, who was a keen collector of prints amongst other things and who had probably known Rembrandt since their Leiden days, enters the story. Only in the previous year to the portrait, Uytenbogaert had assumed the important position of 'Collector of national taxes'. In a letter to Constantijn Huygens he offered to use his good offices

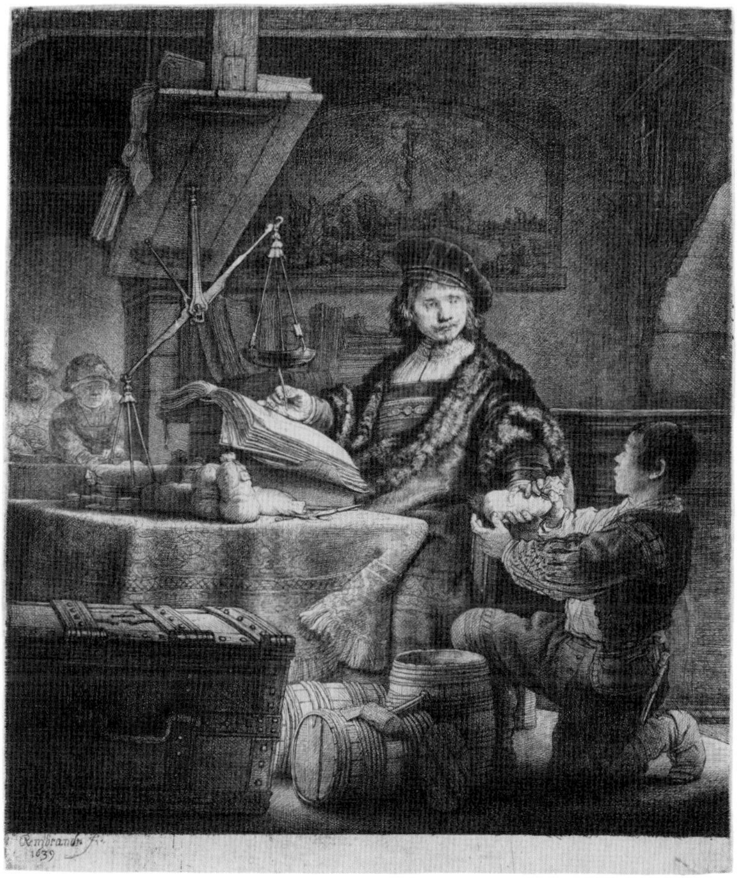

36. *Jan Uytenbogaert (The Goldweigher)*. 1639. Etching and drypoint. 24.8 × 20.5 cm. Rijksmuseum, Amsterdam.

to facilitate the payment to Rembrandt and subsequently acted as an intermediary with Frederick Henry's Treasurer. It may very well be, not for the last time, that the print was made as a token of friendship and gratitude.

One advantage of turning the portrait into a genre scene meant that Rembrandt could largely work on the plate without the sitter in front of him. And so it proved. Rembrandt completed the subject in the first state [Fig. 37], except for leaving the small but important matter of the face, which was only very lightly sketched in. The face was then worked up in the second state which saw the completion of the plate. In a closed interior with no source of light, Uytenbogaert is seated at his desk about to

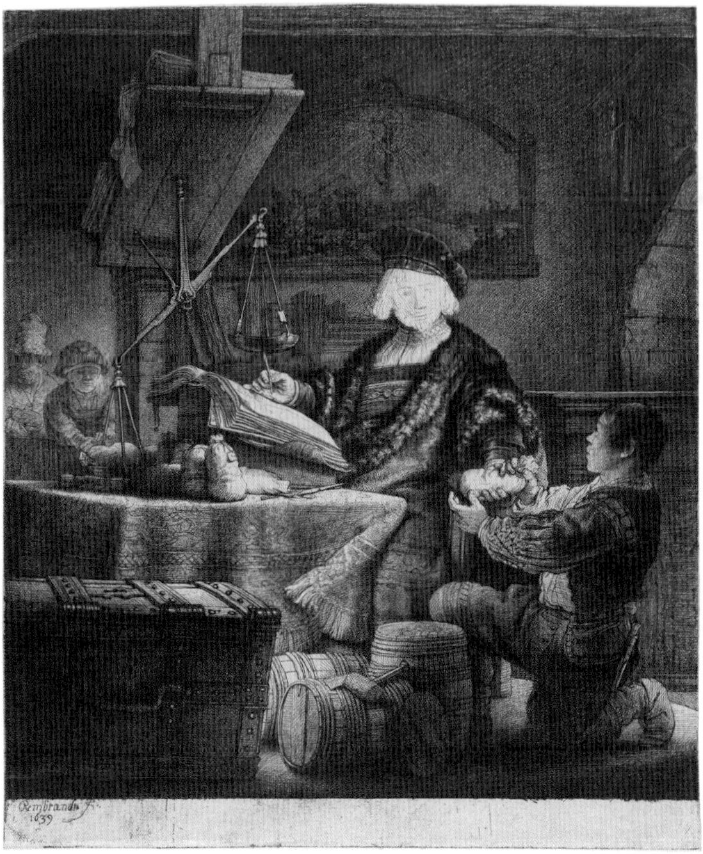

37. *Jan Uytenbogaert (The Goldweigher)*. 1639. Counterproof, etching and drypoint and black chalk. 25 × 20.4 cm. Rijksmuseum, Amsterdam.

write in a large volume supported on a stand before him. A large pair of scales and numerous money bags rest on the table. With his left hand he hands a bag of money to a kneeling servant at his side, while seen through a door in the left-hand background a woman, accompanied by a man, places a bag of money on the scales. We are presented with a crowded scene; an elaborate chest and three barrels fill the foreground, while books on a shelf and a painting of *Moses and the Brazen Serpent* hanging on the wall complete the right background. It is most unlikely that we see Uyenbogaert engaged in daily activity. The allegorical character of the print was acknowledged in the eighteenth century, when the print became known as *The Goldweigher*. The subject recalls sixteenth-century paintings of money changers by such artists as Quinten Massys and Martinus van Reymerswaele and to underline this association with the past the sitter is shown wearing sixteenth-century costume. The idea of portraying him thus may well have come from the sitter who was a great admirer of sixteenth-century art. The high degree of finish employed in creating this lively interior scene recalls his style of etching from the middle years of the decade, such as in the portrait of the other Jan Uytenbogaert previously discussed, but there is one new very prominent technical feature. The rich accents of burr created by the extensive use of drypoint vividly suggest the texture of his fur coat.

After having painted two earlier full-length male portraits, one in a double portrait and the other as one of a pair, Rembrandt returned to this unusual format for Dutch portraiture in 1639 with one probably representing *Andries de Graeff* [Fig. 38]. The two previous sitters were shown standing firmly on their feet but in this instance the man is depicted leaning slightly awkwardly on a plinth, thereby subverting the dignity of the classical contraposto which he adopts. Portraits of men resting a hand or an arm on a plinth are not uncommon in Dutch and Flemish portraiture, but the distinction to be made here is that the sitter is putting part of the weight of his body on the plinth. The man, clearly someone of social standing, wears a black hat on his head and is dressed sombrely but richly in a black silk suit, with the by now fashionable flat white linen collar standing out. He is standing either on his porch or just inside the house, which is a building of some grandeur. This basically formal portrait has been transformed by the nonchalant pose into the art of the casual, which reflects contemporary taste in Dutch portraiture. This would also explain the puzzling detail of the glove lying on the ground, which has sometimes been interpreted as a glove thrown down in a challenge. It can have nothing to do with matrimony since de Graeff never married.

The identity of the sitter is unrecorded, but it is now generally believed to portray a certain Andries de Graeff (1611–1679), who would have been twenty-eight at the time of the portrait. He came from a wealthy family of Amsterdam regents. The portrait may have played a role in the artist receiving the commission for *The Night Watch*, since de Graeff was the brother-in-law of Frans Banning Cocq, whose militia company is the subject of the famous group. The relationship between artist and sitter

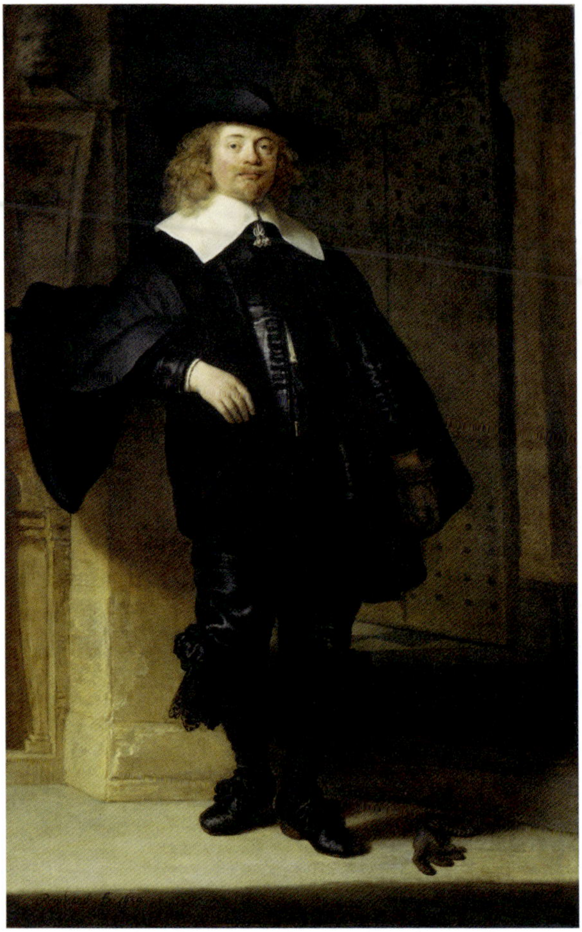

38. *Andries de Graeff.* 1639. Canvas. 199 × 113.4 cm. Gemäldegalerie alter Meister, Museumlandschaft Hessen, Kassel.

did not end well. Twenty years later de Graeff lost a court case for non-payment to Rembrandt for a picture, subject unspecified. From other court cases in which he became involved, it is evident that Rembrandt could stand up for his rights, such as happened with the patron who disputed the likeness in a commissioned portrait only to be met with the artist's refusal to change it until he had been paid in full.

Two years later Rembrandt painted a double portrait of *Cornelis Claesz. Anslo (1592–1646) and his Wife Aeltje Schouten (d. 1657)* [Fig. 39]. The husband was a wealthy trader in cloth who also served as a renowned

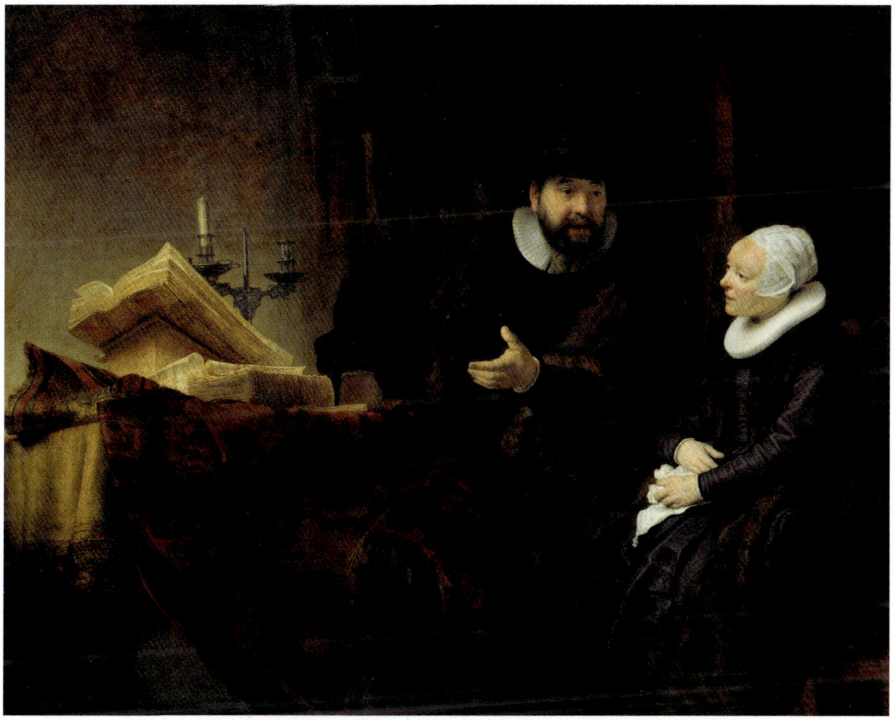

39. *Cornelis Claesz. Anslo and his Wife, Aeltje Schouten.* 1641. Canvas. 176 × 210 cm. Gemäldegalerie, Staatliche Museen zu Berlin.

Mennonite preacher in the more liberal Waterland community, with whose members Rembrandt had numerous dealings. In 1615 Anslo had set up an almshouse in Amsterdam for destitute older women. In the same year as the painting Rembrandt etched a half-length portrait of Anslo seated at his desk. As in the case of the latter, which was also preceded by a signed and dated drawing (British Museum, London), the gestation of the picture went back to the previous year when he made an impressive drawing of Anslo full-length [Fig. 40], sitting on the edge of an arm chair, and sharply turning his head to the left with his left arm outstretched in an eloquent gesture; he is seated beside a table with presumably a copy of the Bible, the source of truth to the Mennonites, propped up on a stand. Infrequently for a drawing, it is a highly-finished work unusually executed in a combination of techniques; over a lay-in of red chalk, the artist worked in pen and brown and black ink, finally heightening and correcting with white bodycolour. Far more fully

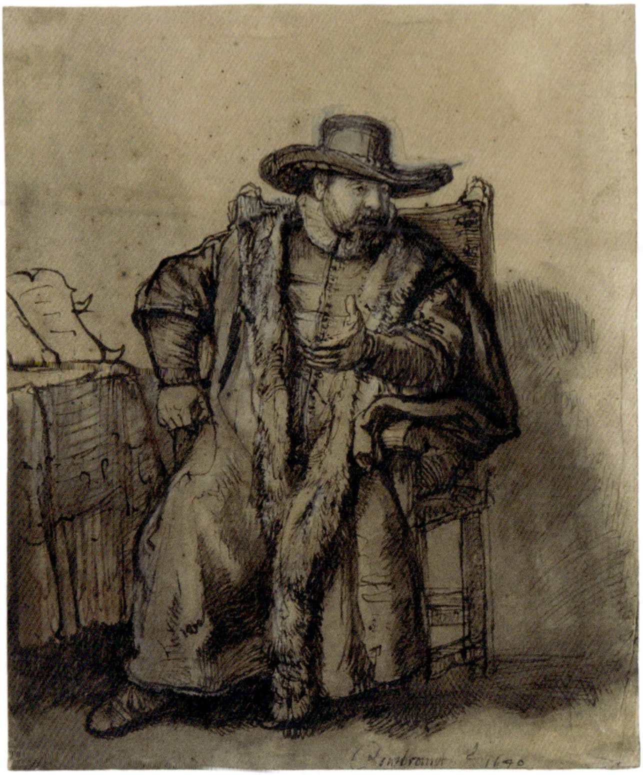

40. *Cornelis Claesz. Anslo.* 1640. Pen and brown ink with brown and grey wash, heightened with white, traces of red chalk. 20.6 × 20.1 cm. Musée du Louvre, Paris.

realised than any of the relatively rare working drawings known for paintings, and unusually signed and dated, its purpose is likely to have been an exemplum of what he had in mind to submit to the patron for his approval. It also reveals that at this stage, the commission was envisaged as a single full-length portrait with possibly a corresponding portrait of his wife. For some unexplained reason, it must have been decided to combine the sitters on one canvas.

The painting is essentially a reprise of the large double portrait of *Jan Rijksen and his Wife, Griet Jans* (see Fig. 31). In the earlier work it was the simple act of delivering the letter which brought husband and wife together, but here, in a similarly domestic interior, a dark study lined with bookshelves, Rembrandt achieves a more cerebral harmony as Anslo speaks, with the authority of the Bible to hand, and she, with rapt attention clearly visible on her face, comprehends what he is saying. It is significant that Anslo chose to be portrayed not as a rich merchant but in his role as a preacher, calling for Mennonite sobriety of costume. With a black, wide brimmed hat on his head, he is dressed in a black, fur-lined *tabbaard*, or gown, over a black suit, while his wife wears a fur-lined three-piece *vlieger*, a fashionable gown with an old-fashioned pleated ruff. In her left hand, she holds a tasselled handkerchief, an accessory indicative of wealth. Seated at a lower level, she exhibits an air of docility and subservience which would make many a modern woman's hackles rise. It is notable that her face is in full light, while his is half in shadow. The low viewpoint gives the sitters an imposing presence and suggests that the picture was intended to hang high on the wall of their house. In its own way the picture is as unique as the earlier work, since most unusually the sitters are confined in close proximity to one another to the right half of the canvas. The left half is entirely given up to a prominent still-life which, seen from a low viewpoint, rather overwhelms the spectator. On a table covered with a Persian rug over a yellowish-green cloth, is a book-stand supporting an open book, probably a Bible, beside which are an unbound book and a sheet of paper. At the apex of the triangle formed by the still-life, there is a large two-armed brass candlestick, with an extinguished candle and snuffing scissors on the left and a stump of a candle on the right, which X-rays show, was originally the same size as the one on the left. No convincing special meaning for the inclusion of candles has been put forward, but it has been suggested that the snuffers can be interpreted as an emblem of the act of cleaning away the sins of the faithful.

The portrait is richly painted with brushstrokes which can be followed throughout the composition. In the case of the woman, her face and hands are executed meticulously in small strokes. In the still-life, the impasto on the curling pages of the books and sheet of paper catches the light, presumably coming from a window on the left, and enlivens the left-hand side of the canvas. With its unconventionality of presentation, it stands out as one of Rembrandt's most striking portraits.

As has been said there was a marked reduction in the number of portraits Rembrandt painted – only three – between 1641 and 1651, years which followed Saskia's death. Whether there was any causal relationship between the two facts, it is impossible to determine. He did, however, make four very finished etched portraits, which showed the sitters 'at home' rather than displayed isolated against a plain background.

In 1647 Rembrandt made an etching of *Ephraim Bonus* [Fig. 41]. The sitter (1599–1665),who might be dubbed 'the doctor with the mournful eyes', was a Portuguese Sephardic Jewish physician, who came from a family of other distinguished doctors. He also wrote poems in Spanish and acted as a translator. He probably came into contact with the artist through his great friend Menasseh Ben Israel, who lived in the same street as Rembrandt and had employed the artist on commissions for his publishing house, which was supported by Bonus. It offers a very plain portrait, without accessories and with little furnishing of the space; it is largely set against a plain background, broken only by the pilaster on the left, which provides emphasis to the figure of the sitter. But what

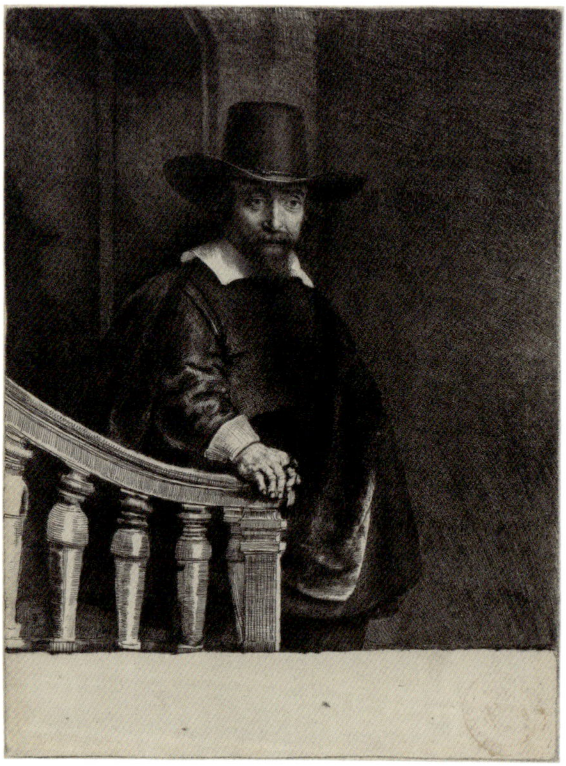

41. *Ephraim Bonus*. 1647. Etching, engraving and drypoint. 24.1 × 17.7 cm. Rijksmuseum, Amsterdam.

gives the print a personal touch and introduces a more intimate note is that he is shown standing at the bottom of a staircase, resting his right hand on a banister, as if he was suddenly caught in thought, a moment of silent contemplation, one might surmise, in the middle of a busy day. The staircase with its curved handrail in the very immediate foreground creates an eye-catching element in the design. The figure is neatly contained within the space between the latter and the dark background wall, but what counters the artificial barrier created by the banisters between sitter and spectator is the motif of his hand falling over the banister into our space. (A hand, in some gesture, breaking the picture plane was a device used by Rembrandt on a number of occasions.) The sitter wears a dark suit, against which the brilliant white collar and cuff stand out; a cloak is thrown loosely over his shoulders, and a high, wide brimmed hat is on his head. He wears a so-called physician's ring, awarded on receipt of his doctoral degree. Initially Rembrandt gave this detail prominence by adding a touch of drypoint burr, which he later removed. At the bottom of the plate there is blank space for an inscription which was never forthcoming.

When on the rare occasions Rembrandt made studies for his etchings, he did so in drawings. But here, perhaps influenced by the pictorial character of the print he was about to create, he began work by producing a small oil-sketch [Fig. 42], confined to the head and the upper part of the body, which though it showed less of the final subject, was nevertheless executed on the same scale. He paid particular attention to the subtle play of light and shadow over the face, which was followed in the print. He did not, however, follow his model slavishly, but made small changes, particularly noticeable in the sitter's expression. In the oil-sketch his gaze at the spectator is direct and uncomplicated, but in the carefully modelled face in the print, the look is abstracted and melancholy, hardly taking in the spectator. There is one curious feature, not noticeable in the oil-sketch, namely that one eye is different from the other. This clearly did not concern the artist, as in the finished second state, illustrated here, he left it as it was.

The whole surface of the plate was fully worked over with etched lines, giving the effect of a monochrome painting; only small areas of highlight – face, collar, cuff and banisters – stand out in the dark interior. The

42. *Ephraim Bonus*. *c.*1647. Panel. 19 × 15 cm.
Rijksmuseum, Amsterdam.

print is notable for the extensive use of drypoint. It is no longer limited to serving as a means of touching up and embellishing small details, as had happened in the portrait of *Jan Uytenbogaert ('The Goldweigher')*, (see Fig. 36), but has now become an integral part in the execution of the print. The extensive use of burr serves to depict the rich black of the shadows on his clothes as well as emphasising the form of the body. Further work on the plate was carried out with the burin to reduce light. The three techniques of etching, engraving and drypoint blended with one another to produce a paralleled translucency and depth, which enhances the feeling of character so strongly evident in the print.

In another of the group of portrait prints executed in the mid-1640s, Rembrandt made an etching of Jan Six (1618–1700), a work which establishes the first known contact between the artist and the man who was to become his most important patron. Six, who came from a Huguenot family, was the son of a successful merchant who inherited a family dye-works and silk mills. At first following in his father's footsteps, he abandoned the family business after undertaking the Grand Tour in Italy.

Thereafter he made a career as a magistrate, eventually serving as burgomaster of Amsterdam. At the same time he devoted himself to art, literature and learning, acquiring a reputation as a dilettante and a poet. In 1654 he married a daughter of professor Nicolaes Tulp, the early patron of Rembrandt, for whom the artist painted the celebrated *The Anatomy Lesson of Dr Nicolaes Tulp* (Mauritshuis, The Hague). He conversed with Spinoza and Descartes, and was a close friend of Vondel. In addition to owning a grand house in the city, he had a small country estate on the Diemerdijk, an area where so many of Rembrandt's landscapes were drawn. Apart from other mutual interests, such as Six's invitation to Rembrandt to contribute two drawings to his *Album Amicorum* (see Figs. 145, 147), their taste for collecting would have given them a topic in common. Whether, however, the bond between them was ever one of close friendship, as has been claimed from the eighteenth century onwards, is much more uncertain. It may have been nothing more intimate than a harmonious relationship between artist and patron, which came apart when Rembrandt's finances took a turn for the worse, and at the same time he was publicly associated with a woman 'living in sin'.

In 1647 Rembrandt received the commission for what became his most famous etched portrait [Fig. 43]. The print was preceded by a broadly-executed drawing with the reed pen of Six, looking out, with his left leg stretched out, leaning very casually, or one could say lounging, on a window sill; a greyhound, a much used hunting dog at the time, leaps up at his side [Fig. 44]. A birdcage stands on a table in the background. The drawing is composed of a flurry of lines with numerous corrections, which show the artist thinking as he was engaged in the act of drawing. It offered the perfect image of the country gentleman that Six unquestionably was. But when after two other preparatory drawings, Rembrandt came to execute the print, there had, presumably at the sitter's request, been a fundamental change in the way he was presented. An image of the *vita activa* was largely replaced with one of the *vita contemplativa*. Gone is the dog leaping up at his side, as Six, stands, for all its informality, in a very studied pose leaning on the window sill. His stance, nonchalant rather than casual, is more upright than it was in the drawing. As Six is absorbed in reading the book held out in front of him, he is prevented by his downward gaze from making contact with the spectator, as he had

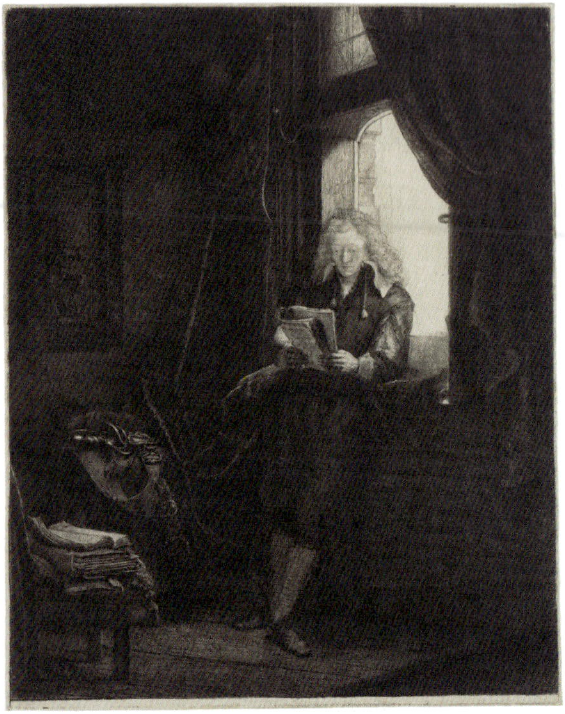

43. *Jan Six*. 1647. Etching, engraving and drypoint, on Japanese paper. 24.4 × 19.1 cm. Rijksmuseum, Amsterdam.

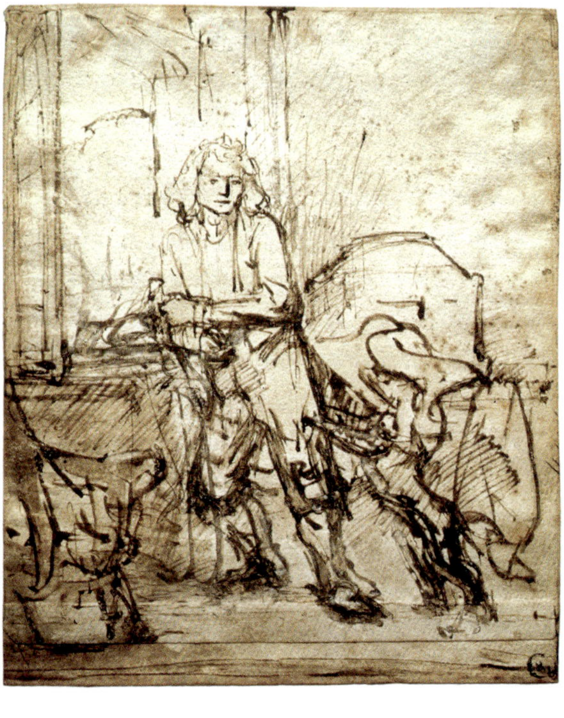

44. *Jan Six*. *c.*1647. Pen and brown ink with brown wash, heightened with white. 22 × 17.7 cm. Collection Six, Amsterdam.

done in the drawing. Bareheaded, he is dressed in an elegant dark suit, with his dark cloak spread over the window sill. With the light coming from the window behind him, he is seen *contre-jour*. It is the only full-length etched portrait in Rembrandt's *œuvre*. Moreover the sitter, unlike in other portrait etchings, is placed back in the composition, with a chair in the left foreground, also seen in the drawing, serving as a *repoussoir*. The room itself becomes an important element in the portrait, displaying the sitter's ambience as well as his appearance. A poem, written in 1661 in praise of the print, describes the sitter 'standing in his Library in the exercise of wise knowledge'.[10] Whether it shows an actual room in Six's house in the Kloveniersburgwal, where he was living at the time, there is no way of knowing.

Much forethought must have gone into the contents of the room, all of which are carefully calculated to allude to the sitter's interests. Unlike the portrait of *Ephraim Bonus*, which showed just the man, *Jan Six* is a print to be read as well as looked at. The book he is absorbed in and the book and folder of manuscripts on the chair indicate that he was a man of letters. The picture on the wall referred to his love of art. The rapier and bandoleer on the table recall his role as an officer in a militia company. But not all vestiges of the country gentleman have disappeared. Discreetly hidden in the shadows in the left-hand background are a game bag, large hunting knife and a hat with a feather. He was known to be a keen rider and huntsman. In an unprecedented manner, the print aims to portray both sides of his character.

The technique is as remarkable as the presentation. Through its play of light and its subtly varied tones, the print achieves an unrivalled degree of finish hardly seen before in Rembrandt's etched *œuvre*. Over an etched basis virtually covering the whole plate, Rembrandt worked with the burin and, above all, the drypoint needle, which produced those wonderfully rich dark tones. As in the *Ephraim Bonus*, the artist melded the different techniques into a perfectly-fused harmony, so that it is difficult to detect the contribution of each. The window, the only unworked area, is the source through which light streams creating a world of shadows of varying intensity throughout the room. Arnold Houbraken, the artist's eighteenth-century biographer, offers an eloquent description of the 'tender, twinkling darks, rendered as finely and softly as can be done by the art of mezzotinting',[11] a technique shortly afterwards to be introduced by other artists. In a plate of such complexity, it is hardly surprising that he artist submitted the plate to four different working states, touching up or changing small details. Both in presentation and in technique, it is a beautifully polished performance, recognised as such at the time. Nearly twenty years later a patron, in search of a portrait by Rembrandt for which he was prepared to pay a large sum, stipulated that it should be etched 'from life, equal in quality to his portrait of Mr Jan Six'.[12]

This work was followed by commissions for a number of varying works, concluding in 1654, when Rembrandt painted *Jan Six* [Fig. 45], producing an imposing portrait set against a plain background which could not be more of a contrast in presentation with his etched portrait. It would have no place in this book, were it not for one small detail. Instead of offering a timeless image, the sitter is shown engaged in pulling on his

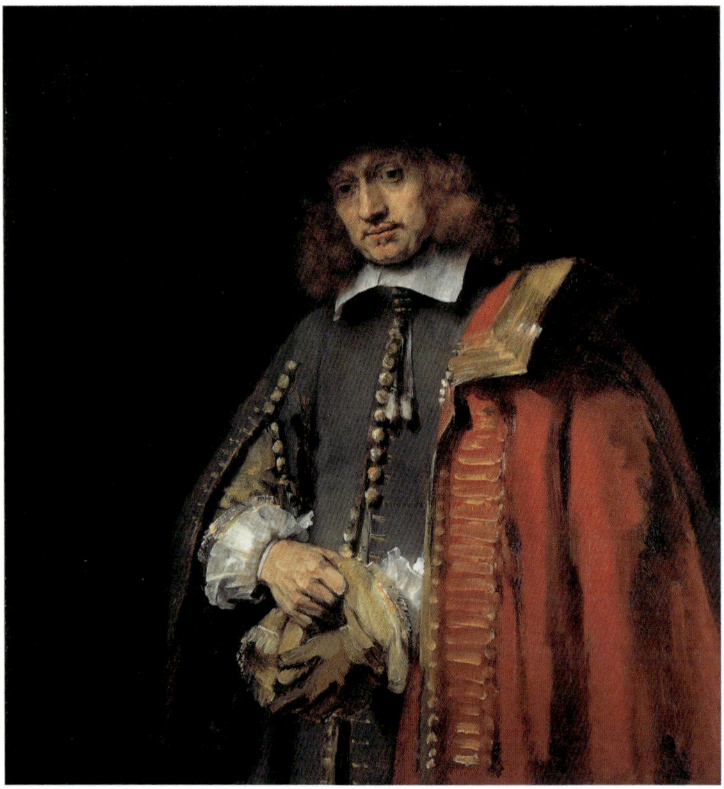

45. *Jan Six*. 1654. Canvas. 112 × 102 cm. Collection Six, Amsterdam.

glove, an action never otherwise introduced by the artist in his portraits. The artist depicts the moment when apparently the sitter has stopped in his tracks on preparing to leave the house, and collects his thoughts as he does so. Jan Six, with his head on one side, wearing a high-crowned hat, is placed almost frontally to the spectator A red cloak, richly decorated with gold braid, is nonchalantly hung over his shoulder, contrasting with the fashionable dark grey coat, opulently buttoned in gold, which has recently been identified as a riding cloak, and therefore to be associated with his country rather than his town life, where dark clothes would have been the norm. Elaborate white cuffs frame the hands. The sitter is studied from a low viewpoint, which makes his intense, questioning gaze all the more imposing. The look is not unfriendly, but he is maintaining his reserve. Although there is suggested action in the hands, the overall impression is of a man suddenly come to rest. The nearly square format and the empty space on the left of the canvas enhances the underlying sense of latent forward movement. There is no question that we are faced by a person of authority and financial well-being.

If his later works are fewer in number, they are more powerful in effect. The sense of personality is profounder, the manner of painting is broader and bolder, and nowhere more so than in *Jan Six*. It is the perfect example of Rembrandt's 'rough manner', which he adopted in his later works. The handling of the brush is extraordinarily free in building up the volume of the figure, and suggests in loose, open strokes the texture and adornment of the costume. The gold braid on the cloak is summarily indicated by repeated strokes with a half-charged broad brush. The most bravura area of painting executed with the maximum economy of brushstrokes is devoted to the hands and gloves, the one area on the canvas where movement, an unusual element in a Rembrandt portrait, occurs. If the work seems unfinished by conventional standards, it did not worry the sitter and the artist had achieved his purpose.

But brilliant as the effect of handling is, we are constantly drawn back to scrutiny of the beautifully-modelled head suggestive of life beneath the outer skin. The shadow cast over the upper part of the face by the brim of the hat succeeds in introducing a depth of meaning in the eyes that detail alone cannot describe. The subtly varying play of light and shadow over the whole surface of the canvas creates a sense of mysteriousness that increases our feeling of contact with the sitter. It is a superb formal portrait for all its country clothing, yet informal in the impression it makes on us by the absence of conscious posing. The present painting represents the last known contact between the two men. If the reasons for the cessation in relations are tantalizingly unknown, it is certainly nothing to do with the reception of this portrait; the sitter, writing in his *Album Amicorum*, expressed his satisfaction: 'Such a face had I, Jan Six, who since childhood have worshipped the Muses'.[13]

In the next decade Rembrandt once again produced a number of highly-wrought etched portraits of people personally known to the artist, either commissioned or intended as gifts in gratitude for help received. It was probably the former which led to the portrait of *Arnold Tholinx* (1607–1679) [Fig. 46], formerly Inspector of the Amsterdam Collegium Medicum, but by now practising as a successful physician. He had married

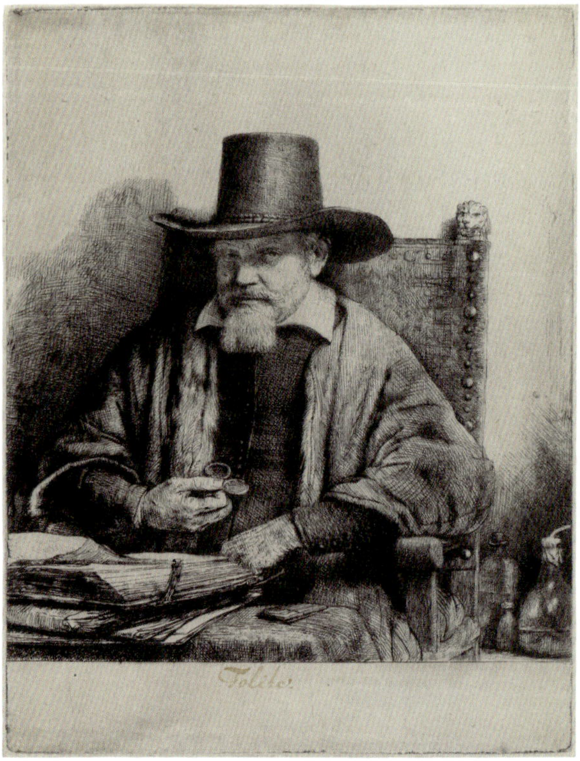

46. *Arnold Tholinx*. *c.*1656. Etching, engraving and drypoint. 19.8 × 14.9 cm. Rijksmuseum, Amsterdam.

the eldest daughter of Professor Nicolaes Tulp, so in 1654 became the brother-in-law of Jan Six and therefore moved in circles sympathetic to Rembrandt. *Arnold Tholinx* was probably etched in the year that Rembrandt's financial problems came to a head in 1656.

With a wide-brimmed hat on his head, Tholinx is seated at his desk in a high-backed chair decorated with lions' heads. He is placed slightly to the left, allowing space for several medicine bottles on the floor, which allude to the sitter's profession. With his arms resting on the arms of the chair, thereby forming a triangle of his body, he exudes an air of comfort and calm assurance. To give depth to the portrait there is some shading in the left and right background. A doubtless medical volume, with the top page curled upwards to give a touch of reality, lies open in front of him, as he looks out, delicately holding his pince-nez by the centre of the frame with finger and thumb. That is all we need to know to get the measure of the man. The spectator, who assumes the role of patient, almost feels uncomfortable by the intensity of Tholinx's gaze, his searching eyes mysteriously veiled by the shadow created by the brim of his hat. The plate was now carried out with what was becoming the usual combination of etching, drypoint and engraving, with the burr of the drypoint creating dark shadows in the folds of the cloak. With only relatively few impressions printed from the plate, it remains one of his most sought after and admired prints.

Whereas Tholinx was probably no more than a patron with friendly intent, Abraham Francen (1612– after 1678) was unquestionably a friend, who was intimately involved in family matters. In 1653 Rembrandt, when in financial trouble, granted him power of attorney; he signed a petition for Titus to be declared of age; and finally acted as guardian to Cornelia, the artist's daughter by Hendrickje Stoffels. Etching a portrait may well have been intended as a token of gratitude, which would have been appreciated all the more since Francen was a keen collector of prints, especially of Rembrandt's, if Edmé François Gersaint, the first cataloguer of Rembrandt's prints (1751),[14] is to be believed, as well as other works of art.

It may be an indication of the informality of the portrait, that Rembrandt started work without having his final goal clearly in mind, which led to no less than seven different working states as he continuously made

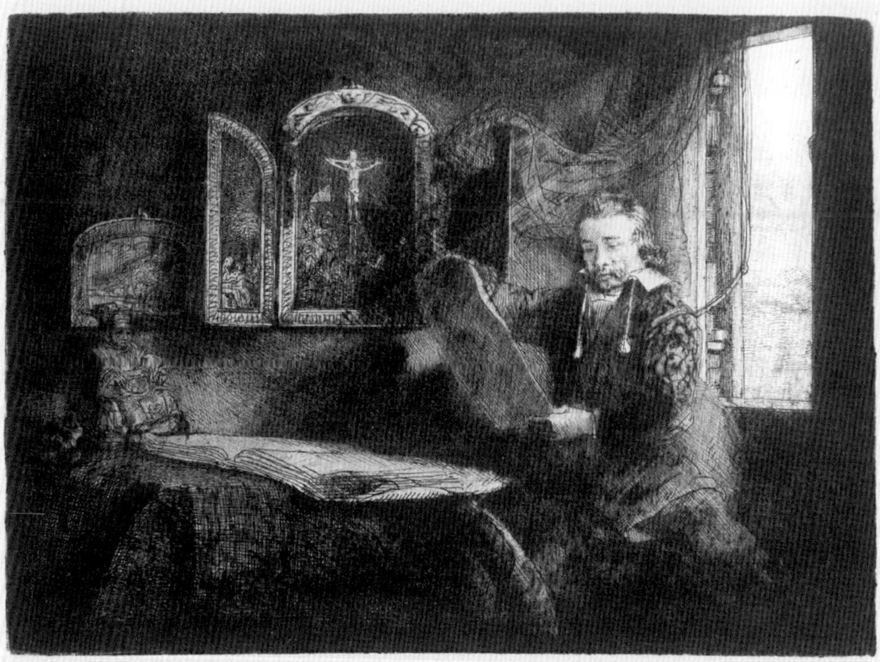

47. *Abraham Francen. c.*1657. Etching, engraving and drypoint, on Japanese paper. 15.8 × 20.8 cm. British Museum, London.

corrections both small and large. As will be seen it was the pose of the sitter and his immediate surroundings, which were the cause of the indecision. The first state [Fig. 47] is a virtually complete subject. The setting is a private cabinet, perhaps the sitter's own, with three pictures hanging on the wall, a triptych with the *Crucifixion* in the centre, flanked by two smaller arch-shaped works; the table in front of the sitter is largely covered by an open album, with a Taoist sculpture, a skull and a pot resting beside it. To give more attention to the room and its contents, with their references to the sitter's interests, Rembrandt opted for a 'landscape' format instead of the usual upright.

Francen, wearing an unbuttoned doublet and open collar cloak, is seen straddled across a stool, admiring a large print or drawing, which he holds up in front of him. The position of the legs was not clearly worked out and there are signs of reworking in this area. Behind him, a curtain is caught up on the wing of the triptych, as light from a bright summer's day floods in from the window creating a world of shadows throughout the room. This was a quality, never more effectively realised, which came to be lost, as the artist worked away at the plate with the drypoint needle and burin. To enhance the softness of the light, nearly all the impressions of the early states were printed on Japanese paper, sometimes with surface tone deliberately left on the plate to reduce the highlights (see below).

By the time Rembrandt reached near the end of his work on the plate [Fig. 48], Francen was seated in a chair, decorated with lions' heads, in a more conventional pose closer to the table. The print or drawing is smaller and his right hand can be seen clearly holding the top of the sheet. The lively image of the first state had been transformed into a calmer, more restful posture, arguably more appropriate for studying a drawing or a print. Behind the sitter, the curtain was removed and the window architecture clarified and sharpened, with a view of trees through the window now added. And finally to enliven the sitter's expression, which

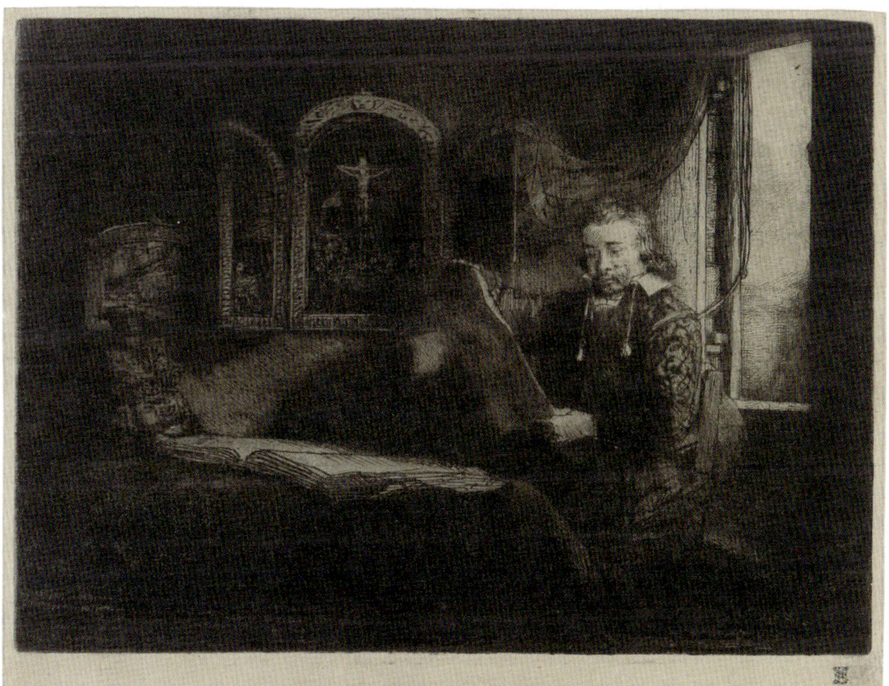

48. *Abraham Francen*. *c.*1657. Etching, engraving and drypoint, on Japanese paper. 15.8 × 20.8 cm. Rijksmuseum, Amsterdam.

by this time was beginning to appear worn, he worked over the hair and face with drypoint. He stands out as one of the artist's most contented sitters, happily absorbed in his interests and free from the melancholy introspection of others portrayed by Rembrandt.

The inventive printmaker that Rembrandt was led him, from the mid-1640s onwards, to vary the way he inked his plates as well as the choice of papers he printed on. Normally the plate would have been wiped clean before printing, but in numerous impressions he obtained a richer pictorial effect by leaving a thin film of ink over much of the plate. It achieved the same effect as the addition of wash to his drawings. In the case of a support, the majority of his prints were printed on white paper, widely differing in weight and texture and coming from a number of different European sources. Occasionally he printed on a rough oatmeal paper. But from the mid-1640s the choicest impressions were printed on imported Japanese paper and more rarely on a thinner Chinese paper. All these oriental papers, varying in thickness and ranging in colour from a dark to pale yellow, are more absorbent than white paper, and give softer and richer effects suited to the qualities of drypoint, which became such an important element in his printmaking. And in addition some impressions were printed on vellum, which produced a similar softer effect. The choice of the paper he printed on was much appreciated by connoisseurs at the time and thereafter.

During the last decade of his life, Rembrandt still continued to receive a number of portrait commissions, which were invariably painted against a plain background without any personal gestures. The same could be said for the *Family Portrait* [Fig. 49], were it not for the behaviour of the children, which gives the portrait such an intimate character. Although Rembrandt had carried out large group portraits during the course of his career, he had never before painted a family ensemble.

An element of mystery hangs over the *Family Portrait*, probably executed in Rembrandt's very last years, which was only first recorded in Germany in the early eighteenth century without, either then or subsequently, any convincing indication of the identity of the sitters. Consisting of two parents with their two daughters and baby son, all dressed in fanciful costume, the canvas posed the problem of how to compose the five sitters in a meaningful and original way. The artist solved it by

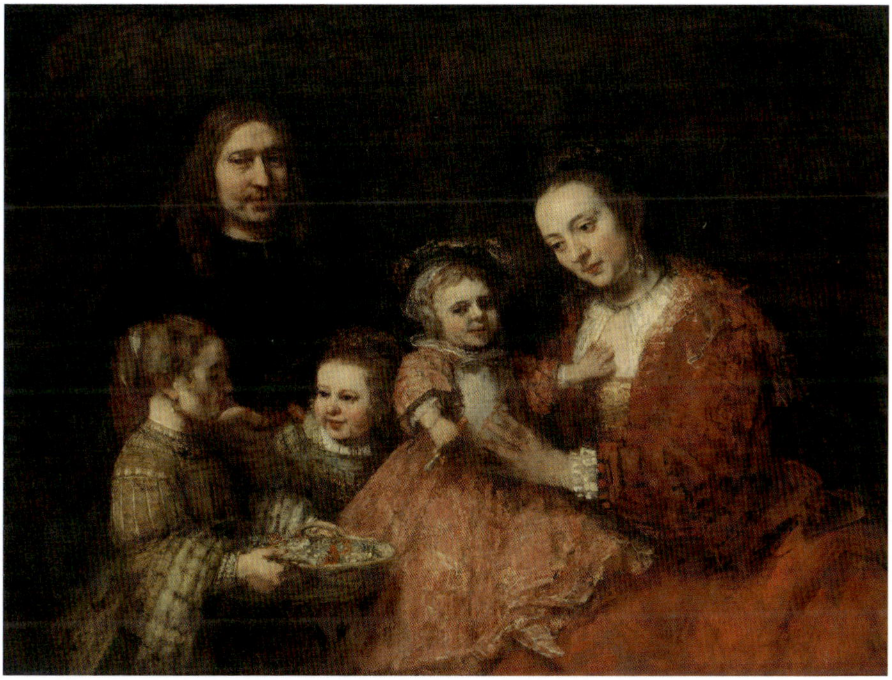

49. *Family Portrait. c.*1665. Canvas. 126 × 167 cm.
Herzog Anton Ulrich-Museum, Braunschweig.

dividing the family into two pyramids interlocking with one another; the father with the two daughters on the left and mother with the baby son on her lap on the right. To bond the two groups, the basket of flowers held by the elder sister is painted over the son's dress, while the younger sister, with whom she is conversing, is placed behind. And then one comes to the individual treatment of each figure, who react in a memorably lively fashion, each in his or her own way. The father, with a benevolent expression, holding a red flower in his right hand, stands behind the two daughters who respond to one another in a touchingly sisterly manner; the younger, with a charming smile, greets the apparent arrival of the elder, face in shadow but seen with reflected light, who proffers her basket of multicoloured petals. On the right, the mother, with a doting expression, places her hand gently on her son's stomach, while the latter, with dark mischievous eyes, has his arms outstretched, one holding a rattle and the other, following the natural instinct of a baby to touch, feels the area of his mother's bare chest revealed by her parted chemise. Whereas the two sisters look at one another and the mother down at her son, only the two males look out directly at the spectator. Not only does Rembrandt portray a moving image of a nuclear family, but he also conveys the sense of happiness enjoyed by these particular members, which enchants the spectator.

No less striking than the artist's portrayal of the family, is the technique which he used in this *echt* example of his 'rough manner'. Obviating any hard outlines, broad brushstrokes of thickly applied paint are visible throughout, so that one area seems to blend into another. But in addition to his very free use of the brush, Rembrandt, ever the technically inventive artist, applied much of the paint with the palette knife. Flat areas of paint applied with the latter can be seen very clearly on the garments worn by mother and son. A transparent black glaze is partially laid over the red of the mother's dress, while pink paint covers a yellow base in the boy's skirt. The red and pink, combined with the green of the girl's dresses and the deep black of the man's costume offer a rich harmony of colours. Never has a picture, following the artist's advice apparently given on another occasion, more needed to be viewed from a distance to bring all the detail together.

Standing alone in his *œuvre* at the end of his career as a monument to his art, the portrait is an extraordinary work in the terms of its technique and psychology. Since people tend to be conservative about portraits of themselves, one can wonder whether the family, who commissioned it, were sufficient connoisseurs of the art of painting to appreciate what had been created for them. And if so, how they dealt with family and friends, the more polite of whom were likely to have declared it unfinished, while the more philistine would have dismissed it as a daub. Today it stands out as an outstanding example of an artist's 'late style'.

CHAPTER 3

Everyday life in Amsterdam

WHETHER INSIDE the house or out on the streets Rembrandt was an inveterate recorder of what he saw around him. This was nothing new in Dutch art but what is particularly noticeable in Rembrandt's studies is the selection of intimate moments or actions, often unobserved by other artists, whether they were done from the life or in recollection. What is impressive is the precision of his observations. But not all is invariably as it seems. Often throughout his life, such studies were inspired by the works of another artist, and then changed into his own personal language, so that without prior knowledge one is unaware that the starting point was another source.

A good example of such dependence is the pair of small etchings, dated 1634, depicting *A Peasant Calling Out: 'Tis vinnich hout'* ('It is very cold') [Fig. 50], and *A Peasant Replying: 'Dats niet'* ('That's nothing') [Fig. 51], which, as has long been recognised, were probably inspired by

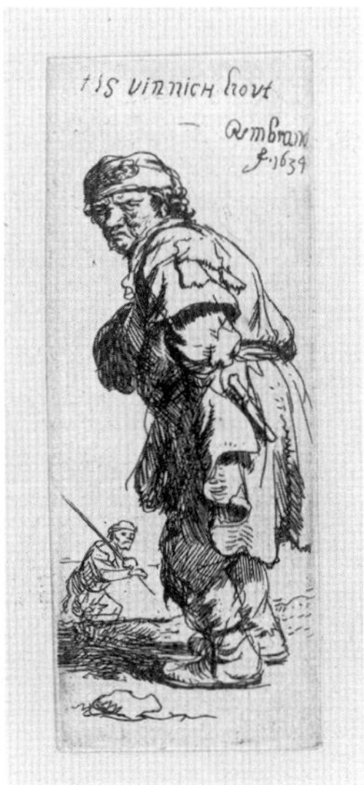

50. *A Peasant Calling Out: 'Tis vinnich hout'*. 1634. Etching. 11.3 × 4.3 cm. Rijksmuseum, Amsterdam.

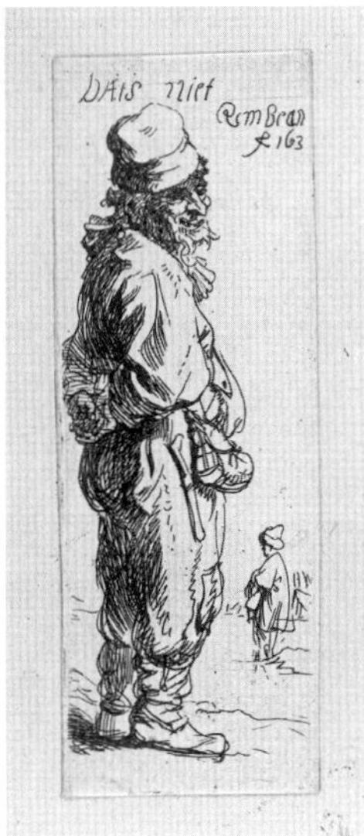

51. *A Peasant Replying: 'Dats niet'*. 1634. Etching. 11.2 × 3.8 cm. Rijksmuseum, Amsterdam.

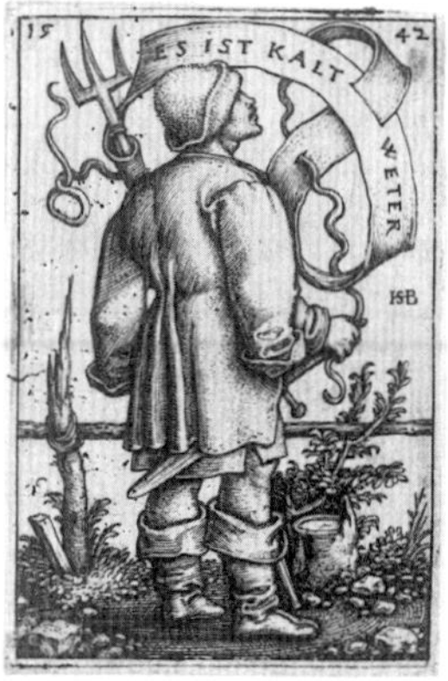

52. Hans Sebald Beham,
A Peasant Calling Out:
'Es ist kalt weter'. 1542.
Engraving. 4.5 × 2.9 cm.
British Museum, London.

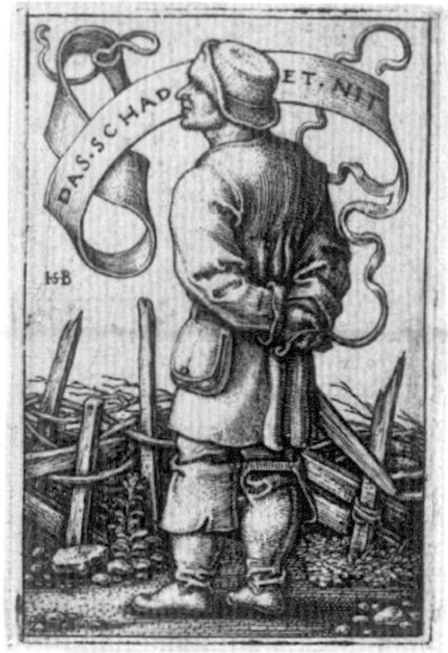

53. Hans Sebald Beham,
A Peasant Replying:
'Das schadet nit'. 1542.
Engraving. 4.4 × 2.9 cm.
British Museum, London.

two small engravings by Hans Sebald Beham (1500–1550) [Figs. 52–3] of peasants, in similar postures, expressing the same thoughts in German. But Rembrandt has transformed their appearance. Instead of Beham's farm labourers, Rembrandt shows two street ruffians, who look out at the spectator rather than at one another. Secondly instead of being shown facing one another, they are depicted with their backs to one another, shouting rudely over their shoulders, thereby sharpening the incident. Rembrandt engages our direct attention to this rough exchange of words on the streets. It is not surprising that this was a very popular image at the time, which underwent no less than four editions in six years. Yet it does reveal that Rembrandt sometimes allowed the ideas of other artists to stimulate him before going out onto the streets to cloth them with his own observations.

Already from his earliest days in Leiden, Rembrandt made numerous general studies, but for the most part they were not place specific. The *Old Woman Seated in a Cottage* [Fig. 54], etched *c.*1629, is an intimate study of the woman probably, but not certainly, seated in her kitchen by the back door, almost out of doors you might say. With her hands clenched, she leans forward as if in deep thought or prayer. Her bare feet rest on a warming stool. A string of onions hang on the wall on the left and the rough wooden door can be seen behind her. Otherwise there

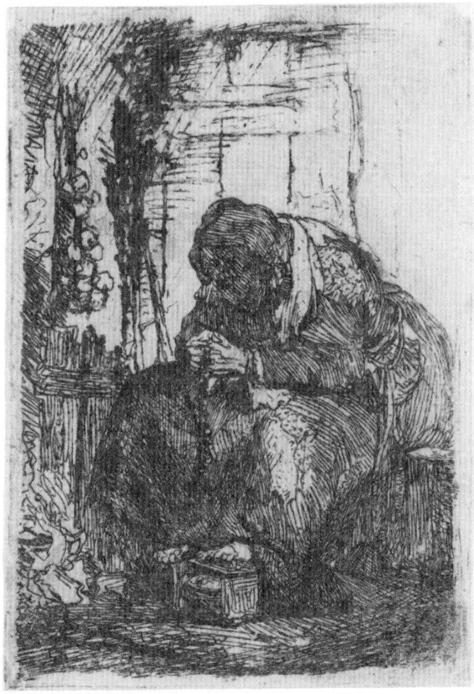

54. *Old Woman Seated in a Cottage.*
c. 1629. Etching. 12.8 × 8.5 cm.
Rijksmuseum, Amsterdam.

are no details which would identify the surroundings. What is unusual is that her face is heavily shaded over like the rest of her body, so that we cannot make out her features or expression. The setting is simple and rustic and there is an atmosphere of poverty, but for Rembrandt it is rather a detached work. The copper plate has been roughly bitten in the acid so that the lines appear coarse, which renders the woman unduly dark against her setting.

Beggars were a common sight at the time, particularly so in cities such as Leiden and Amsterdam, which saw increased immigration from the Southern Netherlands as a result of the religious troubles. In general the subject had already been treated by Jacques Callot (1592/3–1635) in numerous etchings. His influence on Rembrandt was already noted by Edmé-Francois Gersaint, previously referred to. As we know from the inventory of his possessions drawn up in 1656, Rembrandt had an extensive collection of prints and, although none by him are mentioned, it is a reasonable assumption that he had examples by Callot, very possibly some or all of his famous set of twenty-five prints entitled *Les Gueux* ('The Beggars') (1622). But for what Rembrandt actually depicted, he turned to what he could see around him. With their bedraggled appearance, beggars in their various guises probably appealed to the artist because of their picturesque character rather than, as had been the case in earlier times, as objects of satire. They are treated with detachment but with sympathy. Perhaps with Callot's rendering of a similar figure at the back of his mind, Rembrandt came across in Leiden a dishevelled beggar, seated warming his hands over a chafing dish [Fig. 55]; his knapsack and stick are on the ground beside him. His air of self-absorption suggests he is pondering his fate, or more specifically where his next meal is to come from. Seen within a play of light and shadow, the small plate is loosely etched, with clear outlines describing detail with precision. With remarkable sharpness, Rembrandt portrays his expression, which gives life to this image of poverty.

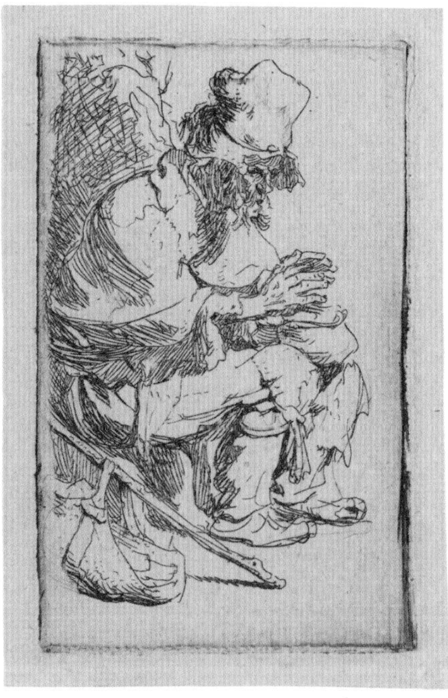

55. *Beggar Seated Warming his Hands.*
*c.*1630. Etching. 7.7 × 4.6 cm.
Rijksmuseum, Amsterdam.

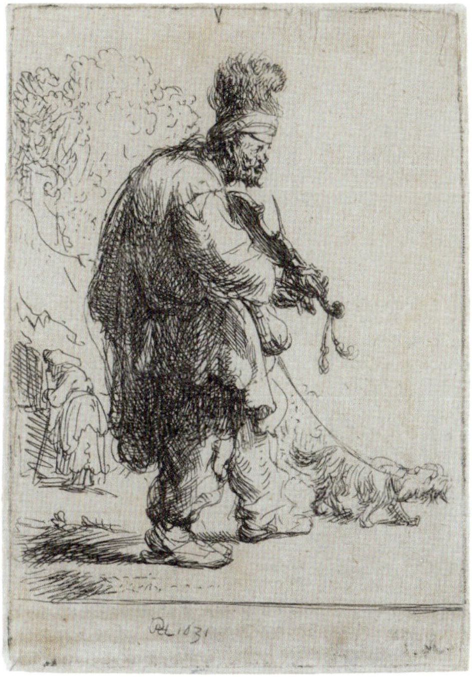

56. *The Blind Fiddler*. 1631. Etching.
7.8 x 5.3 cm. Rijksmuseum, Amsterdam.

In 1631, either still in Leiden or having just moved to Amsterdam, Rembrandt made a small etching known as *The Blind Fiddler* [Fig. 56]. The beggar, walking along the street with his fiddle at his shoulder, has always been described as being blind, but for what reason is not entirely clear. Perhaps the fact that his little dog on a lead precedes him may indicate that the animal is leading his master rather than the other way round. It has been suggested that the faintly-sketched old woman in the background is collecting alms on behalf of what is presumably her husband. Although the plate has been lightly etched, the play of light and shadow over the beggar has been vigorously developed, so that despite its small size the print makes a powerful impression.

For several years Rembrandt had been making individual studies of figures involved in street life, like the previous work, and now for the first time he put several together to create his first etched genre composition. *The Rat Catcher* [Fig. 57], dated 1632, portrays an encounter at the doorway to a house, with the action taking place over the lower half of a

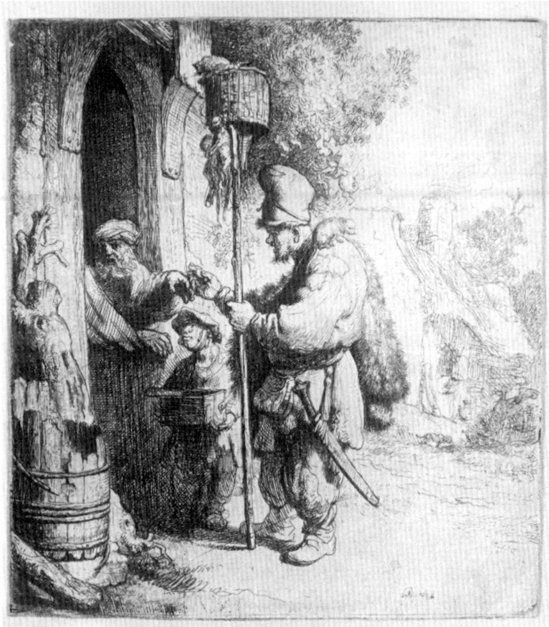

57. *The Rat Catcher*. 1632. Etching. 14 × 12.5 cm.
British Museum, London.

door, a setting which was to provide a favourite framework for a variety of different street events. In a scene filled with picturesque detail, such as the broken barrel and tree trunk in the left foreground, a hunchbacked elderly rat catcher, in a high cap and shabbily dressed, stands with his hand out towards the occupant of the house. In his left hand he holds a long pole with a round basket with dead rats hanging from its underside and live ones inside. A large pelt hangs over his far shoulder while a live rat sits on his near shoulder. The house owner, with his hand out, appears to be turning away in disgust at the whole unsavoury business. The boy assistant, wearing a large cap tied under his chin, stands between the two men, looking up in curiosity and holding up an open box filled with rat poison. Rembrandt's inexperience in composing shows in the way the participants are detached from one another and are not unified in the way that his figures were to become in later works. Only the hands of the two men barely touch. The artist is, however, successful in distinguishing the foreground, more darkly-bitten, from the more lightly-bitten background, containing a farmhouse, similar in character to those seen in his early landscape drawings. The print, clearly popular from the number of copies which were made, established the formula for numerous later narrative scenes.

Rembrandt's artistic interests were, as we have already seen, clearly stimulated by his own family's activities during the 1630s, but from the range of studies he made at this time and continued less frequently later, his concerns went far beyond what was happening in his own home. Apart from the existence of the drawings and etchings themselves, we know that the wealthy marine painter Jan van der Cappelle (1626–1679) possessed a large collection of Rembrandt drawings, including no less than 135 of the life of women and children, which gives an indication of how many he must have made devoted to this theme. Such is his empathy, one might suppose Rembrandt was a child lover, or at least he saw the potential for studying a range of very expressive emotions common to children.

A fraction over ten centimetres square, this snapshot of daily life on the streets [Fig. 58] is remarkable for its precision of observation of a child's reaction. Seemingly on her way from shopping, the mother and child meet an inquisitive dog, which frightens the child. Having put down her basket, in which can be seen the head of a dead duck, the mother, with a look of amusement on her face, puts her arms around the child,

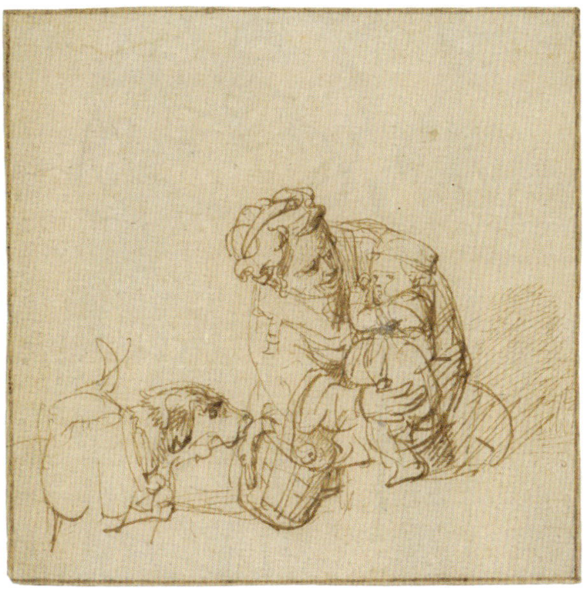

58. *Mother and Child Frightened by a Dog.* *c.*1633/4. Pen and brown ink. 10.3 × 10.2 cm. Fondation Custodia, Paris.

whose fear is eloquently conveyed by its raised left arm protecting itself and by the expression on its face. The dog, with only the head worked up, looks on in a friendly manner, more interested in sniffing the duck in the basket than approaching the child. The tail, added only in outline, is surely wagging. It is remarkable how much sentiment is imparted with the fine lines of the quill pen, of which Rembrandt had become complete master.

In the drawing of *The Naughty Boy* [Fig. 59], executed in the middle of the decade, the fury of a kicking, screaming child is palpable, as the mother or nurse struggles to control it in her arms. A shoe flies through the air. A bent old woman stands there admonishing with a raised hand, while two children look on with great curiosity in the background. All the faces are brilliantly characterised with fine penwork to portray the different emotions they are undergoing. The mother in particular has a look

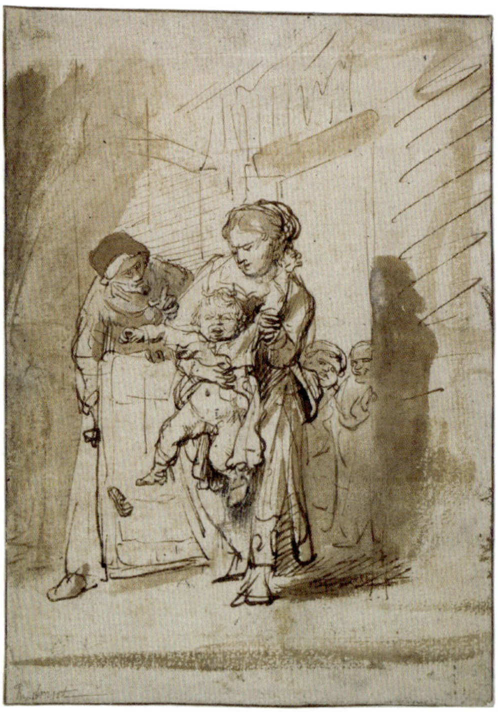

59. *The Naughty Boy*. *c.*1635. Pen and brown ink with brown wash, heightened with white. 20.7 × 14.2 cm. Kupferstichkabinett, Staatliche Museen zu Berlin.

of determination mixed with reluctance at having to overpower the child. It may be a minor domestic event which happened all too often in daily life, but the feeling of drama is as overwhelming as if it were some Biblical story. The execution with the pen is free, but it is a very composed work of art, demanding careful thought, unlikely to have been drawn on the spot. Broad areas of carefully-applied wash frame the subject, as well as creating a pattern of light and shadow which give depth to the scene. It is a perfect example of less is more.

The *Pancake Woman* [Figs. 60–61], dated 1635, was a feature of daily life on the streets, a subject which had been illustrated by other artists going back to the previous century; Rembrandt himself, for example, owned a painting of the subject by the Flemish artist, Adriaen Brouwer (*c.*1605–1638). This relatively small print is noteworthy for its acuteness of observation of the behaviour of small children when confronted with a culinary treat. It can be seen as an amalgam of the numerous sketches of individual women and children Rembrandt drew in these years, brilliantly capturing the different emotions. We are presented with a scene of great animation centred around the figure of the old woman resolutely

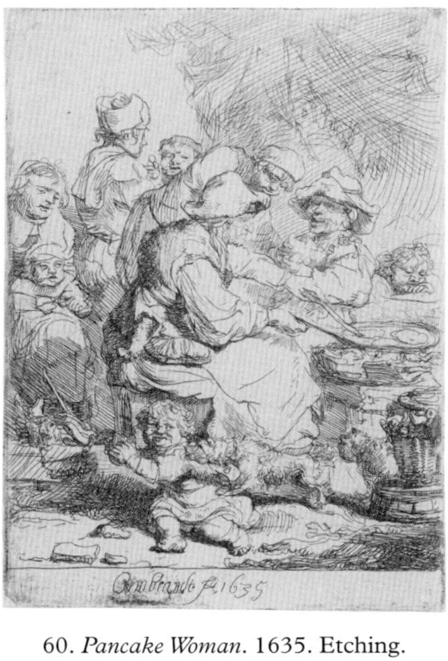

60. *Pancake Woman*. 1635. Etching. 10.9 × 7.7 cm. Rijksmuseum, Amsterdam.

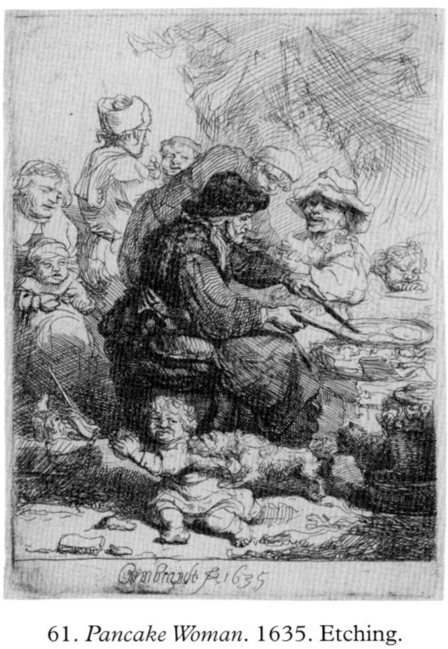

61. *Pancake Woman*. 1635. Etching. 10.9 × 7.7 cm. Rijksmuseum, Amsterdam.

concentrating on turning three pancakes in the frying pan. Arranged around her in a circle are children of different ages and with different reactions. Particularly prominent are the boy, on the right, in a cloche hat, eating his pancake with an expression of joy, the child in the foreground, who is at pains to defend his pancake from an importunate dog, and the expression on the face of the baby seated on its mother's lap. All have one goal in mind – to partake of the delicacy. The loosely-shaded area in the background, it has been suggested, is a canopy protecting the old woman from the elements.

The print is executed in the same loose manner to be found in his drawings of the period. It offers an example how Rembrandt developed his subject on the plate. At first [Fig. 60], he drew in the whole subject largely in outline and bit the plate evenly throughout. He then [Fig. 61], stopping out the remainder, worked up the figure of the old woman so that after further biting of this area she unequivocally becomes the centre of attention, encircled by her more lightly-etched youthful customers. Although finished, it maintains the lightness of touch which gives great sparkle to this everyday scene.

Another very lively version of this attractive subject occurs in a drawing [Fig. 62] made about the same time, although given the differences it cannot be regarded as a preparatory study for the etching. On the

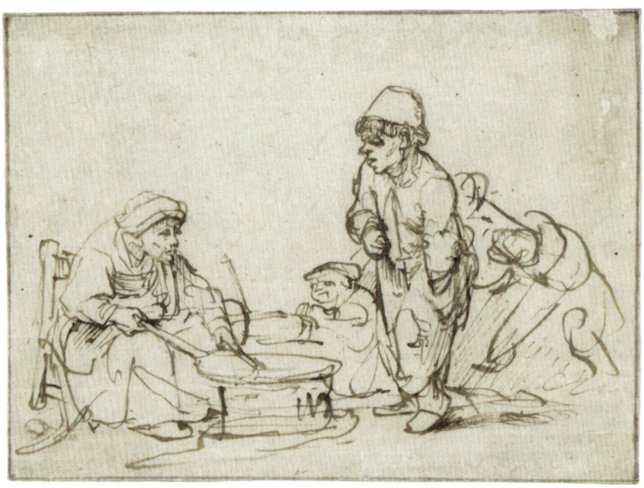

62. *Pancake Woman*. *c.*1635. Pen and brown ink. 10.8 × 14.4 cm. Rijksmuseum, Amsterdam.

left an old woman is hard at work making pancakes, while on the right a small boy, tempted by what is on offer, is seen searching for a coin in his pocket. Between them a baby enjoys a treat, while on the right two boys are ragging with one another. With a remarkable economy of bold line Rembrandt captures the different activities of the participants.

A year or two later Rembrandt returned to the subject of a child confronted by a dog [Fig. 63], but on this occasion the emotion is one of apprehension rather than outright fear. The theme is once again a chance encounter on the street after a shopping spree; the mother's bag, filled with what looks like vegetables, is placed on the ground on the right. She, clearly smiling, puts her arms comfortingly around the child. On this occasion, the long thin dog, of the greyhound type, is curious about the child, as it points its sharp nose forward. The child, with an anxious expression on its face, has its left arm raised, ready to stroke but fearful to do so. Rather than a sketch probably done on the spot, the later drawing has been worked up into a composition, with the encounter taking place

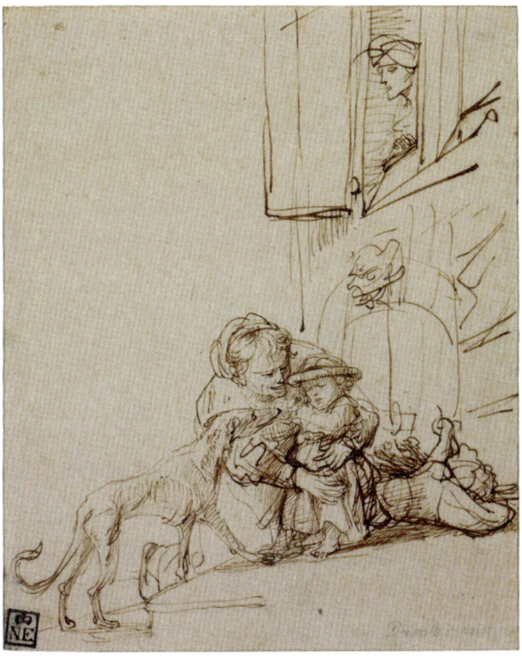

63. *Woman and Child with Dog*. *c.*1635.
Pen and brown ink. 18.2 × 14.5 cm.
Szépmüvészeti Museum, Budapest.

in front of a house. From an upper window, a woman looks out to witness the scene. The sheet may be very loosely executed, but it has a satisfying completeness.

On the threshold of a house, in a combination of both indoors and outdoors favoured by the artist, we are presented with a scene of relaxation and contemplation [Fig. 64], conveyed with a remarkable economy of line. In the foreground, a mother with a child seated peacefully on her lap, is occupied possibly sewing. Immediately behind them, an old woman is seated, leaning forward, looking very much as if she might have dozed off. And finally behind a half door, a younger woman stands abstractedly looking out. Each woman, occupying a distinct position in space, is absorbed in her own world with no contact between them. Despite its seeming simplicity in execution it is a skilfully-crafted drawing. The artist began by lightly laying in the figures, which are then developed to different degrees of finish; the mother and child are schematically sketched in,

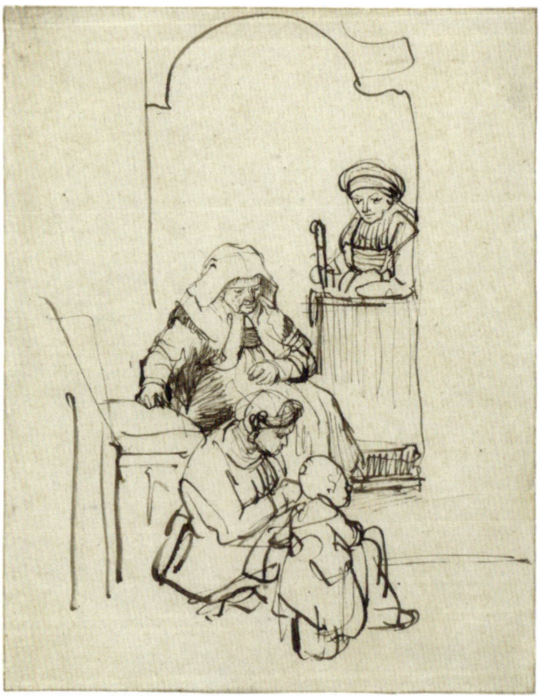

64. *Three Women and a Child Before a House*. c.1640.
Pen and brown ink. 23.3 × 17.8 cm.
Rijksmuseum, Amsterdam.

while the old woman is the most fully worked up of the figures, thereby catching our primary attention as the central figure in the scene. The arch of the doorway, although only indicated by a single outline, plays an important role in providing a framework to the composition and differentiates indoors from outdoors. Recession between foreground and middle ground is gently suggested by the diagonally placed bench on the left with the lower half of the door dividing middle ground from background. With such subtle means, it is remarkable how one senses the precise placing of the figures in three different planes, overall unified but individually separate.

Walking is one of the fundamental skills a child needs to acquire, and learning how to do it became a minor leitmotif in Rembrandt's study of the life of women and children, the repertory of which he explored in several drawings and an etching. The earliest examples, are found in two red chalk studies, representing the later uses of this particular medium for drawing. In one [Fig. 65], a small child, in protective headgear, is led in its first steps by two women both of whom look down attentively at the child, while the left-hand one encouragingly points the way forward. The schematic delineation suggests that it was done from the life. A different aspect of training occurs lightly-etched in the background of the print of a *Male Nude Seated and Standing* [Fig. 66], executed *c.*1646, and known from the eighteenth century as 'The walking frame'. A child in a

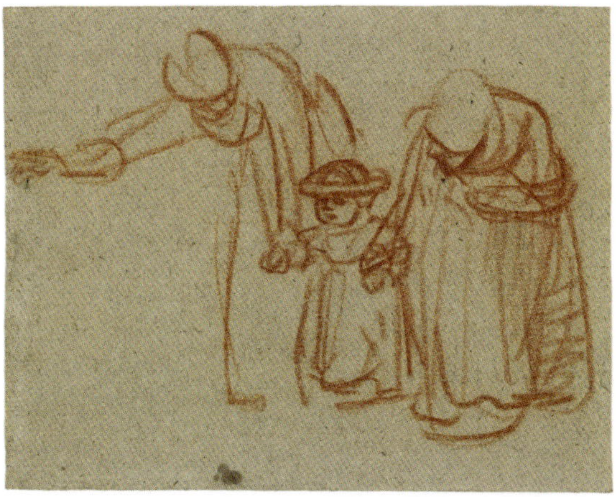

65. *Two Women Teaching a Child to Walk*. *c.*1636.
Red chalk. 10.3 × 12.8 cm. British Museum, London.

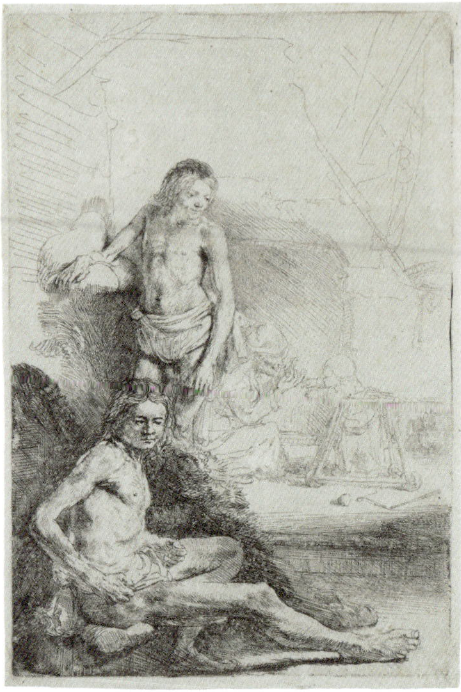

66. *Male Nude Seated and Standing.* *c.*1646. Etching. 19.4 × 12.8 cm. Rijksmuseum, Amsterdam.

walking frame with hands outstretched is coaxed forward with a come-hither gesture by an old woman, kneeling on the ground. In a pen and ink drawing done about the same time [Fig. 67], a child, once again wearing

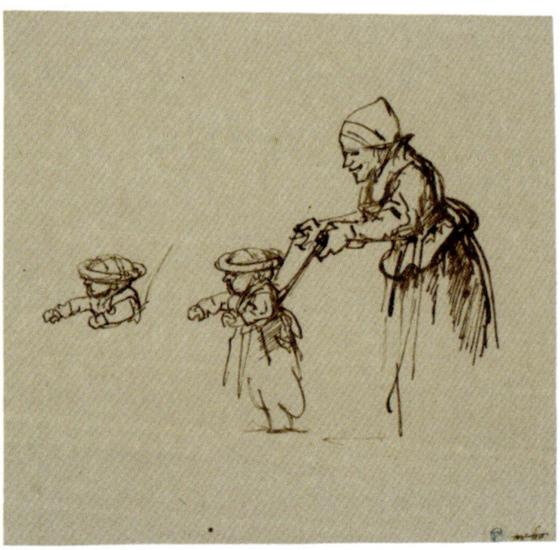

67. *Woman Teaching a Child to Walk.* *c.*1646. Pen and brown ink. 16 × 16.5 cm. Nationalmuseum, Stockholm.

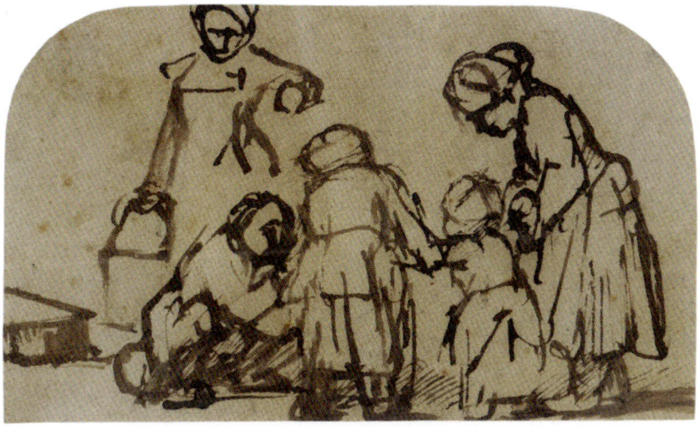

68. *Child Being Taught to Walk*. *c.*1656.
Pen and brown ink on brownish paper. 9.3 × 15.4 cm.
British Museum, London.

protective headgear, gingerly takes a step forward, supported on a leading rein held by a woman in a cap. A repetition of the head of the child is to be seen on the left of the sheet. That this is a study rather than a finished work is established by the fact that Rembrandt has not bothered to work up the lower part of the figures. And finally in a drawing done about a decade later [Fig. 68] Rembrandt basically returns to the incident recorded in the earlier red chalk drawing. A child in a cap, now seen from the back, responding to the coaxing of a kneeling figure on the left, takes a hesitant step forward, supported on either side by a young woman; on the left a man walking by, carrying a bucket, looks on. The thick strokes of the reed pen, characteristic of his late style of drawing, impart a monumentality to this intimate family scene, which belies the simple nature of the event.

……

In the 1630s, the street scene in Amsterdam continued to preoccupy Rembrandt intensively for the whole of the decade. The strolling musicians, once again a traditional subject, seen in this etching [Fig. 69] of around 1635, must have been a common sight. From the chiaroscuro, creating highlights on the figures but leaving the rest in darkness, we must assume that the scene is taking place in the evening. An old man with a hurdy-gurdy and a youthful bagpiper, with a dog at his feet, are

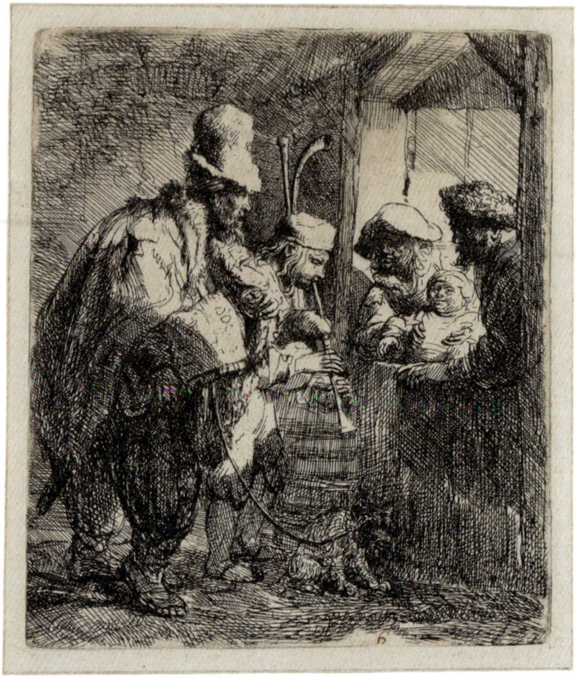

69. *Strolling Musicians*. *c.*1635. Etching. 13.8 × 11.5 cm.
Rijksmuseum, Amsterdam.

playing to a man and woman holding a child at a half-open door. The faces of the parents are shaded, leaving the expression of delight of the baby at what he or she is seeing and hearing to stand out. We are left to guess whether alms were given. Although the plate is extensively worked up with cross-hatching, there is a lightness of touch in the drawing.

Unusual as a subject – he rarely made studies of trade – Rembrandt produced this very lively drawing of *Two Butchers at Work* [Fig. 70], made about the same time. One butcher crouching, with a large meat cleaver in his hand, is furiously working at splitting a pig's carcass in two, while the other, on his feet, with a knife in his mouth, is flaying the carcass of a pig held up against him. To the left, Rembrandt has written: *Its skin is still attached, but it is dangling.* The artist gives the impression that he has just walked into the door of the butcher's premises and found the men hard at work. Drawn with the minimum of pen strokes, the sheet conveys a great sense of energy. We are easily convinced that dealing with a carcass is work only fit for strong men.

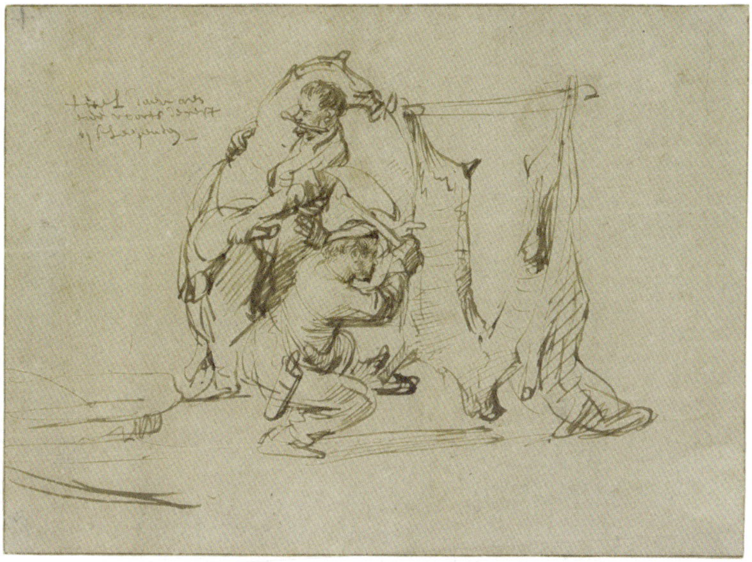

70. *Two Butchers at Work. c.*1635. Pen and brown ink on light brown prepared paper. 14.9 × 19.9 cm. Städel Museum, Frankfurt am Main.

In 1638 a pageant was held in The Hague to celebrate the marriage of Louise Christine van Solms, the sister of Amalia, Princess of Orange, to Wolfgang van Brederode. It may well be that this festive occasion prompted Rembrandt's interest in the event; although he is not recorded as having visited The Hague, he expressed the wish to do so in a letter to Constantijn Huygens in 1636; moreover he painted at least three portraits of Hague residents in the 1630s. It is, therefore, more than likely he made the relatively short journey between the two cities. Probably connected with this occasion, he made four studies of figures in exotic costumes, of which *A Black Drummer and Commander Mounted on Mules* [Fig. 71] is the most spectacular. In the foreground the drummer with raised drumsticks is clearly in action. (A descriptive pamphlet of the The Hague pageant mentions, *inter alia*, the presence of 'a drummer on horseback striking two kettledrums'.[15]) Another black man, seemingly the commander, is seen beyond him, looking steadfastly ahead, with a raised baton in his left hand. The latter wears a Hungarian-style fur cap with a long forked plume. A canopy is held aloft behind them. Both men wear the set expressions induced by the monotony of proceeding in a procession. Rembrandt, who would have few opportunities of seeing a

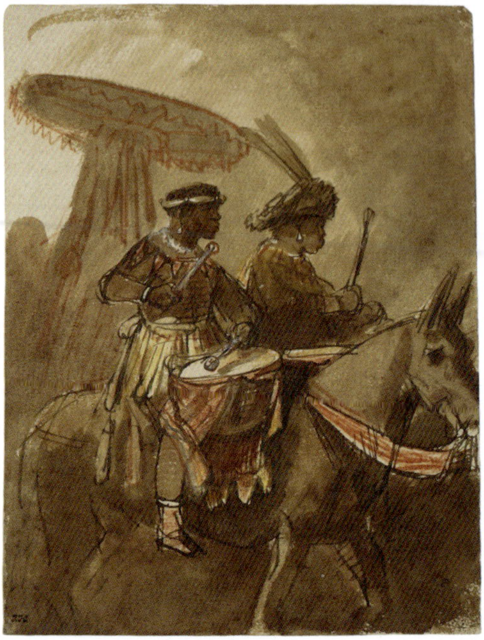

71. *A Black Drummer and Commander Mounted on Mules*. *c.*1638. Pen and brown ink with brown and yellow wash, heightened with white, over red chalk. 23 × 17.1 cm. British Museum, London.

black man, clearly defines the distinctive features of their two faces seen in profile.

Unlike Rembrandt's usual straightforward technique of pen and ink often with wash, here the medium is more elaborate. With the figures established with unusually firm outlines in pen and brown ink, brown wash in two tones was applied to almost the entire sheet, leaving only a small area of untouched white paper upper left. The details of the canopy were then added in red chalk over the wash while it was still wet. The sheet was further enriched with the addition of white bodycolour and touches of yellow in order to pick out various details. The final effect has the character of a largely monochrome painting, which makes considerable impact when framed on a wall.

Ice, frozen canals and winter cold bring out an exuberance in the Dutch character, which is still noticeable today. Something of this spirit is clearly visible in the small print of *The Skater* [Fig. 72], probably

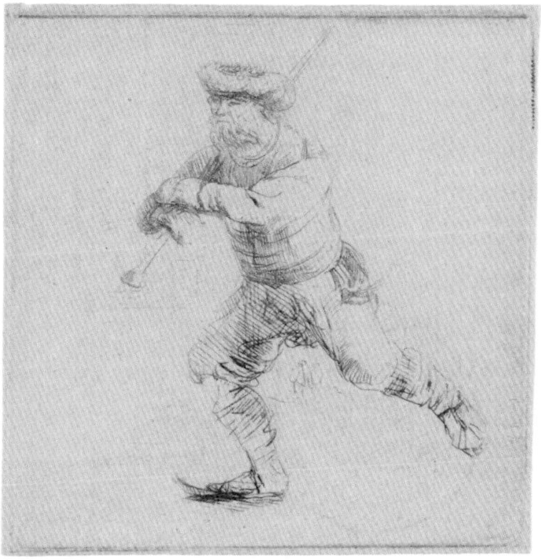

72. *The Skater.* *c.*1639. Etching and drypoint. 6.1 × 5.9 cm. Rijksmuseum, Amsterdam.

executed about 1639. Unquestionably a man of experience with his head held high, he moves across the ice with masterly assurance, left leg raised behind him as he advances on his right. He holds a pole resting on his shoulder, ready to assist him in the unlikely event that he falls through the ice, an occupational hazard for any skater. Entirely drawn very freely in drypoint, with dark accents on the figure created by the burr from the ridges of copper, the print has a wonderful lightness of touch. With such shallow cutting into the copper with the drypoint needle, the plate must have worn down fairly quickly, so that it is hardly surprising only a relatively small number of impressions exist today.

With his omnivorous interest in the world about him, it is hardly surprising that animals, both wild and domestic, should, whether or not essential to the story, appear frequently in Rembrandt's paintings and etchings. Both horses and dogs, for example, are often to be found in narrative scenes, either serving a purpose or providing an extra touch of life. One may surmise the introduction of animals was part of a deliberate policy to give variety to his subjects and incorporate the whole of earthly life in his *œuvre*. It is, therefore, unexpected how few drawings of animals are known today, yet an item in the inventory of his possessions drawn up at the time of his near-bankruptcy in 1656 suggests that there must have been many more: housed in the 'Art Chamber'in his house in the Breestraat was 'One ditto [album] filled with drawings by Rembrandt of animals done from life'.[16] Rembrandt took particular care with such drawings, since, as it has been rightly observed, he varied his technique according to the animal under observation, a detail to be explored below.

The drawing of *Two Horses at a Resting Place* [Fig. 73] is perhaps Rembrandt's earliest study of a domestic animal, possibly done as early as during his Leiden period. Two rather exhausted-looking horses are standing side-by-side with traces of the cart they are pulling on the right. A man in a high hat leans over the foremost horse, seemingly either laying a blanket on its back or drying it. On the left another figure, impossible to say whether male or female, is feeding the rear horse, only the head of which is visible. Rather than a limited animal study, the subject is a fully-fledged genre scene, probably, in view of the apparent hastiness of execution, done from the life. In getting the subject down on to paper, Rembrandt imbues the black chalk lines with a remarkable vigour and certainty, a quality which he acquired very early on and is, for example, very notable in the summary definition of the rear legs of the nearer horse. One feature which is typical of drawings done during the Leiden period is the combination of black and red chalk, seen here in the way he has used the latter to impart further detail to the head of the nearer horse. The sheet stands as the only known representation of a horse done from the life.

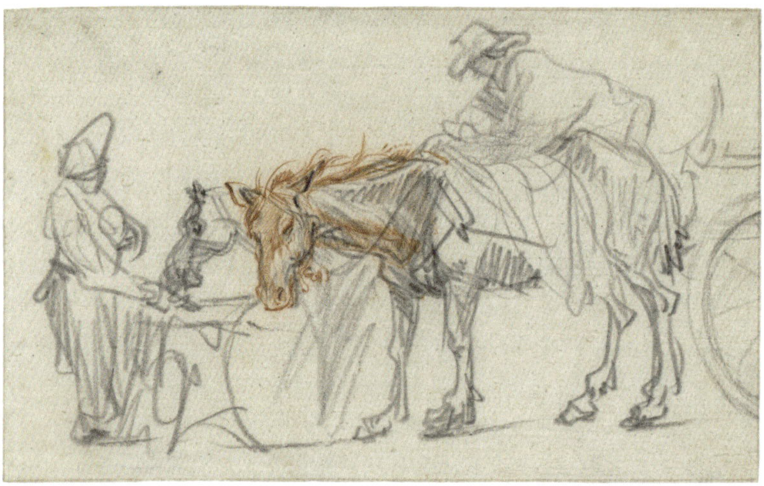

73. *Two Horses at a Resting Place*. *c.*1637. Red and black chalk. 17.3 × 27.1 cm. Rijksmuseum, Amsterdam.

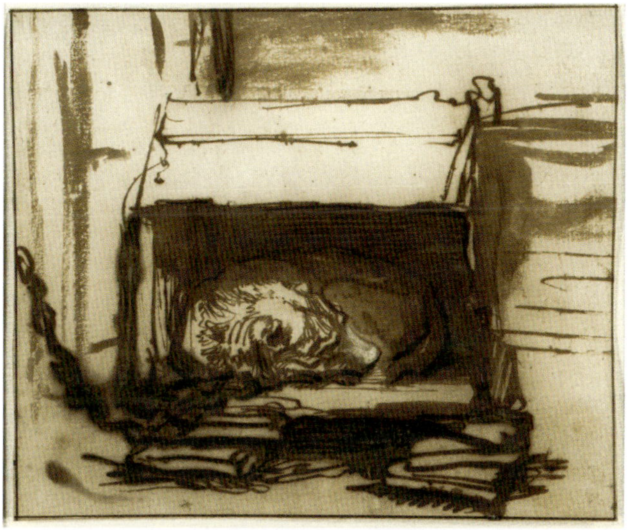

74. *Watchdog Sleeping in its Kennel. c.*1638/9.
Pen and brown ink with brown wash. 14.3 × 16.8 cm.
Museum of Fine Arts, Boston.

A *Watchdog Sleeping in its Kennel* [Fig. 74], executed around 1638/9, has the distinction of being shown as part of the everyday scene and not limited to an isolated study of the animal itself. Dogs, as has been said, appear regularly in Rembrandt's paintings and etchings, but this watchdog, with cropped ears taking a kip, appears to be a work in itself and not preparatory to another work. Roughly constructed, the kennel rests on loosely-piled wooden blocks to counter the damp. An imposingly large chain for such a small dog limits the animal's movement within a narrow space. This is a farm dog with no frills to his life. The iron-gall ink, which turns from a cool grey to a warm brown in the course of time, was used by Rembrandt for a small group of drawings in the 1630s, maybe because it was cheap. Drawn on paper prepared with a light brown wash, the pen work varies between the fine drawing of the dog itself to the broader description of the chain, kennel and supports. Once again touches of white bodycolour have been used to introduce a highlight, in this case on the dog's nose. The dark shadow within the kennel is strongly conveyed with wash, while broad strokes made with the brush adumbrate the shape of the background wall. The drawing stands as another example of Rembrandt's penchant for a strong chiaroscuro at this date in his career.

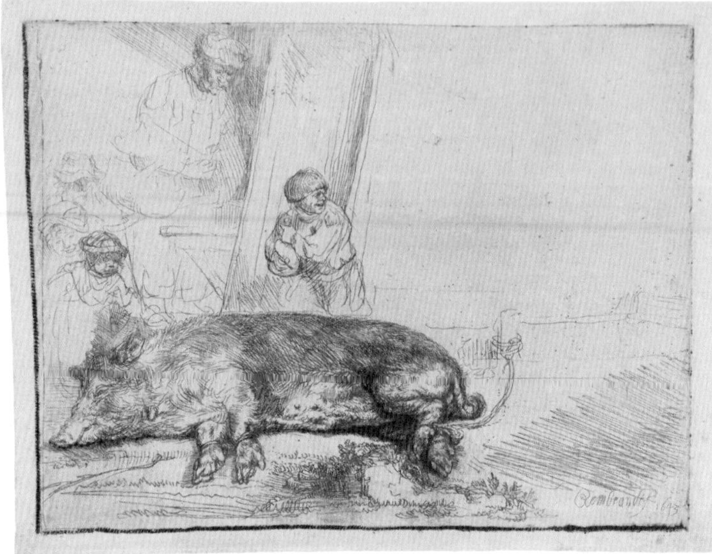

75. *The Hog*. 1643. Etching and drypoint. 14.3 × 18.3 cm.
Rijksmuseum, Amsterdam.

Pigs were the subject of three drawings, an etching, and apparently a painting or possibly an oil sketch, recorded in the 1656 inventory of his possessions as 'a little painting of a hog',[17] which was hanging in the entrance hall. The etching of *The Hog* [Fig. 75], dated 1643, shows the animal, legs tied and tethered at the back to a post, slumbering peacefully on a patch of grass in the left foreground. Happily unaware of its impending fate, it bears an expression of bliss on its face. The coarse bristly skin is brilliantly suggested by the manner of shading, enriched with touches of drypoint to give darker accents. Lightly etched behind the hog are, crammed in at the top, a man, the key figure in the story, standing with a basket on his arm and, in his hand, an axe and a curved yoke from which to hang the carcass; lower centre, a grinning boy joyfully blowing a pig's bladder; and lower left, a baby, looking on in wonderment, supported by its smiling mother, with a boy seen beyond. This part of the plate was etched with remarkable freedom and certainty, as he placed each figure in its own allotted place.

Given the notable difference between the deeply-etched animal and the various figures in the lightly-etched background, it may be that Rembrandt began with the hog, possibly done from the life, and only added the latter at a later stage to enlarge what had been an individual study into a genre scene. Characteristically Rembrandt did not follow tradition by showing either the act of slaughtering or the subsequent display of the strung-up carcass, but picked an earlier moment, when the animal was still alive, but with its demise clearly foretold by the presence of the butcher with his tools to hand. One might argue that the boy blowing a pig's bladder, alluding to the brevity of life, was out of sequence since the animal was still alive.

Rembrandt did not pay much attention to birds. Apart from two unusual painted still-life paintings, one with a dead bittern and the other with a pair of dead peacocks, he drew a bird of paradise on two occasions. In the more significant and particularly beautiful of the two [Fig. 76], he drew two versions of the same bird. One item in his collection of exotica, recorded in 1656 as 'a paradise bird and six fans',[18] may have provided the model. The two studies, one above the other, show the bird without legs, reflecting the habit of the natives of New Guinea, who removed them, as well as the guts, before mounting them, to be brought back to

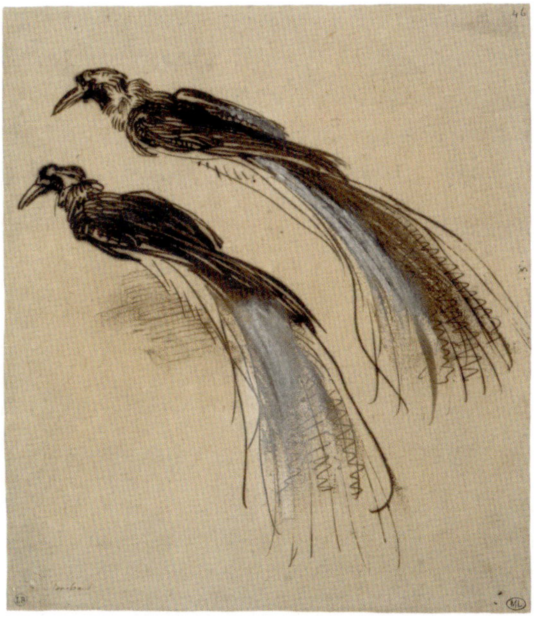

76. *Birds of Paradise*. *c.* 1638. Pen and brown ink with brown wash, heightened with white. 18.1 × 15.5 cm. Musée du Louvre, Paris.

the Netherlands by the Dutch East India Company for sale. They are studied as specimens in isolation, with, apart from some light shading beneath the lower bird, no indication of any background. The sheet has the appearance of a work made for reference, but in fact never used. With exquisitely applied long strokes of the pen, the artist builds up the body of the bird with its exotic plumage, with lines placed together so closely that they seem to merge. Over this he worked in white bodycolour, heightening the the effect of their attenuated tail feathers, and giving some semblance of colour. With the dark iron-gall ink, he is able to suggest the gloss of the plumage. The birds may be dead but there is a lightness and airiness of touch which seems to defy their defunct state.

Rembrandt would have had an opportunity to study wild animals at fairs, markets and festivals, where they were regularly exhibited. If he went to The Hague, as has been said seems probable, he might have taken the occasion to visit the renowned zoo belonging to the Stadholder Frederick, which was situated outside the city. Elephants were a regular feature at public events and the most celebrated of the four studies of the beasts, is the signed and dated drawing of 1637 [Fig. 77]. Although there were other elephants on display, which could have served as models, the present animal has somctimes been identified as the well-recorded female elephant from Ceylon called Hanske, which arrived in Amsterdam on a Dutch East India ship in 1633. This was possibly the animal seen by the diarist, John Evelyn, in Rotterdam in 1641: 'It was beast of monstrous

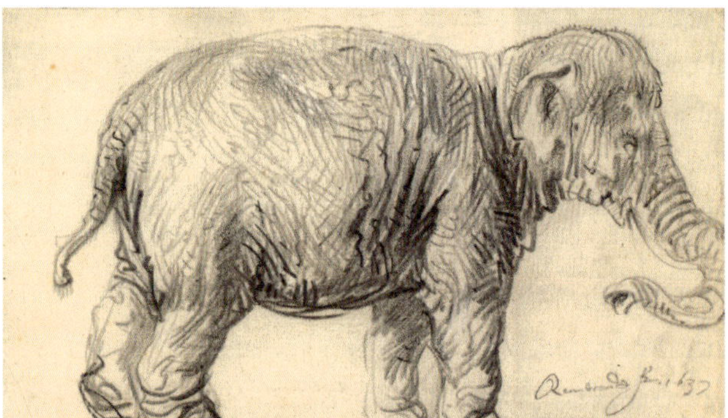

77. *Elephant*. 1637. Black chalk. 23.3 × 35.4 cm.
Albertina, Vienna.

size, yet [as] flexible and nimble in the joints ... but I most of all admired the dexterity and strength of its proboscis, on which it was able to support two or three men, or by which it took whatever it was offered it'.[19]

The elephant is seen in profile, seemingly trying to communicate with the spectator as it holds his trunk out towards him or her. Although the animal is stationary, this action gives a sense of movement and vitality to the sheet. It is very much a study of nature alive and not of a detached specimen. Some slight shading on the ground beneath the beast, emphasises the immense solidity of the animal as it stands on terra firma. Even allowing for Rembrandt's dexterity as a draughtsman, it is remarkable how he is able to suggests the animal's rough skin with two shades of black chalk. The animal is predominantly described with lightly-coloured, loosely-hatched lines, over which he has worked in darker chalk giving emphasis to the lower half of the animal's body. There is a nice touch in the way he has depicted the shadows on the wrinkled trunk with a series of circles drawn in dark chalk; the open end of the proboscis, ready to receive any offerings, is emphasised by a small area of dark shading. His drawings of elephants came to hand, when, as will be seen, he made an etching of *Adam and Eve* (see Fig. 128) in the following year.

If elephants only made a rare appearance in Rembtandt's *œuvre*, lions were more frequently to be seen, such as the very prominent example which is reclining majestically in the limelight in the allegorical grisaille painting of *The Concord of State* (Museum Boijmans Van Beuningen, Rotterdam). In the no less than eight etched and one or two drawn representations of St Jerome, the saint is appropriately accompanied by his attribute. The animal itself attracted the artist's interest at two different periods of his career, the first sometime around 1640 and then some years later in a group executed with the pen. Belonging to the former, four studies of lions and a lioness, is the *Lioness Devouring a Bird* [Fig. 78]. The animal, with raised shoulders, is stretched out on the ground in profile, her tail laid out behind her. Her length is impressive. She has an almost human expression of supreme satisfaction on her face as she ponders, before taking a bite of the bird clutched firmly between her paws. As with his drawing of an elephant, there is a sense of latent movement.

Of particular interest is the technique Rembrandt used for this and the other two studies. On paper applied with a yellow wash, he drew in

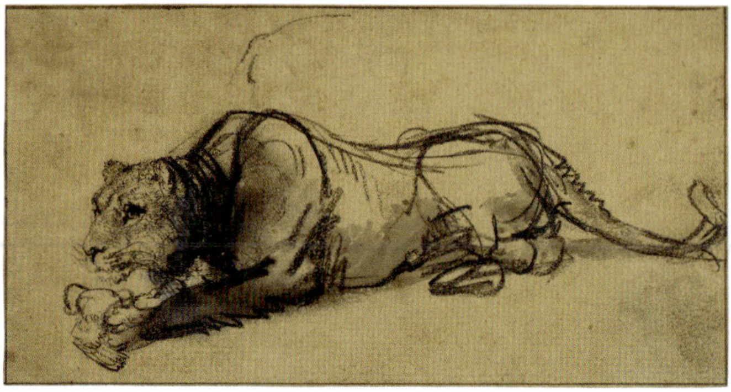

78. *Lioness Devouring a Bird*. c.1640. Charcoal, with grey wash, heightened with white, on brown prepared paper. 12.6 × 23.9 cm. British Museum, London.

what appears to be charcoal, adding grey wash and white body-colour to heighten the effect. Over careful delineation of the animal, Rembrandt has worked with bold freely-applied strokes to give emphasis to the outline of the body. The use of charcoal would have been most unusual in Rembrandt's *œuvre* and can perhaps be regarded as an experiment abandoned even more rapidly than with what happened in the case of his use of iron-gall ink.

Some ten years later Rembrandt returned to the subject of lions and made several studies abandoning chalk for pen sometimes with wash. In the most freely drawn of the group, a lion, seen in profile, is lying on the ground, with its head raised in the act of contemplation [Fig. 79]. This

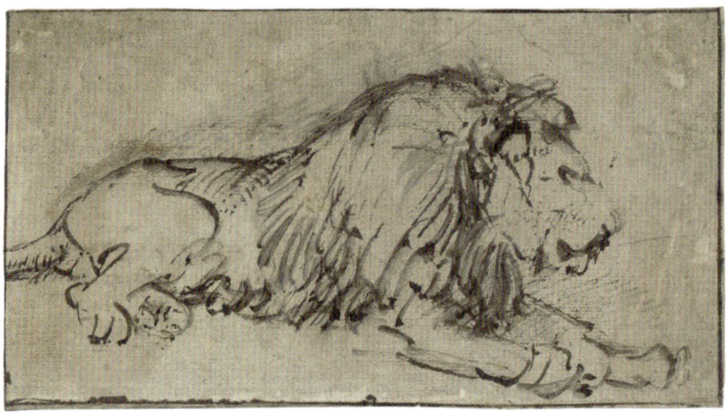

79. *Lion Resting*. 1650s. Pen and brown ink on brown paper. 12.2 × 21.2 cm. Rijksmuseum, Amsterdam.

study, which marvellously conveys the majesty of the beast, was executed solely with the reed pen, the broad strokes of which might suggest it was drawn with the brush. Such studies came to hand when Rembrandt was designing his last etching of his favourite saint, *St Jerome Reading in an Italian Landscape*, *c.*1563, in which the animal, seen from behind, assumes a no lesser role than the man.

......

Compared with the previous decade, there are from 1640 onwards fewer studies of the everyday scene, but nevertheless Rembrandt's sharp eye for what was going on around him did not desert him. On the feast of the Epiphany on 6th January, commemorating the story of the three wise men from the East who followed the star of Bethlehem, it was the custom for children accompanied by adults to process through the streets bearing a lantern in the shape of a star ('The star of the kings'); going from house to house they sang songs – after each verse the star was rotated – and asked for small gifts.

In this rare example of a signed drawing [Fig. 80], indicating that he regarded it as a finished work of art, Rembrandt illustrates just such an

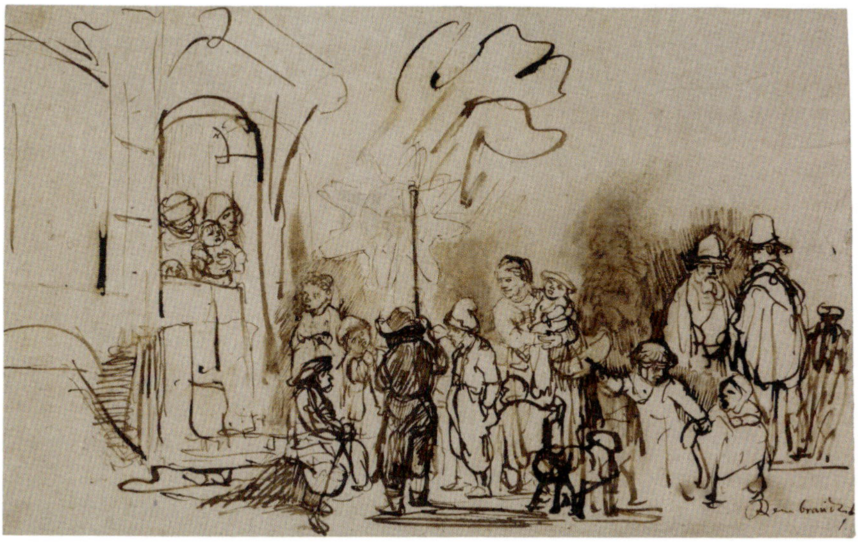

80. *Star of the Kings*. *c.*1646. Pen and brown ink with brown wash. 20.4 × 32.3 cm. British Museum, London.

occasion. It is a scene of great animation with a wide variety of children and adults all shown in a range of stances and each reacting in his or her own way. On the left leaning out of a half door, two women holding up a baby look out at their unexpected visitors. Moving from left to right, one can pick out the child sitting on the steps looking up, one elder boy, seen from the back, holds up the star while another boy beyond him rotates it by pulling a string; in the centre a boy with his hand in his pocket stands in front of a woman holding a baby in her arms with a dog at her feet; on the right a young child, pointing out the star as she leads a baby towards the action; and on the right two men in conversation, while another walks off. The vivacity of the event, studied on this relatively large sheet of paper, is conveyed by the flexibility of the quill pen, which expands and contracts across the page in a beautifully fluid line. Light and shadow, denoted by hatching or areas of wash, are carefully balanced to suggest depth. Sketchy it may appear but intended as a finished work it merits the imprimatur of the artist's signature.

1648 saw the signing of the Treaty of Münster marking the end of the Thirty Years War and the cessation of hostilities between the Dutch and Spanish. This led to a decline in immigration from the Southern Netherlands to the north. But if peace had broken out, there were still plenty of beggars to be observed on the streets of Amsterdam. In the year of the Treaty Rembrandt etched the scene of *A Blind Hurdy-gurdy Player and Family Receiving Alms* [Fig. 81], his most monumental rendering of the subject of beggars. In a scene in which the householder is engaged with a group of humble visitors at his front door, it represents a reprise of the setting of his first genre etching of *The Rat Catcher* (see Fig. 57). But whereas the latter showed a certain inexperience in bringing the figures together, here the elderly bearded man in his house hat greets a harmoniously integrated group of family members, standing on the doorstep. And in sentiment, there is a also contrast between the two works. In the earlier, the householder turned away in disgust at the rat held out, while here his counterpart exudes benevolence as he hands over a coin; the motif of his hand giving and the woman's hand receiving establishes a focal point. Although the figures are brought together in an act of charity, the gutter running in front of the house serves to divide the world of the giving from that of those receiving.

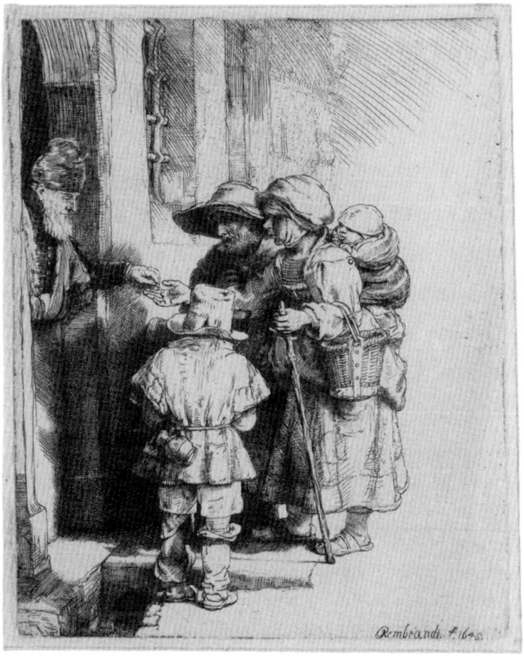

81. *A Blind Hurdy-gurdy Player and Family Receiving Alms*. 1648. Etching and drypoint. 16.5 × 12.8 cm. Rijksmuseum, Amsterdam.

Arranged in a tightly-composed circle, the family consists of the striking figure of a boy in a high hat, seen from the back with his jug attached to his waist, a youngish woman, a stick in hand and a basket on her arm, and carrying a tightly wrapped baby on her back, and finally an old man in a wide-brimmed hat, holding a hurdy-gurdy. The last, with his curiously blank stare, has the appearance of blindness, which would accord with the pictorial tradition going back to the previous century of blind peddlers depicted as playing the instrument. Unlike the artist's earlier studies of ragged beggars, the riff-raff on the streets, this family, though shabbily dressed in patched clothing, convey an aura of quiet dignity, suggesting that there is nothing satirical in the artist's approach to the subject. They are clearly representatives of the deserving poor, impoverished through no fault of their own, rather than the undeserving poor; this was a distinction relating to the moral duty of practising charity, which was much discussed at the time. To give to the former would be rewarded in heaven, while to give to the latter was merely wasteful.

The print, mainly etched but with some drypoint, is masterly in the way that it varies from the high finish devoted to what is important, namely the figures. Their faces are strongly individualised, which are emphasised by the heavy shading in cross-hatching, creating a play of light around them. This contrasts with the lightly-etched architecture. The wall of the house gradually peters out with no background beyond. There are no distracting picturesque details, everything is concentrated on the central act of giving.

In July 1652 the destruction by fire of Amsterdam's Old Town Hall, by that time considered out of date for the city's booming economy and in the course of demolition, greatly excited curiosity in the city. Rembrandt, like many other artists, did not lose time in visiting the site and two days after the event had made a drawing of the still smouldering ruins [Fig. 82]. The sheet was executed in broad simple lines with the reed pen, which gives the impression that it might have been done with the tip of a brush. On the back of the sheet he wrote, 'seen from the weighing house, the town hall of Amsterdam after it was burned down

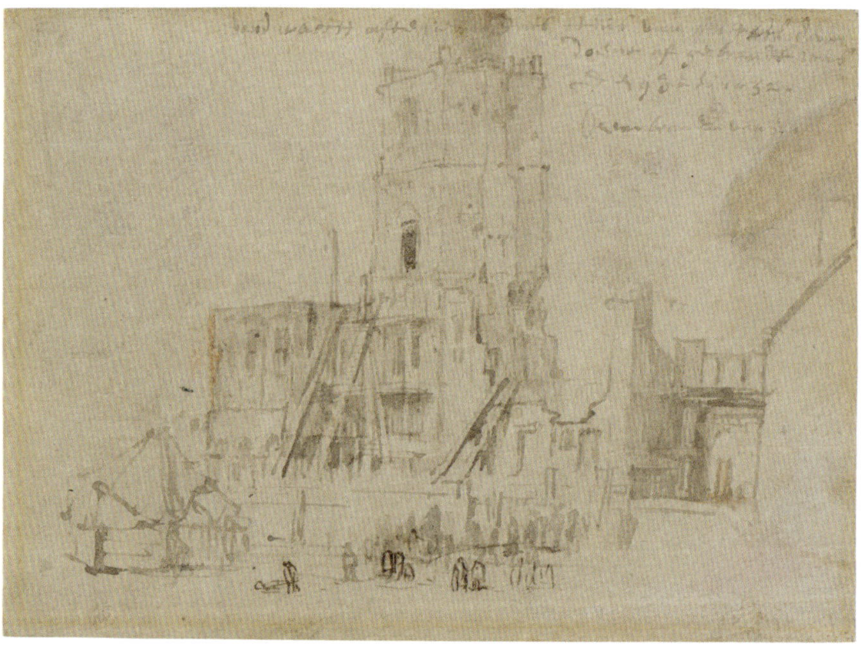

82. *Old Town Hall after the Fire*. 1652. Pen and brown ink, some red chalk. 15 × 20.1 cm. The Rembrandt House Museum, Amsterdam.

9 July 1652, Rembrandt van rijn'. Since he did not normally annotate his drawings, it suggests that on this occasion he was making a record for posterity. Long ladders are propped up against the ruined building and a fence had been put up protecting the site from the numerous sightseers; a wooden and canvas tent, which had been hastily erected to serve as a temporary Exchange Bank, stands in the left hand foreground. The artist, an admirer of medieval architecture, would have regretted the Old Town Hall's demise; he seems not to have been interested in the new magnificent classical building, hailed with much fanfare as the Eighth Wonder of the World, that replaced it. Doubtless increasing the artist's distaste is the fact that the palace was to have been the site of his rejected painting of the *Feast of the Batavians* (Nationalmuseum, Stockholm).

A drawing executed about this time of a young man in a high-crowned hat [Fig. 83] is, most unusually for a genre scene, site-specific. Seated in the corner of a room probably of an inn, his head is bent as he occupies himself writing or drawing. An inkpot can be made out beside the paper he is working on. The table is placed near a window, through which a small boy peeps, curious to know what is going on. The scene was drawn in a combination of pen and brush, with a few corrections made in white bodycolour; the rich play of light and shadow in the room, contrasting

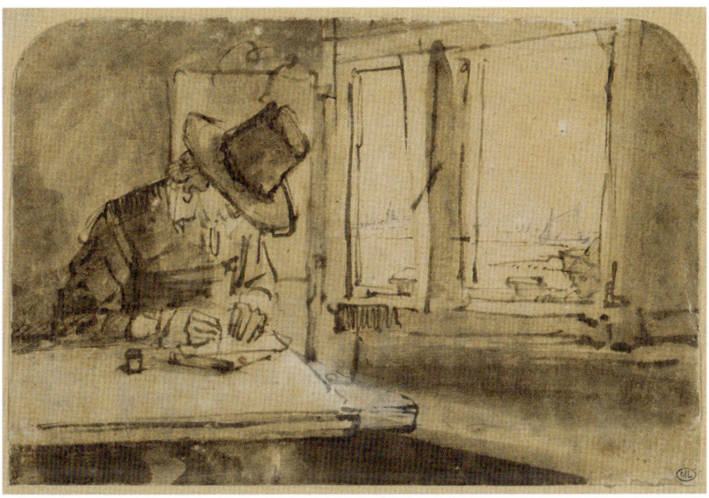

83. *Man Drawing or Writing at a Desk*. *c.*1652. Pen and brown ink with brown and grey wash, heightened with white. 13.5 × 19.7 cm. Musée du Louvre, Paris.

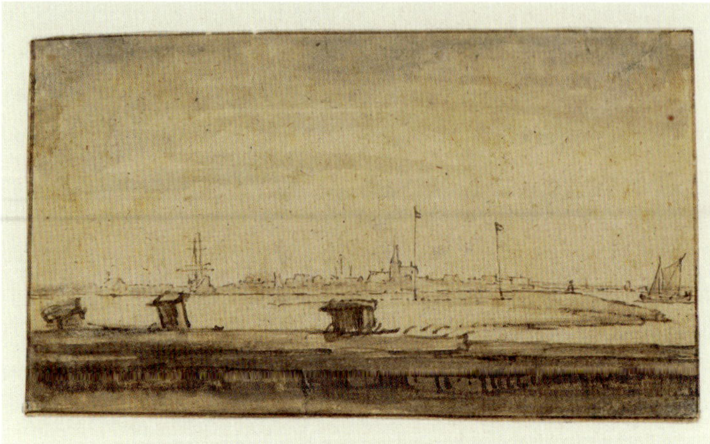

84. *View from Diemerdijk*. *c.*1652. Pen and brown ink with brown wash, with later additions in grey wash. 7.8 × 13.8 cm. Museum Boijmans Van Beuningen, Rotterdam.

with the bright daylight coming through the window, is carefully worked out to present a very finished work of art, almost certainly done in the studio rather than *in situ*.

A carefully depicted landscape can be made out through the window, consisting of probably two mooring posts, bordering a stretch of water with a sailing boat, and a church and other buildings on the far shore. By chance Rembrandt made either at the same period or on some other occasion a study of this particular view [Fig. 84], identifiable as a particular bend on the Diemerdijk with the village of Schellingswoude on the far shore. Situated in an isolated spot outside Amsterdam, with fine views over the water and the location of several inns, it was a favourite subject with the artist on his walks in the countryside around the city.

In 1655 Rembrandt painted *An Old Woman Reading* [Fig. 85]. Both Biblical and classical figures have been suggested as the subject, but the artist offers us no clues as to her identity, so probably we must regard the picture as another example of the *tronies* or heads which were so popular in his youth. The elderly had been a favoured subject with Rembrandt from the start. As the German author and artist, Joachim von Sandrart had written in his *Teutsche Akademie* (1675), 'In the depiction of old people, particularly their skin and hair, he [Rembrandt] showed great diligence, patience and practice'.[20] In a frontal pose, the woman

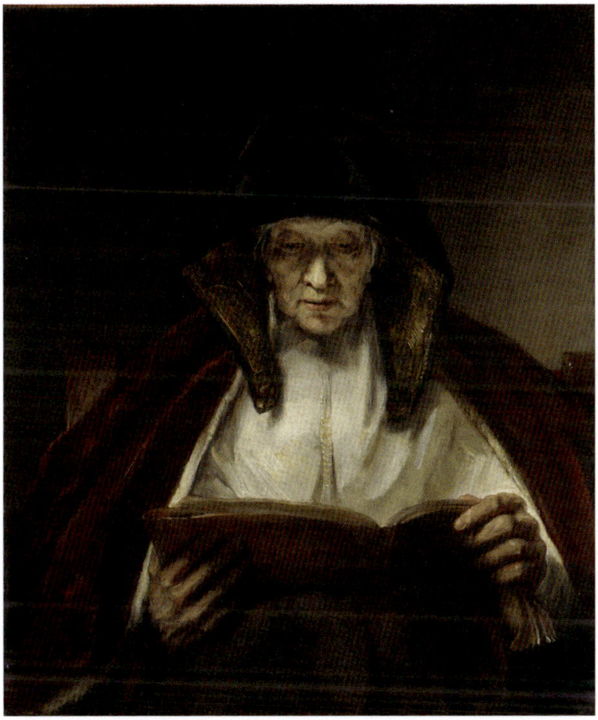

85. *An Old Woman Reading*. 1655. Canvas. 79 × 65 cm.
Duke of Buccleuch, Drumlandrig Castle.

is depicted, head bowed and displaying a peaceful expression of great dignity on her face, while she intently reads a large book held out in front of her, the subject of which we are left to guess. She has a long bony face with strong features powerfully modelled with broad brush-strokes. As so often with the artist, the hands holding the volume are rather perfunctorily adumbrated. The figure, which spreads out on either side of the canvas, creates a simple triangle outlined by the silhouette of her red velvet cloak. Both by virtue of her being seen from close at hand combined with the subtle play of light, the painting makes an immediate impact on the viewer. In fact the painting might be seen as an exercise in treating the varying sources of light. Coming from above it falls with intensity on her white undergarment from where it is reflected up onto her face, so that, for example, we can make out the dark shadows under her eyes and the glittering gold brocade lining to the inside of her hood. Seen from a distance, the picture positively glows.

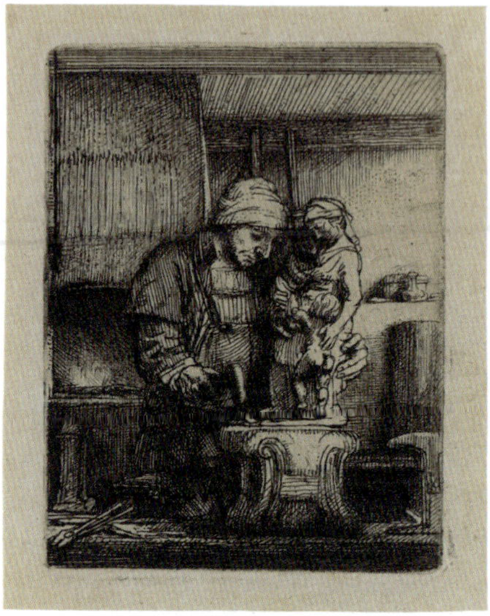

86. *The Goldsmith*. 1655.
Etching and drypoint. 7.7 × 5.6 cm.
Rijksmuseum, Amsterdam.

In the same year Rembrandt, for his last genre print, produced an etching usually known by its eighteenth-century title, *The Goldsmith* [Fig. 86], but in fact more likely to represent a sculptor. Set beside other prints of this period, the print stands out not only for its small size but also for its subject matter, namely the artist in his studio as opposed to the usual biblical scenes or portraits. Whether or not Rembrandt picked up the idea for the subject from an earlier representation of *The Smith* by Dirck Vellert (*c.*1514 – *c.*1547), as has been suggested, it is a totally personal creation. The scene is set in a studio with a fire burning beneath a large shield on the left, a ladder set up against the wall in the centre and an anvil in the foreground with a flask and pot on a shelf on the right. The very apparent verticals and horizontals of the background provide a foil to the irregular shapes of the figures. The standing sculptor, head draped and wearing a craftsman's apron, lovingly puts his arm round a personification of *Charity*, here represented as a woman with one child at her shoulder and the other clasped to her skirt. Rembrandt makes a telling contrast between the sculptor's large masculine hand and her delicate fingers. With his right hand he hammers the sculpture to a pedestal decorated with scrolls. He wears a melancholy look. One senses the artist's empathy for the sculptor handling his statue in the same way that Rembrandt caressed his copper plate as he produced such a jewel of a print. Although the setting is realistic, the work is probably intended to be allegorical, possibly illustrating the artist's love of his craft.

Compared with the freedom of execution of other etchings of the period, it is a highly wrought piece, with extensive fine hatching and cross-hatching, which conveys the delicate play of light in this dark interior. Darker accents are added in drypoint, and to enhance the preciousness of the image all the impressions are printed on Japanese paper which gives a softness and yellow tone to the print, and which is particularly sensitive to the work in drypoint, a tool which had become increasingly popular in Rembrandt's printmaking.

In April 1664 a young woman from Jutland, called Else Christiaens, arrived in Amsterdam to find work. For non-payment of her rent, her landlady beat her with a broom. In retaliation Else killed her with an axe. She was sentenced to death with the stipulation that she should be hit on the head with the axe. Her body was then to be 'brought to Volewijk and fastened to a pole with an axe above her head, to decay in the air and to be devoured by birds'.[21] If this tragic event is rightly associated with two drawings of a *Woman Hanging on a Gibbet* [Fig. 87, and Metropolitan Museum of Art, New York], which seems likely, it would establish the two

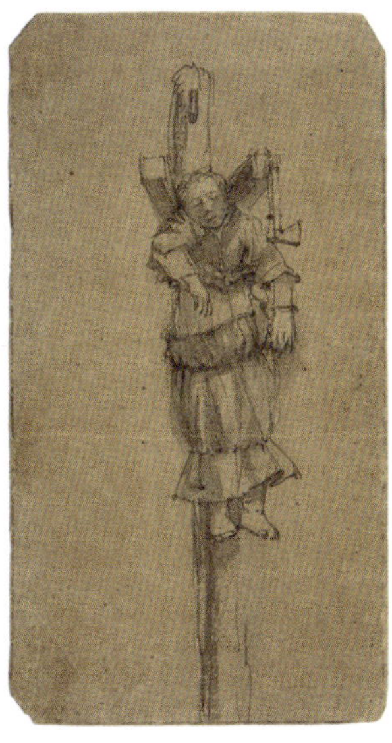

87. *Woman Hanging on a Gibbet. c.*1664. Pen and brown ink with brown wash on light brown paper. 17.2 × 9 cm. Metropolitan Museum of Art, New York.

studies as the latest documented drawings in Rembrandt's *œuvre*. The isolated spot, where the execution took place, was situated on a headland to the north of Amsterdam, accessed by ferry across the river Ij. Although we know from a landscape drawing Rembrandt had visited the place earlier, by the time these drawings were made he had given up his regular walks around Amsterdam, so that one can presume he made a special visit to study this macabre spectacle.

Taken from the low viewpoint of the observer at ground level, the young woman is seen strung up to a post, with her axe hanging accusingly beside her. To avoid any unseemly exposure of the lower parts of her body, her skirts are tightly tied around her legs. There is an air of detachment about these two drawings which make it impossible to divine whether Rembrandt felt any sympathy for the mournful end of this newly-arrived immigrant. Yet the lifeless expression on the girl's face, squeezed between her hunched shoulders and with her arms hanging feebly down beside her, induces a feeling of pity on the part of the viewer. The studies are freely drawn with the pen, so that one might suppose that they were executed on the spot, with the wash added in the studio. As the last dated drawings, they testify to the artist's continuing interest in all aspects of the Amsterdam scene, whether life enhancing or the opposite.

CHAPTER 4

Landscape and the bucolic scene: life in the countryside

THE LANDSCAPE of Holland poses a particular problem to the artist. From the eastern borders with Germany to the North Sea in the west, there is not a single mountain or high hill. There are limitless views on all sides. The most elevated terrain is to be found in the dunes bordering the coast. In the countryside around Amsterdam, which for a time became Rembrandt's regular stamping ground, the most noticeable features are farm buildings or cottages, usually surrounded by trees, church towers and small villages; even cattle and the sails of boats stand out against the skyline and provide variety to an otherwise largely featureless scene. In selecting his subjects the artist was spoilt for choice. Dykes and waterways stretch in a network across the landscape, but the viewpoint is so low that it requires a masterly precision in the rendering of tone and linear perspective in order to suggest distance. It was precisely this quality which Dutch artists made so much their own.

Led by a number of artists emigrating from the Southern Netherlands, there was by the second decade of the seventeenth century an established tradition of realistic landscape painting, drawing and printmaking in Holland. One popular speciality were prints of actual views both within the town and outside. It was a trend of which Rembrandt was fully aware, when he began to treat landscape as a serious subject; but he followed with one important difference. His interest was rarely if ever topographical. He may have taken the same walks outside Amsterdam as other artists – they tended to be along the medieval dyke roads leading to outlying villages – but he almost never identified his works with inscriptions; and when an etching was of an identifiable view, he was unconcerned that the image would be printed in reverse. And faced with a building, which had been modernised but not to his taste, he did not hesitate to remove the later additions. But despite his lack of interest in topography, there are numerous prints and drawings, which contain features, although sometimes modified by the artist, which can be identified. From these it is possible to reconstruct specific walks around Amsterdam, to some of which he returned on numerous occasions. In treating landscape Rembrandt varied his procedure, it would seem sometimes working outdoors 'from life', carrying either a sketchbook or a grounded copper plate with him. The 1656 inventory of his possessions makes mention of 'an album full of landscapes drawn from life by Rembrandt' and 'a parchment book full of landscapes drawn from life by Rembrandt',[22] which might possibly support this contention. On other occasions he worked in the studio, relying on existing knowledge or with relevant sketches beside him. It is not easy to establish a hard and fast dividing line between the two procedures and frequently it remains a matter of guesswork.

In Holland the landscape artist was faced with a choice of subject. Unlike a good number of Dutch artists, who had their own speciality, Rembrandt did not limit himself to one kind; whatever he saw around him could and did engage his interest. It is remarkable how varied his landscapes were, both in approach and choice of motif. Underlying the former was the basic artistic challenge of harnessing the multiple forms of the natural world into a coherent whole, without getting lost in detail. On the one hand he could depict a wide panorama, in which the sky was necessarily an important component, or a receding view along a river into the distance. On the other hand he could concentrate on one of the details of the landscape, such as farm buildings, often with hay barns attached, or cottages, frequently surrounded by trees, or more secluded parts of the scene. There are numerous of examples of the latter category, which is a principal focus of this chapter.

One other aspect of Rembrandt's landscapes, also discussed here in depth, is how often the human figure is part of the scene. Although less apparent in his drawings, almost every print contains a human element. This varies from what can be called 'staffage', usually on a very small scale so that sometimes the figures are difficult to make out, to figures engaged in some activity which is part of the subject. And this approach can be expanded to genre or narrative subjects, in which the all enclosing landscape becomes an important ingredient.

Rembrandt's engagement with realistic Dutch landscape was short and sharp, approximately stretching from the first dated etching in 1640 to the latest dated 1652. How intensive this study was is illustrated by the number of works still existing. One of the problems of studying his landscape drawings is that it is very difficult to date them, so that when he made them largely remains a matter of guesswork. It should also be borne in mind that the span of his activity may have been wider than we think. Earlier in the 1630s he began by painting a number of landscapes with imaginary scenery, usually overcast with dramatic cloud effects. Even in the one painting related to an actual site, *The Stone Bridge* (Rijksmuseum, Amsterdam), one is more conscious of the weather, rather than what lies below the dark storm-laden clouds promising a downpour. At the other end of the time scale his intense interest in the subject waned sometime after 1652, when he seems to have abandoned walking in the landscape.

Among the earliest landscape drawings to be considered is one which is nothing more rural than the rear view of a farm building [Fig. 88]. So typical of the artist, his interest was engaged by the variety of detail to

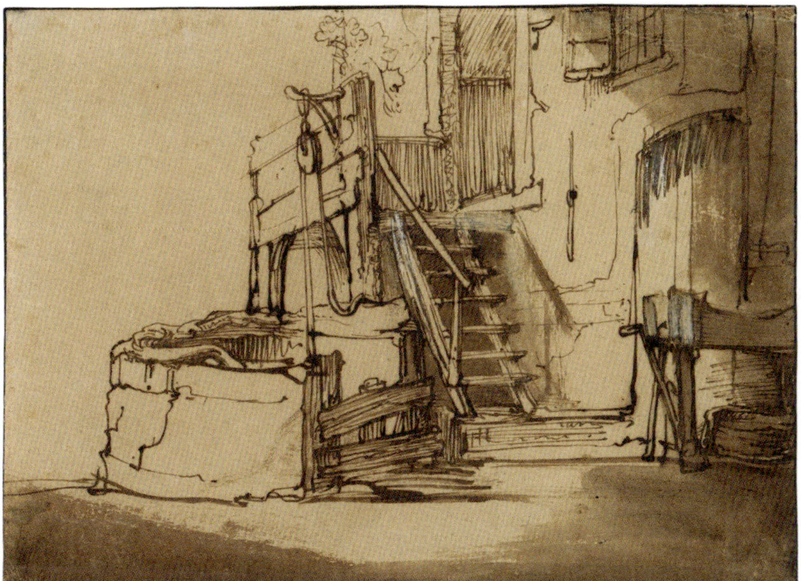

88. *Entrance to a Farm*. *c.*1638/9. Pen and brown ink with brown wash, heightened with white on light brown paper. 17.9 × 23.5 cm. Kunsthalle, Hamburg.

be found of this farmhouse, which had seen better days; broken wooden steps leading to the back door; at the bottom a well, closed with a makeshift wooden gate and overhung by a pulley attached to a bucket to collect water; a trestle table can be made out on the right. It is an image of bricks and mortar at its most basic, with the surfaces lovingly described with the quill pen and iron gall ink, so that stone is clearly differentiated from wood. The whole is brought together with the addition of wash in the foreground, so that it can be regarded as a finished work of art.

Humble cottages, such as those seen in the drawing of *Two Thatched Cottages* [Fig. 89], were a constant theme. Side by side, the two homes are sited diagonally beside a track. The foremost cottage is constructed in a jumble of stone, clay and wooden supporting boards, covered with a thatched roof, over which a vine has spread itself. The study would appear to be unfinished, since the roof of what was presumably to be a third cottage can be seen on the right. Once again the quill pen is brilliantly accurate in describing the different surfaces, at the same time conveying the volume of the structures. Indicative of how much thought Rembrandt gave to a seemingly simple study, he took the trouble to suppress a small area of vine to the left of the foremost chimney by covering it with white bodycolour. Although the lines are freely drawn, the drawing has the impression of high finish. And on this occasion a human element has been added with the introduction of two very small figures

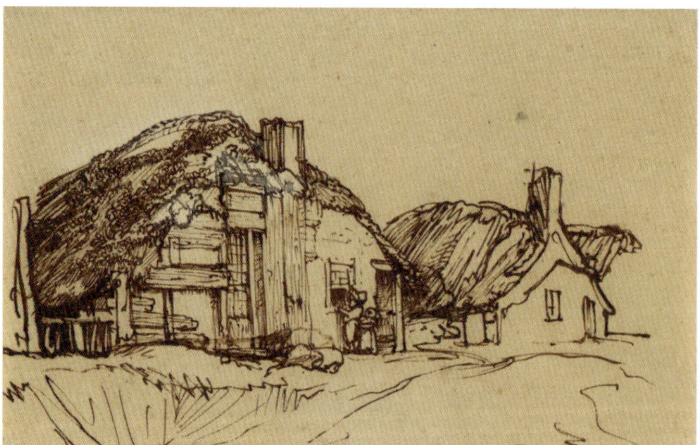

89. *Two Thatched Cottages*. *c.*1640. Pen and brown ink, heightened with white. 13.2 × 20.2 cm. J. Paul Getty Museum, Los Angeles.

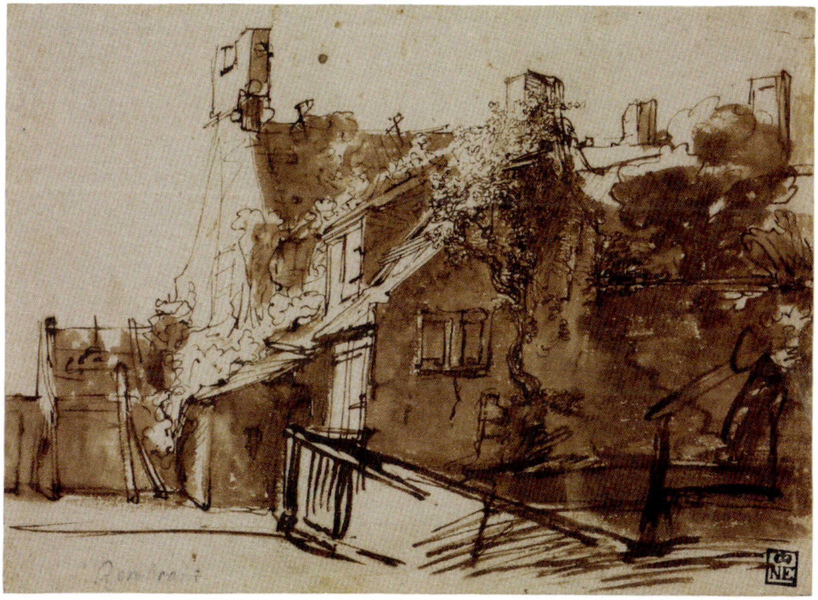

90. *Inner Courtyard of a Farmhouse*. *c.*1640. Pen and brown ink with brown wash. 15.4 × 22.3 cm. Szépmüvészeti Museum, Budapest.

of a woman accompanied by a child standing by the cottage door; the woman is clearly engaged in conversation with the inhabitant. It enlivens what otherwise would have been a detached study of buildings.

In another drawing [Fig. 90], done about the same time, Rembrandt has portrayed the effects of sunlight falling on the rear quarters of a farmhouse. The roofs of the extensions to the main building are covered with a vine tumbling over the tiles, which almost becomes the main subject. The backdoor, hidden in shadow, is protected from the elements by a roof, under which a bench and bucket can be made out. In few other landscape drawings is light and shadow so strongly portrayed with extensive areas of brown wash overlaying the underlying penwork. It is yet another representation of country picturesque, which engaged the artist so forcibly at this time.

A *Cow Standing in a Shed* [Fig. 91], executed in the late 1630s, has the distinction of an animal being shown as part of the everyday scene and not limited to an isolated study of the creature itself, as has already been seen in other depictions of animals In this drawing, an unusual variation on his studies of country buildings, a cow is munching hay in a manger,

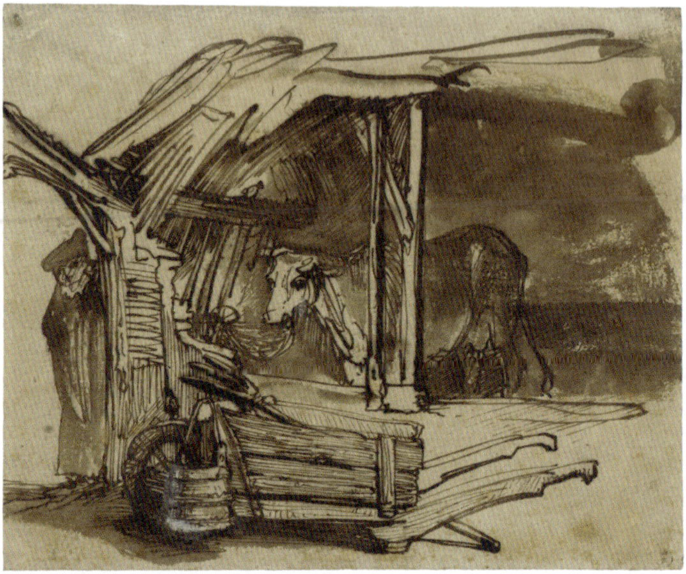

91. *Cow Standing in a Shed. c.*1638. Pen and brown ink with brown wash, heightened with white, on light-brown prepared paper. 15.3 × 18.2 cm. Rijksmuseum, Amsterdam.

while, on the left, a man in a flat cap, an active participant in the scene, leans forward to peep round the outside of the building on the left, presumably to see what the cow is up to. In the foreground, neatly arranged together, as if in a composed still-life, are a wheelbarrow, a pitchfork and a milk-pail. The roughly-constructed shed supported by timbers and covered with straw has unquestionably seen better days. Rembrandt has drawn on paper which has been given a light brown wash to provide a basic tone. Similar to a number of other drawings of this period, Rembrandt has used iron-gall ink (see p. 91). The technique here varies from the fine lines describing the objects in the foreground to the summary description of the roof of the shed. The cow's mouth and the pail have been highlighted with small touches of white bodycolour. To portray the darkened interior, the artist has applied wash freely, so that the sheet offers a strong contrast of light and shadow, not dissimilar in effect from the previous drawing.

Executed about 1640 or possibly a few years later – the date is a matter of dispute – the *Small Grey Landscape* [Fig. 92], as it is called, is unique both in size and treatment compared to the other landscape etchings.

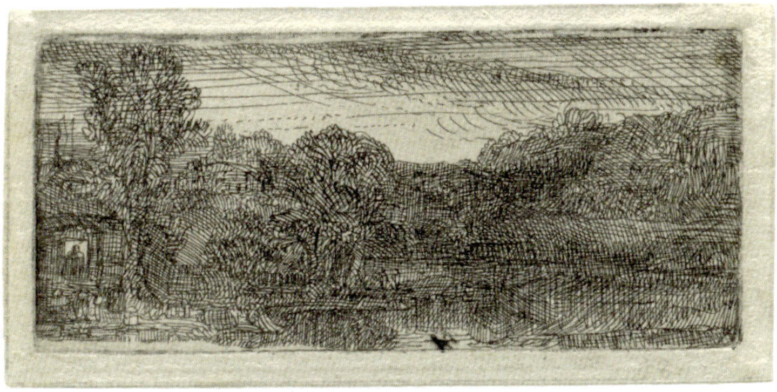

92. *Small Grey Landscape*. *c.*1640. Etching. 3.8 × 8.2 cm. Rijksmuseum, Amsterdam.

Measuring no more than 3.8 × 8.2 centimetres, it is one of his smallest etchings, and might, one could suppose, be the case of the artist using a piece of copper left over from cutting down another plate. Without any clear definition of individual features, the landscape is made up of a web of uniformly etched lines, offering a study in tone within a limited range. As its name implies, there are no strong contrasts to create a sense of great distance. Through the penumbra a cottage with a large tree beside a lake, bordered by trees, emerges from close study. The long shadows cast over the water indicate either the advent of morning, or, more likely, evening. There is an overwhelming feeling of calm and quietness. Unobtrusively humanising the scene. a man standing against the light looks out of the cottage door, watching a woman, barely visible, doing the washing, while two men walk beside the tree-bordered lake, with hills in the background; a partly drawn boat can perhaps be spotted in the immediate foreground. It is not a realistic scene but offers the type of crepuscular wooded landscape, which was the forte of the German artist, Adam Elsheimer (1578–1610), whose paintings Rembrandt knew from the reproductive engravings of Hendrick Goudt (1580/5–1648). Intimate in its closed-in setting and poetic in its rendering of light, it is more an expression, in miniature, of mood than a record of fact, and stands alone among Rembrandt's landscape prints.

After this exquisite small print, a study of another country building, in this case a *Farmhouse with Artist Sketching* [Fig. 93], might seem more down to earth, but it has its own special interest. Unlike the *Two Thatched*

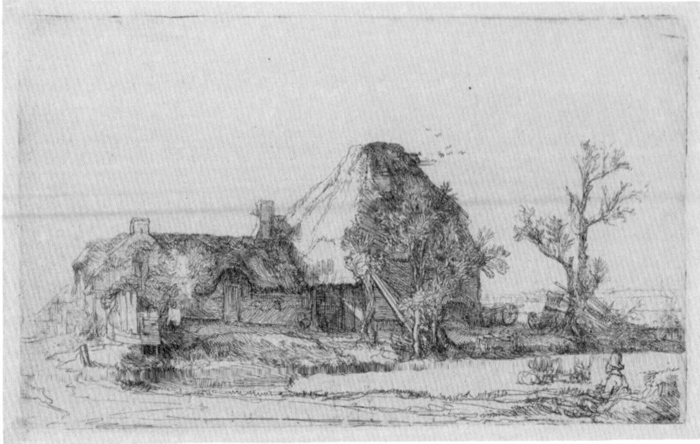

93. *Farmhouse with Artist Sketching*. *c.*1641. Etching. 13 × 20.8 cm. Rijksmuseum, Amsterdam.

Cottages (see Fig. 89), which are firmly rooted to the earth, the farm sits proudly on slightly raised ground, with an upright tree to one side playing the role of a flagpole and giving the building status. Distances on either side are barely delineated, yet there is a sense of air encompassing the building, which stands firmly on its own in the round. The evenly-etched lines serve a dual purpose. The contrasts of sun and shadow are clearly depicted on both the roof of the living quarters on the left and the higher stable roof on the right. At the same time it conveys the detail of the thatching and the varied materials used in the rough and ready construction of the building, as well as such items as the laundry hanging next to the extension on the left and the birds hovering above the dove hatch on the stable roof. What appear to be cattle but with long ears like rabbits are grazing in the field in front. Suggesting that the artist was studying a specific building, the chimney, as has been pointed out, is placed on the divide between dwelling and stable, rather than in the middle of the former, as is found in other Rembrandt farm buildings. In the immediate right foreground an artist sits drawing or etching, a feature to be found in a drawing to be discussed later (see Fig. 102) as well as in minuscule form in the etching of *The Three Trees* of 1643. The reasons for its inclusion are not clear. Here the artist is bearded so is not intended to be a self-portrait, but its presence might suggest Rembrandt is giving us a hint that he was working on his copper plate before the motif rather than in the studio, that is if Gersaint is correct in asserting that Rembrandt carried prepared copper plates with him on his walks around Amsterdam.

Surely with lingering memories of childhood, windmills make a frequent appearance in Rembrandt's *œuvre*, with such works as his renowned painting of *The Mill* (National Gallery of Art, Washington), and before that one of his first dated landscape etchings, *The Windmill* of 1641. About the same time or shortly after the latter, he made a close-up study in *The Mill on the Bulwark 'Het Blauwhoofd'* [Fig. 94]. The site, a dead-end for the walker, which Rembrandt visited on more than once on his excursions around Amsterdam, was a promontory on the outskirts of the west side of the city, offering wonderful views overlooking the river Ij, a chain of lagoons, with its constantly moving shipping. Standing in isolation were a grain mill, known as *De Bok* (Billy Goat), and two adjoining cottages, protected by several cannon, which can just be made out on the shore on the left. In front of the latter are two figures, one of whom is seated and may be an artist at work with a sketchbook resting on his lap; another figure is just beyond them.

Although the mill looms high on the sheet, the artist's main preoccupation were the two cottages, which by the application of darker chalk

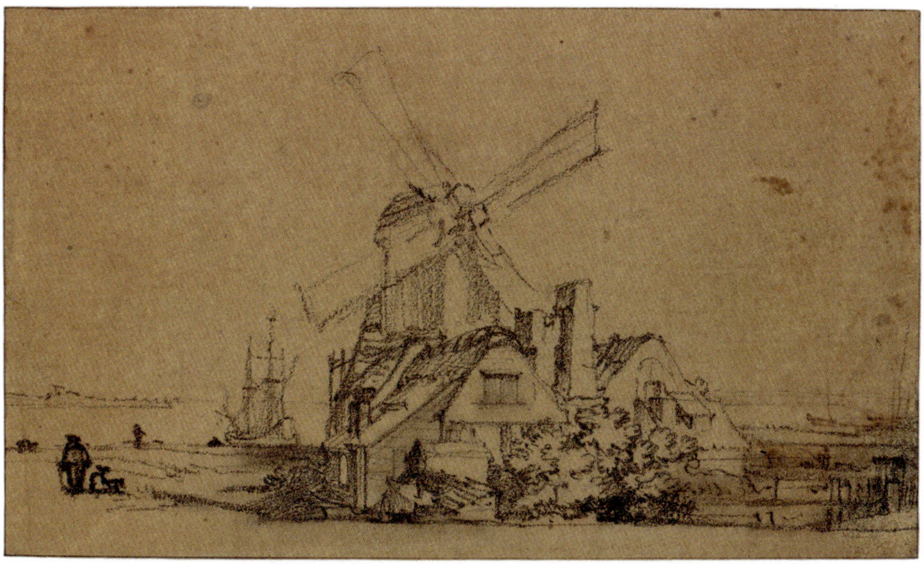

94. *The Mill on the Bulwark 'Het Blauwhoofd'*. *c.*1645. Oiled charcoal on light-brown paper. 16.6 × 27.5 cm. Museum Boijmans Van Beuningen, Rotterdam.

lines establish their place in the foreground. The artist varied the pressure on the chalk throughout to create a sense of aerial perspective, diminishing in the distance to the faint indication of the flat landscape on the north shore. Chalk was less often used for his landscape drawings, and here, Rembrandt ever the experimenter with his media, has used oiled charcoal – i.e charcoal fixed with linseed oil – on a brown tinted paper. The overall result of his technique employed here is to produce a soft atmospheric effect, appropriate for the depiction of landscape, but one which curiously he never used again.

In another chalk drawing [Fig. 95] of this period, Rembrandt made one of his most intimate studies of nature, unparalleled in the work of other Dutch artists. Standing on a wooden drawbridge, which can be seen in the immediate foreground, the artist looked along a backwater, bordered by trees, with a view of a windmill faintly discernible in the

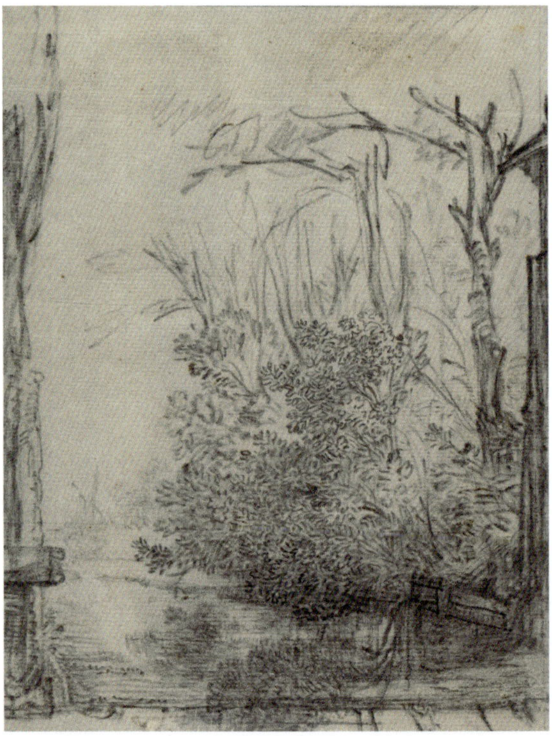

95. *Canal Between Bushes*. *c.*1645. Black chalk.
14.5 × 11.5 cm. The Museum of the Lubomirski
Princes at the Ossoliński National Institute, Wrocław.

distance. The view is neatly framed by wooden posts at either side. In the foreground, the foliage on the bushes casts a strong reflexion in the water, while the upper branches of the trees stand out bare against the sky. The handling of the chalk shows his appreciation of the different elements in the landscape, which he had mastered by this time. Particularly to be noted is the differentiation between the broken strokes conveying the soft foliage with the stark outlines of the tree trunks rising behind them. Compared with the wide views seen in so many of his drawings and etchings, this simple subject to be seen throughout the Dutch landscape must have caught his eye on one of his walks in the polderland around Amsterdam, where houses were frequently separated from the road by a ditch, covered by a bridge. It is surely a sketch made on the spot.

If not exactly a preparatory study, the drawing must have served as an *aide-memoire* when Rembrandt came to his etching of another very intimate landscape known as *The Boat House* or, in the eighteenth century, as *The Grotto* [Fig. 96], dated 1645. The two works share the motif of trees and bushes bordering a closed-in stretch of water. In the print, the viewpoint is the near bank with the diagonally-placed water leading the

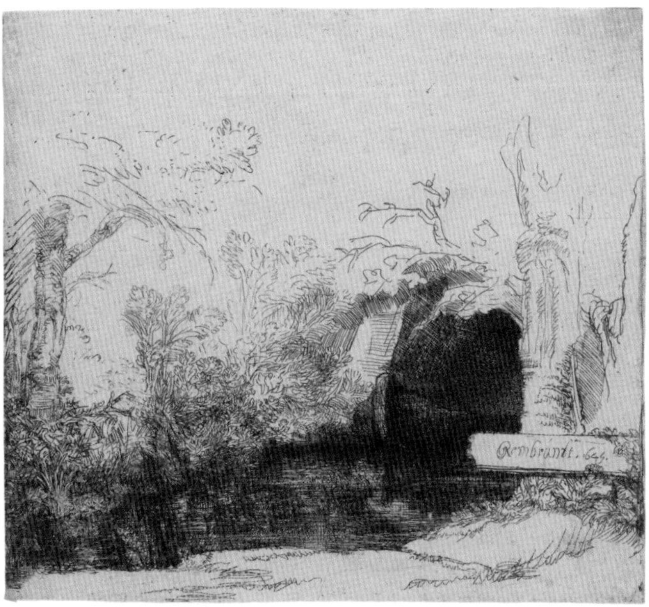

96. *The Boat House*. 1645. Etching and drypoint. 12.5 × 13.2 cm. Rijksmuseum, Amsterdam.

eye gently to the grotto on the right, from which the prow of a boat is emerging. Rembrandt's signature in the right hand foreground is placed very deliberately on a wooden plank serving no other particular purpose. Once again the plate offers the kind of hidden scene that one might come across by chance wandering through the landscape. The foliage and tree trunks are sketched in with finely-etched lines, achieving the same freedom and spontaneity as his handling of the chalk in the drawing. To make it stand out, the artist darkened the water with drypoint, working heavily over the area of the boat and the grotto, which, as a result, steal the limelight. In a change of technical procedure to be discussed further below, this landscape and *The Omval* (see Fig. 99), executed in the same year, are the first landscapes to include extensive work in drypoint In fact, on this occasion he must have concluded that he had made the grotto area too dark from the ink held by the burr and in a second state he removed much of the burr on the prow of the boat and the grotto, leaving an unsatisfactory scraped appearance.

It is unwise to try and interpret Rembrandt's work through his life, yet nevertheless a phase of eroticism became apparent in Rembrandt's etched work in the years just after Saskia's death and during the time the ensuing *menage à trois* was developing between Rembrandt, Geertje Dircx and Hendrickje Stoffels. Whether or not there is any connection between life and art remains an open question. In two etchings, one euphemistically called *'Le lit à la française'* (The French Bed) and the other *The Monk in the Cornfield*, probably of the same date, the couples are unashamedly depicted in *flagrante delicto*. More covert eroticism is at play in *The Flute Player* [Fig. 97] of 1642. At first sight nothing could be more innocent than a young shepherd, with his crook at his side and holding his flute, lying on the grassy bank next to a young shepherdess wearing a wide straw hat by the side of a brook, while, untethered in the background, sheep and goats tumble over one another to quench their thirst. An unexplained woman's head, later removed, appears in the trees upper right. The thick boscage behind the figures provides the appropriate setting for, it would seem, an innocuous pastoral scene, popular both in Rembrandt's work and Dutch art at the time.

But on closer examination, the shepherd can be seen, not only playing his flute, a recognised phallic symbol, but holding it with his fingers on

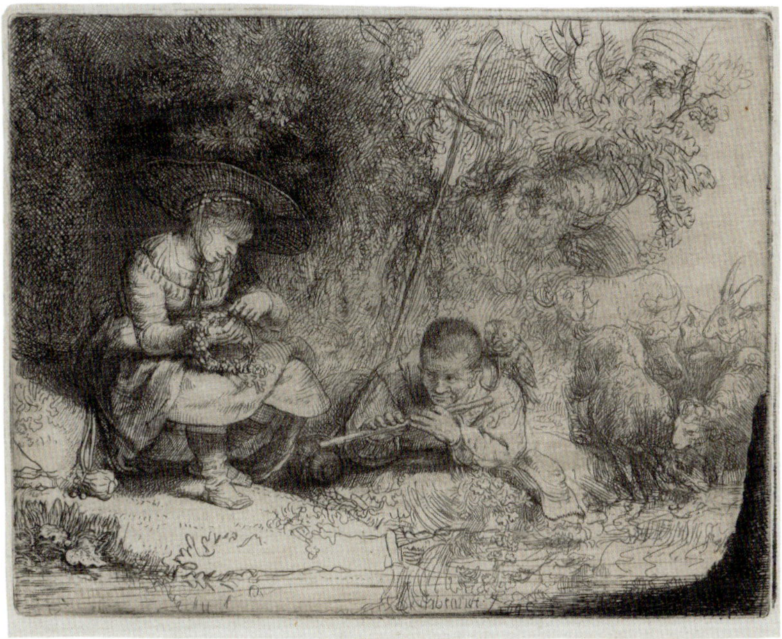

97. *The Flute Player*. 1642. Etching and drypoint. 11.5 × 14.3 cm. Rijksmuseum, Amsterdam.

the stops as he furtively glances up the skirt of the indecorously seated shepherdess; the placing of the flute follows the direction of his gaze. The tame owl sitting on the shepherd's shoulder, with collar and bells around its neck, was associated with folly and sinfulness. The floral garland she is weaving so lovingly can be interpreted as a symbol of female genitalia, as can the purse beside her, while sheep and goats were often considered as symbols of sexual excess. The entire scene is charged with an understated sensuality. Although, following the trend of much contemporary Dutch art, it is possible Rembrandt's intention might have been moralistic or satirical, it seems more in character that his approach to the subject was more straightforward.

The print was executed in what was becoming his usual procedure of starting with etching and then reworking certain details or areas with dry-point to embellish or emphasise. Undergoing no less than four working states, it was a plate which caused the artist some difficulty in achieving his end. Since the watermarks on the paper on which all four states were printed are the same, we can be certain that one stage quickly followed another. Apart from altering or removing some details, he had most concern in defining the girl's straw hat against the shaded background, at first over strengthening and then reducing the contrast. The etching is an example of his perfectionism, never hesitating to try and attain an ideal end, but occasionally, as was seen in the previous print, going too far.

Several years later Rembrandt produced a very small etching of the *The Sleeping Herdsman* [Fig. 98]. In the eighteenth century, the work was known as 'the courtly print'. While the elderly herdsman, with his head resting on his right hand, supported by his stick, is seated on a bank in deep slumber, a young couple beside him are engaged in advanced dalliance. The young man's joyful gaze follows the actions of his hands at work beneath the girl's skirt, while she keeps a keen weather-eye on the old man, who is perhaps her father or grandfather. Behind in a densely-wooded setting, two cows are peacefully munching, observing what is taking place. Suffused with eroticism, the plate offers an idyllic pastoral scene. The composition was established with loosely-etched lines, after which areas of shadow around the figures and the animals were created with drypoint. Although very small in size, it is a work rich in content.

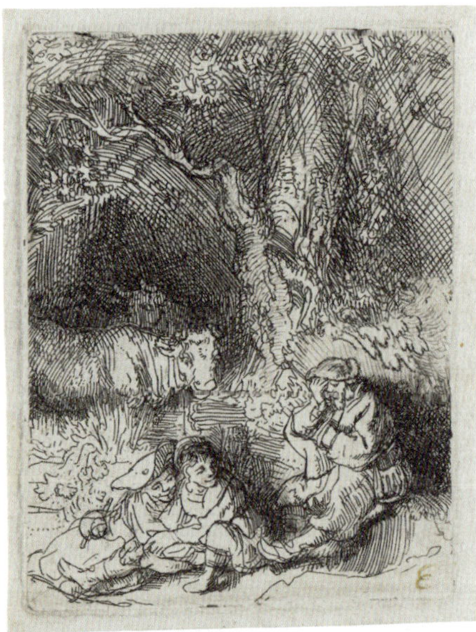

98. *The Sleeping Herdsman. c.*1644.
Etching and drypoint. 7.8 × 5.7 cm.
Rijksmuseum, Amsterdam.

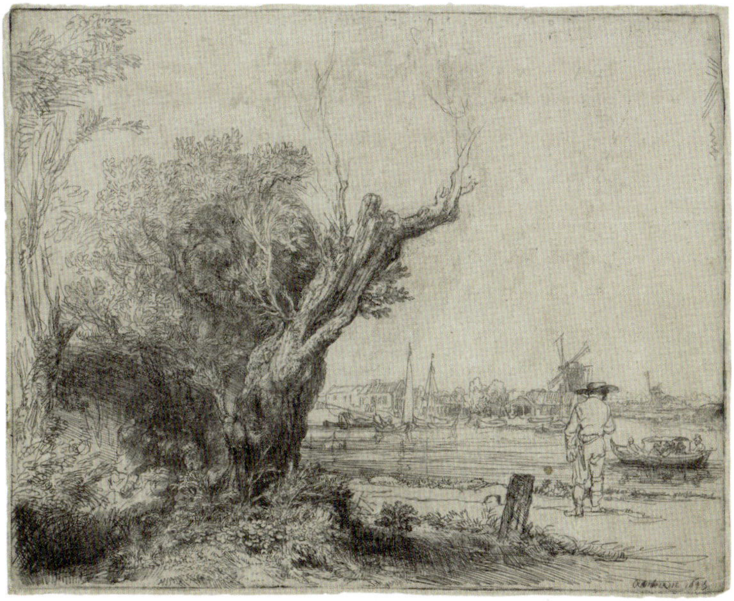

99. *The Omval*. 1645. Etching and drypoint. 18.4 × 22.5 cm.
Rijksmuseum, Amsterdam.

More innocent love-making can be found in the etching of *The Omval* (Ruin) [Fig. 99], dated 1645. The name *Omval* recalls the ruined building which once stood on the site, which was situated on a spit of land, bordered on one side by the river Amstel (seen here) and a tributary known as the Ringvaart on the other side. It was the scene of much activity on the river, since it was at this point that the Amstel coming from Amsterdam divided in two. As well as a series of windmills, the place was known for its tavern, which was very popular with Amsterdammers and was to be the subject of at least three drawings in the years to come. (For more on the artist's later walks along the river Amstel, see below).

The print divides roughly, and somewhat uneasily, into two subjects. On the right we see the Amstel with the Omval on the far side, with buildings and the shipyard with boats and yachts moored in front, all suggesting a lively scene of a local watering hole. On the right a man, whose purpose is unclear, stands looking at a canopied boat, filled with people, who are presumably taking a trip along the river or, perhaps, crossing to go to the inn. A wooden post on the near bank followed by the figure of the man and the boat create a diagonal which leads the eye towards a distant windmill. On the left of the composition is a copse with the gnarled trunk of a dead willow standing prominently in the foreground. In the shadows within the foliage, a young couple can just be made out lying on the grass, he crowning her with a garland of flowers. Totally wrapped in themselves, they are unaware of all the activity taking place around them. The print offers a contrast in mood between the inner private world of a couple of romantic young lovers and the bustle of everyday life on the river.

The year 1645 marked a technical turning point in Rembrandt's landscape etching. The earlier landscapes were limited to etching, but now, having etched in the basic subject, he turned to drypoint for embellishment and refinement. This allowed him to make changes directly on the plate, without having to put a new ground on the copper plate and submit it to a second biting in the acid. But at this stage he had yet to achieve a perfect blending of the two techniques. In earlier impressions of *The Omval* (seen here), before the burr had either worn down or having been scraped away, there is a conflict between the over-dark work in drypoint compared with the comparatively lighter-etched lines. This tonal imbalance is particularly apparent on the willow trunk and the nearby foliage. If one can regard it as a fault, it was soon remedied.

In the following year Rembrandt painted a very small panel of a *Winter Landscape* (Fig. 100), which was unique in his *œuvre*. In scale, treatment and theme, it is quite unlike his other painted landscapes and has the fluency and spontaneity that we normally associate with an oil-sketch by Rubens (1577–1640). Part landscape, part genre scene, it follows the subject matter of the artist's elder contemporary, Esaias van de Velde (1587–1630), who was a specialist in such scenes. The setting here is a stretch of frozen canal, crossed by a bridge seen on the left. The clear bright light of a winter's day is evident, as one senses the cold crispness of the air. In the left-hand foreground, a skater, wearing a wide brimmed hat, is seated resting; in the centre, followed by her dog, a woman gingerly makes her way across the ice towards two men, both holding poles, one, a seated skater, and the other, wearing a fur cap, standing. A grey horse(?) can just be made out on the far bank, where a farm building, flanked by a bare tree and a haystack fill the background. In the distance, on the left, a windmill and a church tower with a crowning spire are silhouetted.

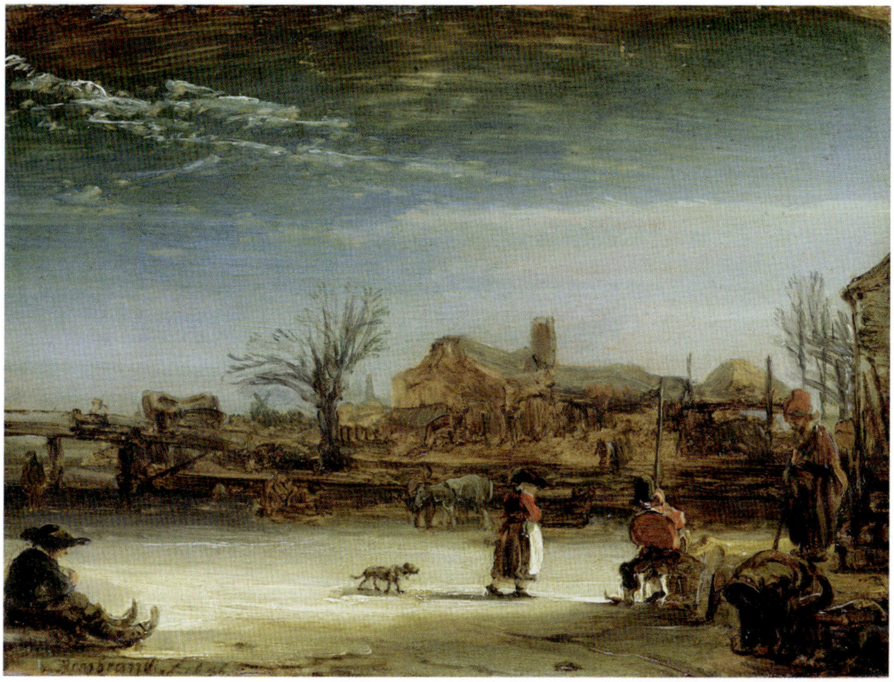

100. *Winter Landscape*. 1646. Panel. 17 × 23 cm. Gemäldegalerie alter Meister, Museumlandschaft Hessen, Kassel.

Scudding clouds, which partially catch the sunlight, fill the sky. Rich in colour contrasts, heightened by the use of a white ground instead of one of the artist's usual darker grounds, the bright blue sky and the white ice are divided by the neutral brown of the terrain. Touches of red enliven the clothing of the woman and the seated skater on the right. For all its informality, it is a beautifully composed little landscape, a perfect image of a country scene on a cold, frosty day in winter. That he added his signature and a date, painted into the still wet surface, must indicate that he considered it a finished work.

The freedom of execution gives it the character of one of those works, referred to at the beginning of the chapter, that were supposedly executed outdoors before the motif. From an examination of the paint layers, one can determine that the technique was sufficiently straightforward to allow of such a procedure. It might well be identified with either 'A landscape from nature by the same (i.e. Rembrandt)' or 'A small landscape painted from nature by Rembrandt', both of which were recorded in the 1656

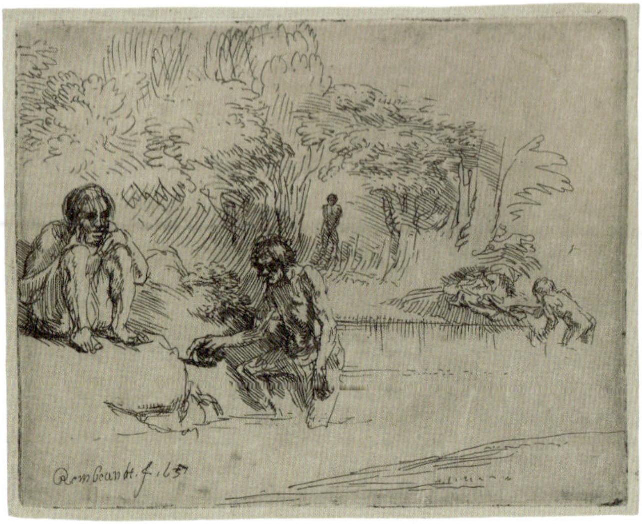

101. *The Swimmers*. 1651. Etching. 10.9 × 13.5 cm. Rijksmuseum, Amsterdam.

inventory of his possessions. This small panel has the immediacy of a drawing rather than a carefully considered painting.

The etching of *The Swimmers* [Fig. 101], dated 1651, offers a subject that was rarely treated in Dutch art. The setting is a river bordered by trees with four men, presumably friends who have gathered to refresh themselves on a hot summer's day. One, on the left, sits huddled on the bank while beside him another makes his way out of the water. A third man is seen on the right reaching for his clothes on the river bank. And the fourth, in the centre background, appears to be relieving himself. It is a vivid snapshot of daily life, studied for itself without any other significance, such as illustrating a mythological story. It is a scene which the artist might unexpectedly have come across walking in the landscape. Certainly the men display no embarrassment over their naked state. Sharing the character of a line drawing, the plate is so freely and lightly etched, with the foliage so summarily suggested, that one might suppose it was done from the life. Artfully placed areas of loosely drawn parallel hatching create a pattern of light and shadow, giving depth to the scene.

The ancient village of Diemen, situated to the East of Amsterdam, was Rembrandt's favourite motif, which he studied from both within and without. From where the artist lived, he was soon out of the city and walking, no doubt bracingly, along the Diemerdijk. The dyke, which bordered the stretch of water known as the Ij with fine views of shipping (seen clearly in the background of an etching to be discussed later (see Fig. 107)), soon reached a point called Diemen Afstop (Turning-off), where Rembrandt turned right inland, soon arriving at Diemen. On at least three occasions he drew the village from the approach road. In one of which [Fig. 102], the most lightly-drawn of the group, an artist, in hat and jacket, can be seen seated on a hillock, drawing the view before him in his sketchbook. It is almost the only occasion on which he included the figure of an artist in a drawing, and recalls the figure in the etching discussed earlier [Fig. 93]. His presence, firmly establishing the foreground, might, if it is not imaginary, suggest that Rembrandt was not always alone on his walks. The diagonal road, establishing distance, leads to a broken wooden bridge, with the village beyond. The medieval church with its spire stands out with farm buildings nearby, with a distant view of trees and a village across the open polder to the right. Despite the free but delicate execution with the reed pen, which suggests it might have been drawn on the spot, the placing of the village in the landscape is carefully calculated, with touches of wash added at strategic places to give emphasis.

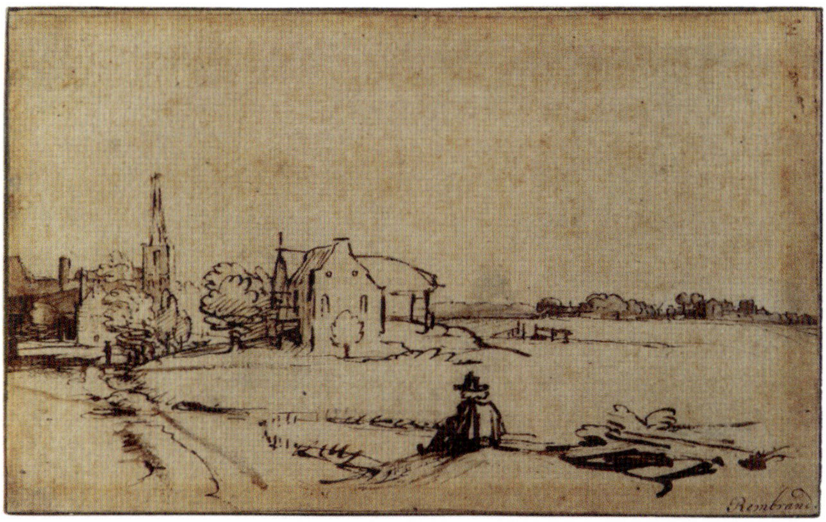

102. *View of Diemen with an Artist Drawing*. *c.*1649/50. Pen and brown ink with brown wash. 11.1 × 17.4 cm. Private collection, Netherlands.

A direct connexion between a drawing probably made standing before the motif and one made afterwards in the studio can be found in two studies of *The Amsteldijk at Meerhuizen* [Figs. 103–4]. The site of the two drawings was situated about halfway along one of Rembrandt's favourite walks, starting in Amsterdam and following the bends in the river Amstel as far south as the ancient village of Ouderkerk. The river, already seen at a point further north in the etching of *The Omval* (see Fig. 99), was a busy waterway, bordered by farms, houses, windmills and taverns, which, until recently within the writer's memory, retained much of its rural character. The whole route was studied in numerous drawings by Rembrandt, which, when placed together, offer a beautiful conspectus of views along the river.

What must be the first sheet [Fig. 103] was essentially a line drawing executed with the reed pen, handled with great dexterity in defining the different textures of the varied elements in the landscape. One can admire the way the density of the foliage is suggested by the curling strokes of the pen, which never become mechanical. The artist took his viewpoint on the road looking ahead towards a clump of trees set to the right, which are the principle subject of the drawing, while the road and river, lightly adumbrated, curve away to the left, echoing the line of the trees. The

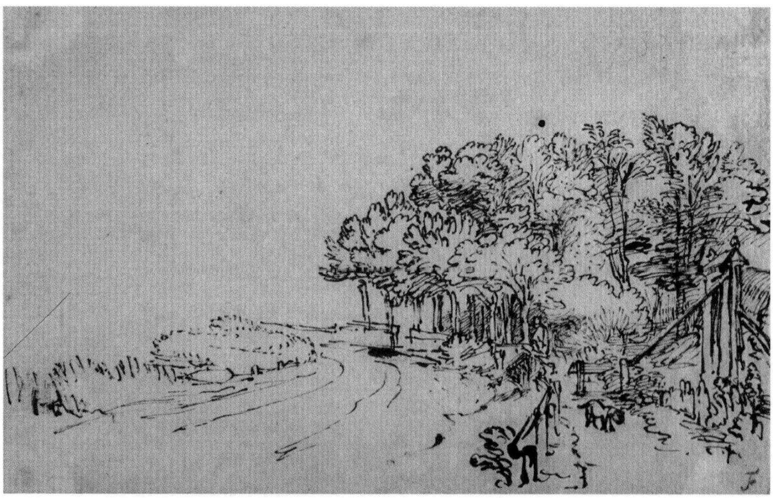

103. *The Amsteldijk at Meerhuizen. c.*1649/50. Pen and brown ink. 13.2 × 20.7 cm. The Duke of Devonshire and the Trustees of the Chatsworth Settlement, Chatsworth.

right foreground, given emphasis by touches of the loaded pen, includes a wooden fence, leading the eye into the landscape, and a gateway providing access to an unseen house. Rembrandt adds life to the scene by the inclusion of a dog wandering beside the road and a man beyond, standing or walking inconspicuously in front of the trees.

When Rembrandt returned to the subject in the studio [Fig. 104] he repeated the composition. With only a few minor changes, such as removing the dog and adding the end of a house beyond the gateway, he left the right hand side of the landscape unchanged. He now focused his attention on the landscape on the left, clearly defining the outline of the river with its tall rushes and enriching the scene with various details. On the road in the centre, a horse, with an attached rope, is pulling a boat laden with passengers, while further on a hay wagon is rounding the bend in the river, with two diminutive figures beyond. On the river a sailing boat can be seen midstream with a view of the 'Little Mill', the site of an inn, standing out in the background. The amount of detail shown on each side of the landscape are now carefully balanced, with the play of light and shadow creating a unity. But while the artist in this second version of the subject produced a more finished result with the addition of brown wash and touches of white bodycolour, seen notably on the clump of

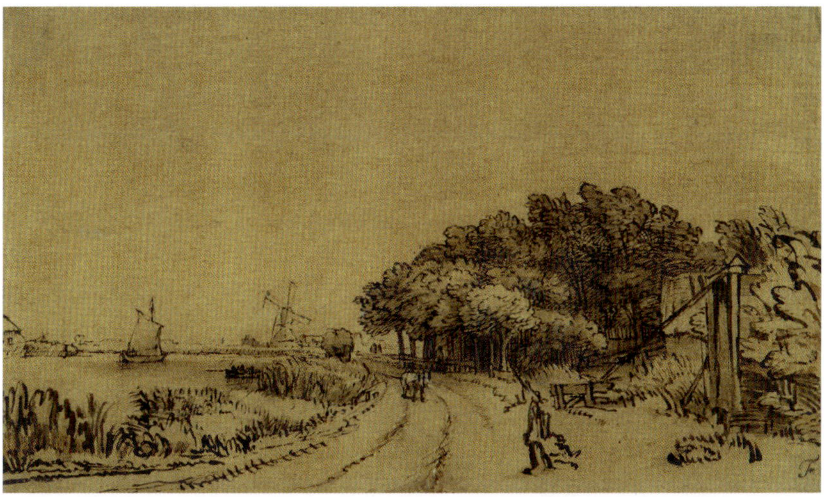

104. *The Amsteldijk at Meerhuizen. c.*1649/50. Pen and brown ink with brown wash on light-brown paper. 13 × 21.7 cm. The Duke of Devonshire and the Trustees of the Chatsworth Settlement, Chatsworth.

trees, his penwork remains remarkably free without losing precision when it comes to detail. Rembrandt retains all the subtle variations in pressure on the pen seen in the preliminary drawing, which gives the sheet a feeling of a sparkling summer's day on which the landscape, bathed in sunlight, is alive and lived in.

We know very little about the marketing of Rembrandt's drawings except there were collectors eager to acquire them, such as, the marine painter Jan van der Cappelle (1626–1679), already mentioned. In the case of his landscape drawings, a large group of twenty-four, including some of his finest sheets, such as the previous two drawings as well as a third to be discussed (see Fig. 106), belonged to Nicolaes Anthonis Flinck (1646–1723), of Rotterdam. He had inherited most if not all of them from his father, Govert Flinck (1615–1660), who had been a pupil of Rembrandt and who had presumably acquired them directly from the latter. (In 1723 they were acquired from the younger Flinck by the 2nd Duke of Devonshire and many still remain at Chatsworth.) It is to be noted that both earlier collectors were artists.

Although by far the majority of his landscapes were based on the countryside around Amsterdam, he did on at least one occasion venture further east, visiting Rhenen, for what purpose is unknown. Situated on the river Rijn, south-west of Utrecht, its picturesque setting on a slight hill beside the river attracted other artists, such as Jan van Goyen and Jacob van Ruisdael, who painted or drew the town seen from a distance. For Rembrandt the interest was not apparently the view but the medieval gateways, which were largely destroyed by the French in 1673, shortly after the artist's death. As proved by other studies he made of buildings, Rembrandt's taste in architecture was directed towards the past and not the present. In one of the most beautiful landscapes that he ever made, he drew the West or Utrecht Gate [Fig. 105], seen from within and from close at hand. The central tower block, massive and forbidding, surmounts the tunnel-like entrance at the end of which can be seen a vista of the outside with a pair of minuscule figures, who set the scale of this monumental architectural ensemble. On either side of the tower there are simple dwellings, with large chimneys looking like small towers with viewing points. In the right hand foreground, there is an empty stall waiting for an occupant.

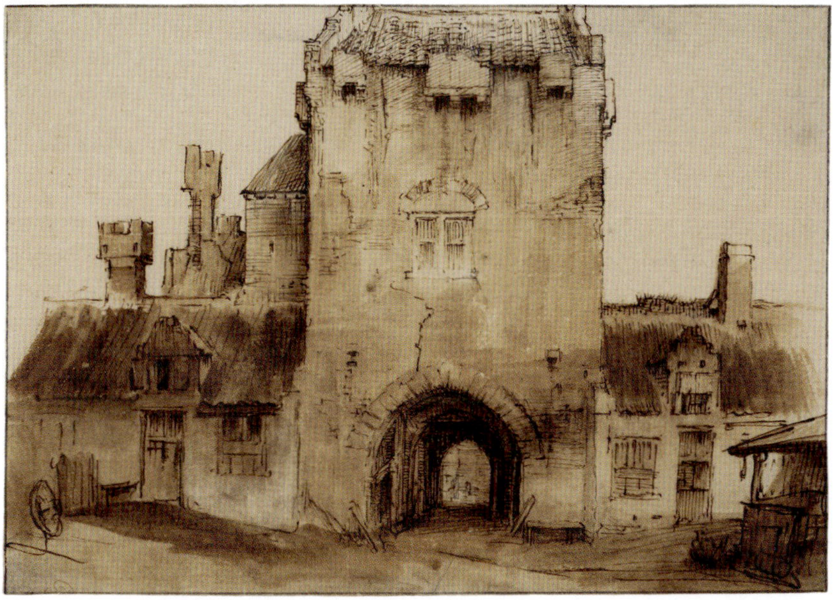

105. *Westpoort (Utrechtgate) at Rhenen*. *c.*1648–50. Pen and brown ink with brown wash, heightened with white. 16.3 × 22.6 cm. Teylers Museum, Haarlem.

What is so remarkable about this drawing is the degree of finish, achieved with a subtle combination of pen and brush with touches of white bodycolour. The delicate outlining of architectural detail forms the basis of the extensive washes carefully applied to suggest both depth and the play of light over the buildings. The eye is particularly caught by the bright vista of the outside of the town at the end of the dark tunnel. With its exceptionally varied shades of wash, it is the most technically elaborate of all his landscapes, clearly made as a work of art in its own right, to be sold or kept as a memento of his travels.

The human figure as a feature in the landscape, found far more frequently in etchings rather than in drawings, can be seen never more assuredly than in the drawing of *The Amstel near Ouderkerk with a Man Rowing a Boat* [Fig. 106]. Rembrandt's viewpoint was beside the river on the far side of the village, from where most artists proceeded no further. Perfectly composed, the landscape, drawn in pen and brown wash with some touches of white bodycolour, shows the river, bordered by reeds, receding diagonally towards the background where the village of Ouderkerk fills the horizon. The ostensible subject, a farmhouse partially

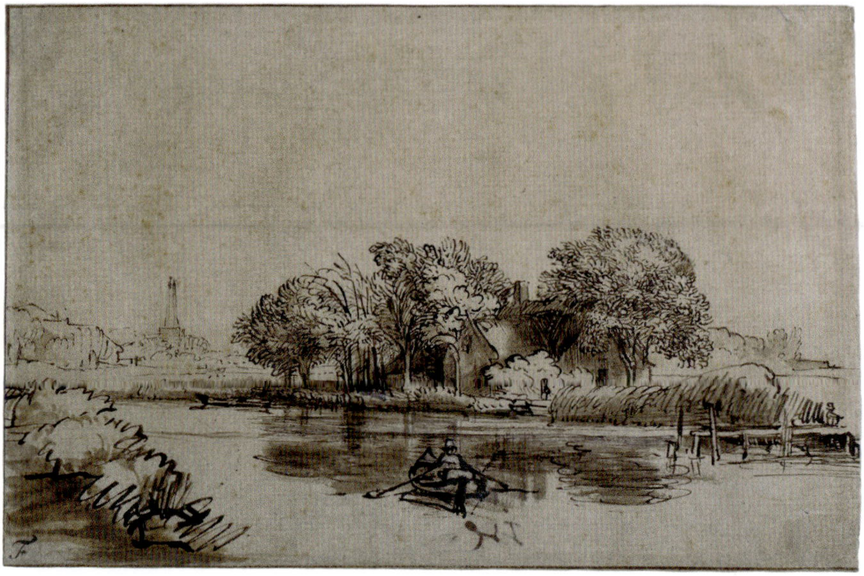

106. *The Amstel near Ouderkerk with a Man Rowing a Boat*. 1648–50. Pen and brown ink with brown wash, heightened with white. 13.2 × 19.8 cm. The Duke of Devonshire and the Trustees of the Chatsworth Settlement, Chatsworth.

hidden in the shadows of surrounding trees, emphasised by the richly applied wash, fills the middle ground. On the left, there is a rowing boat tethered to the bank and a very small figure before the bushes in front of the farm and another sitting on the jetty on the right can just be made out. Yet what catches and holds the eye is the man, his figure firmly outlined with the broad strokes of the reed pen, rowing midstream away from the spectator, as the boat emerges from an area of shadow cast on the water by the trees in full growth. His oars rest on the surface of the water. The drawing, which combines two of the artist's favourite motifs, a farmhouse amongst trees and a river view, conveys the atmosphere of a balmy summer day spent languidly rowing on a gently flowing river.

Man steals the limelight more obliquely in the etching of the *View of the Diemerdijk with a Milkman* [Fig. 107], where the human element is to be found on the far right. We experience a beautiful depiction of a characteristic stretch of identifiable polder landscape around Amsterdam through the eyes of the milkman. Carrying a yoke with pails and with a dog at his side, he walks along the raised Diemerdijk (see p. 125) towards the so-called Taverns in the Bend, namely several inns, in the distance.

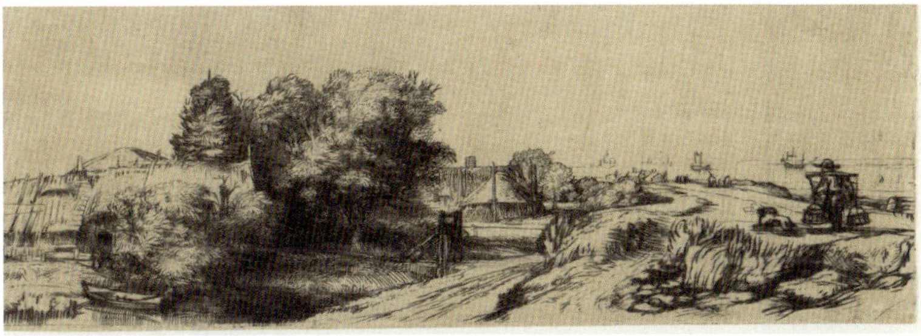

107. *View of the Diemerdijk with a Milkman. c.*1650. Etching and drypoint, printed on Japanese paper. 6.4 × 17.5 cm. Rijksmuseum, Amsterdam.

On his right he has a wide view of the Ij busy with shipping, and on the left down below the dyke, the sight of farm buildings nestling protectively amongst trees against the winds beside a road. A rowing boat is moored on the bank before a large farm building, constructed of wood and with a thatched roof; beyond the trees is a covered hayrick in front of another farm. In the final state, reproduced here, the artist added low hills in the left hand background, nowhere present in actuality, proving that his interest in the subject was not topographical. It is another example of Rembrandt's habit of combining the real with the imaginary in his landscapes, which might have puzzled his more literally minded admirers used to accurate topographical views.

On account of the pails he is carrying, the man has sometimes been identified as a fisherman, but this seems unlikely. Apart from the print's eighteenth-century title of 'Het melkboertje' ('The milkman'), it has been pointed out that a poem celebrates the milk and cream from a nearby village, which was popular with walkers; moreover, a drawing of the same farm (Ashmolean Museum, Oxford) shows a rack of milk churns standing at the back of the building.

By the time Rembrandt made this print, probably about 1650, he had mastered the technique of integrating etching and drypoint to produce a harmonious result, unlike his experience with *The Omval* (see Fig. 99) five years earlier with its tonal imbalance. Here he used etching to establish the basic outlines of the subject, describing, for example, the foremost building in great detail, so that the different building materials can be made out. And then he went to work with the drypoint needle adding both detail, such as the figures of the milkman and his dog, as well as areas of dark shadow beneath the trees and on the stretch of water below. From this subtle blending of media, Rembrandt produced a beautifully balanced composition, establishing depth as well as the play of sunlight over the scene.

Although it is sometimes disputed, the first stage of the *Clump of Trees* [Fig. 108], dated 1652, has all the appearance of a work started before the motif. It is one of two landscapes created solely in drypoint. Since drawing into the plate requires greater pressure than drawing on a grounded plate with an etching needle, it would have required a firm hand or some other support to hold the plate steady The motif, a farm building, made out only with difficulty, set amongst a solid clump of trees, must have been a favourite, since around the same time as the print he made two drawings, both showing different aspects of the subject and none serving directly as a preparatory drawing for the print. Two drawings and a painting by followers show it must have been a gathering spot for the faithful. In this first state, hardly more than the lightest of sketches dashed down on the plate, a tree, briefly outlined in jagged strokes, stands on the left, and leads to a clump of trees, hardly more clearly defined, in the centre middleground, in the centre of which a wooden outbuilding

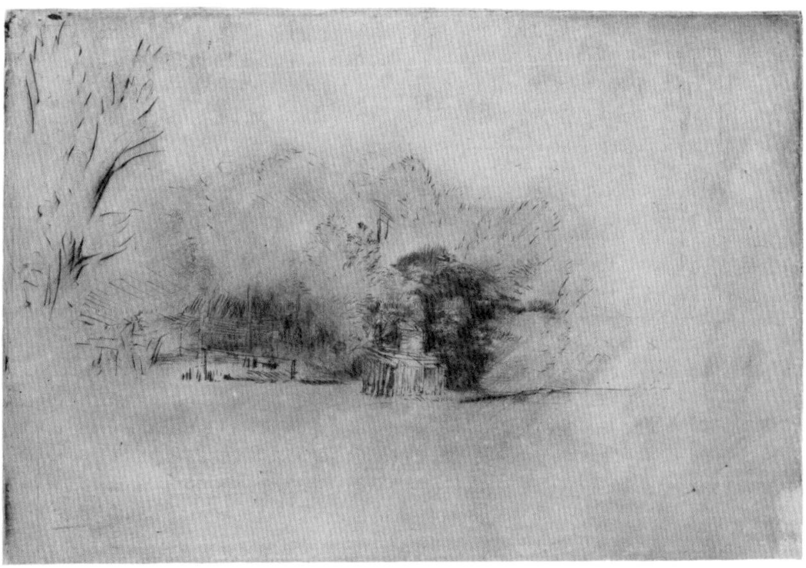

108. *Clump of Trees*. 1652. Drypoint, with surface tone. 15.6 × 21.1 cm. Rijksmuseum, Amsterdam.

nestles. From a drawing (Fitzwilliam Museum, Cambridge), it can be determined that a stream runs in front of the trees, suggesting that the building might be a boathouse. Despite its summariness, this first state contains the whole essence of the finished composition.

Since there are no less than seven impressions of this first state known today, it suggests that, slight as his first work might seem, Rembrandt regarded it as more than just a preliminary working stage. One impression, illustrated here, reveals the unusual inking of the plate he began to employ extensively around this time. Here he obtained a richer pictorial effect by leaving a thin film of ink over much of the plate; the marks of the material or his hand, which served to wipe the copper, are visible. He then inroduced one or two highlights, so that, in the same way that he employed wash in his landscape drawings, he is able to suggest the play of sunlight and shadows over the trees.

When he returned to his print [Fig. 109], presumably back in the studio, the first thing he did was to cut three centimetres from the bottom of the plate, to give a size more consonant with his subject. It significantly altered his depiction of space. The tree at the left now fills the height of the plate and stands out by virtue of the drypoint burr evident on the spiky branches. He then built up the the abundant foliage growing on the clump of trees, the subject of his print. Cut through the blanket of trees at the left, a circular vista into the field beyond creates a sense of

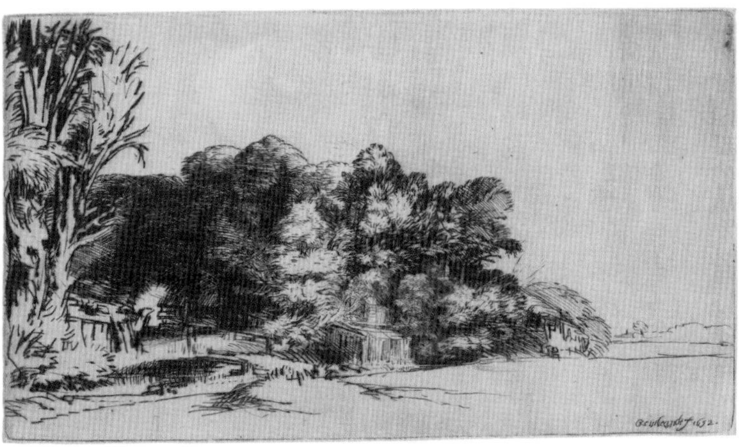

109. *Clump of Trees*. 1652. Drypoint. 12.4 × 21.1 cm.
Rijksmuseum, Amsterdam.

air flowing through and, to one side, reveals the end of a farm building. And to give a further illusion of space, he adds a distant horizon, before which a man can just be made out standing over a stream, the only mortal in the landscape. With that work completed, he signed and dated his print 1652. The intense black from the drypoint, which corresponds to his increasing use of the reed pen about the same time, creates a beautiful pattern of sunlight playing over the foliage. Never before had he captured so well the shimmering quality of the trees on a breezy day. Without losing the spontaneity of his first sketch he created a balanced, composed landscape.

As he came to the end of his landscape years, Rembrandt's drawings changed in character. Gone is the love of detail and the sense of infinite space, to be replaced by a more impressionistic study of the scene, built up with the broad strokes of the reed pen in horizontal lines across the landscape, and enriched with an extensive use of wash. He took the final step in one unique drawing, *River with Trees* [Fig. 110], which was executed entirely with the brush. It is such an unusual work that one might doubt its authenticity, were it not for a recipe for a stopping-out varnish, written in Rembrandt's hand, on the verso. Devoid of the usual detail, we

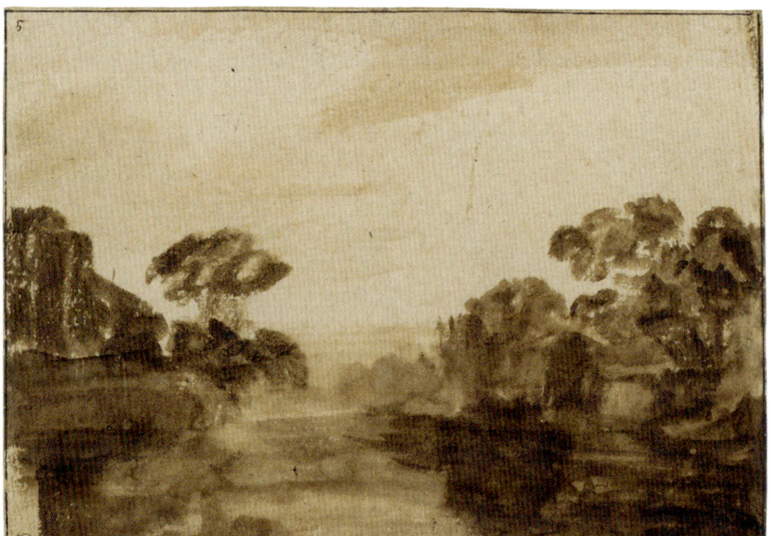

110. *River with Trees*. *c.*1652/1656. Brush in brown wash. 13.6 × 18.6 cm. Musée du Louvre, Paris.

might be looking at the scene at dusk, when the forms of the landscape seem to merge together into an indissoluble whole. With summary, broad brush strokes, Rembrandt suggests the trees and their reflexion in the water as, without any marked division between them, they seem to fuse into one another. We cannot be sure whether the subject is imaginary or whether it is based on an actual experience.

It is illuminating to juxtapose such a dreamy scene with the work of Rembrandt's contemporary, Claude Lorrain (1604/5?–1682), the master of landscape drawings executed solely with the brush, and another artist who produced a memorable image of the landscape in which he lived. With similar free brush strokes, Claude portrays, in the *View of the Tiber, Rome* [Fig. 111] the dark trees contrasting with the brilliant glow of the water, creating a dramatic play of forms and light over the Campagna. But at the same time, he establishes a wonderful sense of space as the river winds its way back towards the Tiburtine Hills in the distance. No less atmospheric, it is a measurable landscape compared to Rembrandt's two-dimensional vision.

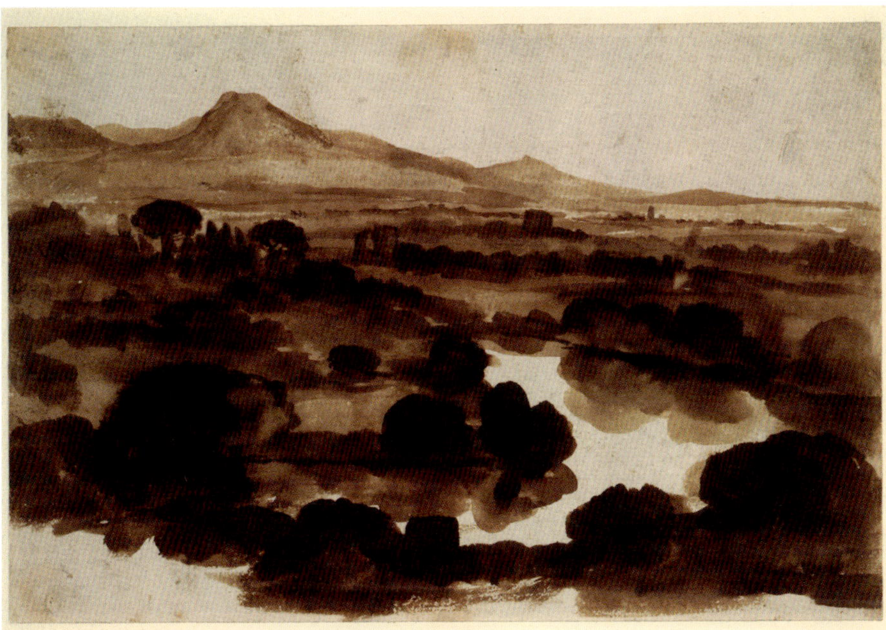

111. Claude Lorrain, *View of the Tiber, Rome*. *c.*1640. Brush drawing in brown. 18.5 × 26.8 cm. British Museum, London.

Well over a decade before his death, Rembrandt abandoned realistic landscape. When he required an appropriate setting for, say, St Jerome, his favourite saint, or St Francis, the inspiration tended to come from Venetian sixteenth-century landscape, notably that of Titian, rather than from what the artist could see around him. Whether there was any personal reason for such behaviour we do not know, but it is far more likely that his decision was an artistic one. He had explored the landscape around him so thoroughly that there was nothing more to say. But in those twelve to fifteen years his involvement was as intense as that of any other great landscape artist. To speak of Rembrandt's Amsterdam is as meaningful as to speak of Cézanne's Aix-en-Provence.

CHAPTER 5
Narrative subjects

REMBRANDT'S PREOCCUPATION with narrative themes stands at the centre of his art. His subjects were primarily Biblical – seventy-four paintings, seventy-one etchings and about double that number of drawings – with classical and historical following behind with twenty-five works in his *œuvre*. In the case of drawings of narrative subjects, irrespective of their degree of finish according to conventional standards, many were intended as finished works in their own right; only remarkably few were conceived as preparatory studies for paintings or etchings. So much is he renowned as an interpreter of the Bible that one tends to forget that when at the beginning of his career in 1625 or 1626, he went to Amsterdam to study under Pieter Lastman (1583–1633), he found a number of narrative painters with similar ideas, a group coming to be known appositely as the Pre-Rembrandtists who were already treating a wide range of lesser known subjects from the Bible as well as scenes from mythology and secular history. Among the circle Pieter Lastman stands out as *primus inter pares*, favouring small pictures with numerous figures, the subjects of which often involved the interaction between individuals; not infrequently they were, as will be seen, exactly those to which Rembrandt was to pay such attention. They offered the Dutch artist a new range of iconography, which was only, if at all, previously to be found in printmaking.

But if in choice of subject matter Rembrandt was often preceded by his master and his contemporaries, his interpretations, often favouring the intimate and the domestic, became increasingly personal, raising narrative art on to an altogether more exalted plane. Whereas Lastman and others took pains to set out all aspects of the story, Rembrandt more and more went to the heart of what he was illustrating, eliminating extraneous detail and concentrating on the basic theme underlying the subject. By omitting figures and iconographical details normally associated with the subject and largely avoiding the use of symbols, he sometimes plays his cards so close to his chest that we struggle to recognise his subject. In earlier works gestures and expressions would bring out the essence of the story, whereas in later works the basic emotion invoked by the story gradually was isolated from the narrative aspects and became dominant. It is the very intimate and contemplative aspect of his story-telling which is at the heart of this chapter.

When approaching a subject, one asks to what degree Rembrandt's starting point was visual or literary. It is perhaps surprising for such an original artist, how often a work by another artist served as a source of inspiration, which he would then transform into his own language, leaving only the skeleton of the original. At the same time he had, as will be seen, a propensity to alter the moment in the story being illustrated. The principal source for his knowledge of the work of other artists was undoubtedly his very extensive collection of works of art, particularly prints and drawings, which were not just there for pleasure, but played an active role in his composing in a good number of cases. Compared with his art collection, the contents of his library were decidedly meagre. In the inventory of his possessions taken in 1656, no more than twenty two books are mentioned, only five of which are identified by title, including, most importantly, 'an Old Bible' as well as 'A "Flavius Josephus" in High German';[23] the latter, presumably referring to the author's *A History of the Jews*, provided an essential exegesis of the Bible and was much read at the time not only by Rembrandt. These two books might be regarded as all that he needed in Biblical themes but in coping with mythology or history the artist, even if we do not know what he actually read, almost certainly turned to other books in addition to pictorial tradition. His profound approach to his subject matter was a quality already appreciated by his contemporaries, as is illustrated by the comment made by the artist and writer Philips Angel (1612–1683). Discussing the painting of *Samson's Wedding Feast* (Gemäldegalerie, Dresden) in his published lecture, *In Praise of the Art of Painting* (Leiden, 1642) he lauded it as an example of the 'the fruit of a most natural and well trained understanding, and intelligent reflection on its meaning'.[24]

Although Rembrandt was an inveterate draughtsman, it is notable how few preparatory drawings for etched or painted compositions exist. Unlike

Rubens, for example, who used numerous drawings and oil-sketches as part of the process in working out the composition, Rembrandt appears to have had the desired image clearly fixed in his mind before he started work. It is true that X-rays and infra-red reflectography have revealed that Rembrandt sometimes changed his mind after he had laid in the subject on the canvas or panel, but is fair to see these, not as part of the realisation of his original idea, but more a change of mind carried out in retrospect. With the arrangement of figures already apparently decided, it is pertinent to speculate what was in the forefront of the artist's mind as he sat working away. Since, as has already been seen, technique, with a wide range of alternatives at his command, was such an essential part of his art, one might hazard a guess that he was primarily preoccupied with technical processes, bending the paintbrush, pen or etching needle to his purpose to achieve the desired pictorial result. Amongst his other qualities, he was essentially a very practical artist.

1. The early years.

The painting of *Tobit and Anna* (Tobit 3:11) [Fig. 112] is one of Rembrandt's very first narrative pictures, executed in 1626, either in Amsterdam or just after he returned to Leiden. The domestic drama illustrated here stands as a perfect example of unusual Rembrandt iconography. It was taken from the *Book of Tobit*, one of the Apocrypha associated with the Old Testament, which served as a frequent source for Rembrandt. So inspired was he by the events related in the Book of Tobit that over the course of his career, it has been calculated, he illustrated them in no less than fifty-five paintings, etchings and drawings. In a later part of the story, the aged Tobit, formerly a rich man but now blind and impoverished, has unjustly accused his wife Anna of having stolen the kid which she has appeared with under her arm; forced to go out and work spinning cloth, she had in fact been given it as part of her wages. Both figures are shabbily dressed, revealing the distressed circumstances under which, on account of their faith, they are now forced to exist. We see Tobit, deeply mortified, at the moment he has realised his error, and accepting his wife's berating as a sign of God's anger, he expresses the wish to die. Looking up in aguish, he wrings his hands, while she stares at him still

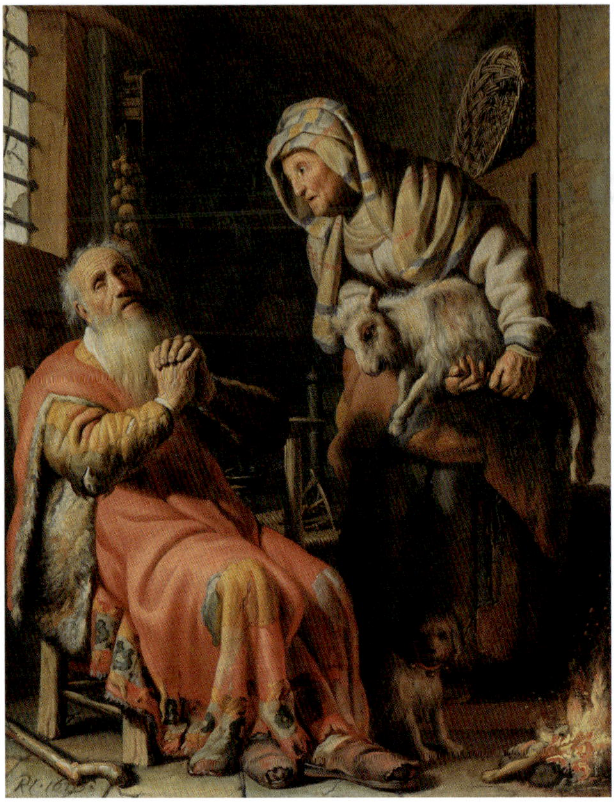

112. *Tobit and Anna*. 1626. Panel. 40.1 × 29.9 cm. Rijksmuseum, Amsterdam.

stunned by the blatant injustice of the accusation. Although the emotions of both figures are strongly expressed, Rembrandt nevertheless illustrates what was to become his increasingly psychologically revealing interpretation of narrative themes.

The event takes place in the corner of a panelled room, the construction of which is not entirely clear. The lack of space within the room with two large figures filling the foreground emphasises the intimacy of the scene. To give a cosy atmosphere, it is filled with homely detail. Beside the window in the left background, a string of garlic attached to the side of a small birdcage hangs on the wall; in the corner two shelves are filled with domestic objects, while, on the right above a door, a wicker basket is set into an alcove. Between the two figures, a chair with a rush seat and a candleboard stand can just be made out. A small dog sits warming itself in front of the briskly-burning fire in the lower right-hand corner. The strong highlight from the window is cast on the two figures, picking out the bright red of Tobit's cloak and the garment tied around Anna's waist, while further illumination is provided by the glow from the fire. As with other contemporary works, Rembrandt employs bright bold colours contrasted with one another, a manner of painting soon changed to a preference for broken colours subject to the play of light and shadow to give a more realistic effect. Painted on panel, his usual support at this time, the application of the varied brushwork is carefully calculated to reflect the texture of what is being described. It is a highly thought out and executed performance, reflecting the artist's early ambition.

As a point of departure, it seems likely that he had turned to an etching by Jan van der Velde the Younger (1593–1641) after the Rotterdam artist, Willem Buytewech (1591/2–1624) [Fig. 113]. There is a strong similarity in the figures, particularly Anna holding the kid, and the timbered interior, as well as such details as the birdcage. But whatever he may have

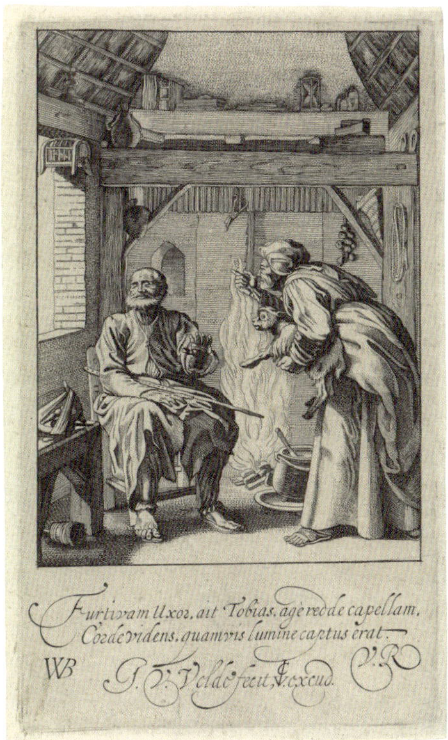

113. Jan van der Velde II, after Willem Buytewech, *Tobit and Anna*. *c.*1620. Etching. 19.3 × 11.2 cm. Rijksmuseum, Amsterdam.

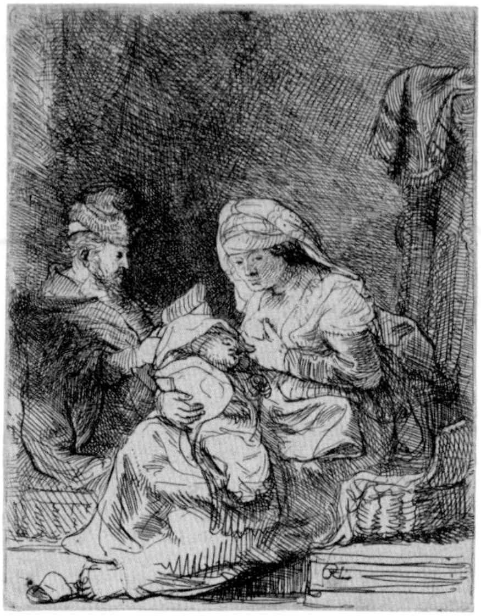

114. *Holy Family*. *c.*1632. Etching.
9.4 × 7.1 cm. Rijksmuseum, Amsterdam.

taken from Buytewech, he made one important change by illustrating the later moment in the story, when Tobit has realised his error and repents, rather than, as in Buytewech's design, the earlier occasion when Tobit has made his accusation and Anna reacts with indignation; he rather than she becomes the principal exponent of emotion. This is typical of Rembrandt's refinement when starting ftom an existing prototype.

The Holy Family was a subject he turned to throughout his life. What is very apparent is how much he, depending more on pictorial tradition than any account in the New Testament, varied the activities and situations in which the Holy Family found themselves. In Rembrandt's work they are usually depicted as engaged in some form of down-to-earth domestic life. Here [Fig. 114] the seated Virgin, with her workbox beside her, is offering her breast to the infant Christ held firmly in her right arm, while St Joseph is reclining behind them, reading a book. The latter detail may, attesting to the artist's early knowledge of Italian art, have been inspired by an etching by Annibale Carracci (1560–1609) of the same subject [Fig. 115], although otherwise the two images differ. (Prints by Annibale are listed in the 1656 inventory of Rembrandt's possessions.)[25] What is noticeable is how much expression on the faces the artist is able

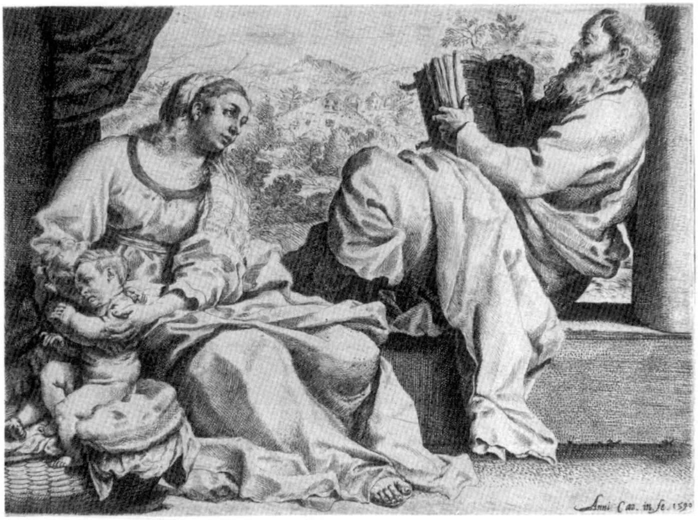

115. Annibale Carracci, *The Holy Family*. 1590. Etching and engraving. 16.2 × 21.7 cm. British Museum, London.

to conjure up with a few lines; St Joseph intent, Mary abstracted and the Child sleepy. The whole scene exudes an air of intimacy and peace.

The light, coming from a window on the left, falls strongly on the three figures, who stand out from their shadowy background, empty apart from a piece of drapery hung over the top of a high object. The plate is worked up in a combination of freely-drawn outlines defining the figures and extensive areas of loosely-executed shading. The latter is unlike the more mechanical cross hatching found in larger plates of this period. One has no sense of effort as he makes the etching needle distinguish between outline and shadow. Pictorially rich, this small print has a satisfying completeness.

In 1633, shortly after he settled in Amsterdam, Rembrandt painted a very small panel, devoted to an unusual subject from the Apocrypha of the Old Testament, *The Prophet Daniel and King Cyrus before the Idol Bel.* [Fig. 116]. Taken from the Book of Daniel (Bel and the Dragon 16–21), it illustrates the theme of the mighty brought low by a young man, who is traditionally regarded as a prefiguration of Christ, a story which clearly appealed to Rembrandt. Daniel, challenged by the Persian king to say why he did not worship Bel, replied that he did not worship 'idols made by human hand'. Cyrus defended Bel as a living god on the grounds that Bel

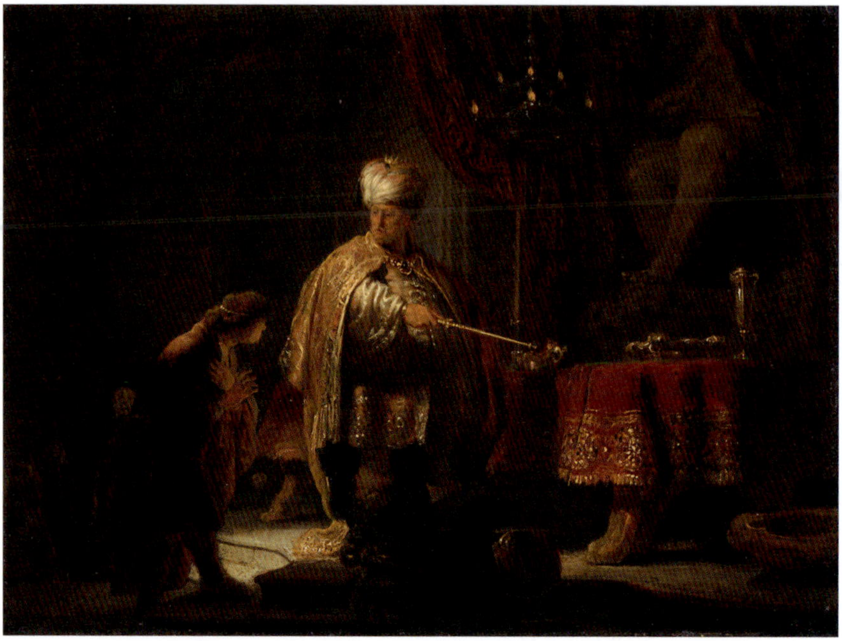

116. *The Prophet Daniel and King Cyrus before the Idol Bel.* 1633. Panel. 23.5 × 30.2 cm. J. Paul Getty Museum, Los Angeles.

ate the food regularly laid out at the foot of the statue. By putting ashes on the floor to reveal footprints, Daniel was able to prove to Cyrus that in fact it was the priests, stealthily entering the locked temple at night, who were responsible for consuming the food and not Bel. Enraged at having been duped, Cyrus put the priests to death and ordered Daniel to destroy both the idol and the temple in which it was housed.

It is a complicated story to illustrate in one composition and it took Maerten van Heemskerck, the only previous Netherlandish artist to treat it, two prints to encompass all the events. But Rembrandt successfully makes reference to all aspects in one scene. In the temple the young Daniel bows reverentially in front of an indignant-looking Cyrus, wielding a sceptre with a commanding gesture directed towards the metal dish and chalice on a table, which are placed before the lower half of the seated statue of Bel. A high priest, staff in hand, makes his way up from the lower left. The hole in the floor which gave the priests access to the building is seen lower right. Despite its size, it is very freely painted, so much so that some underdrawing on the ground can be made out. The highlights sparkle within a limited colour range. It is an eloquent interpretation of an involved story, but carried out on such a small scale it seems like a curious commission. By chance it can very probably be identified with 'A small painting of Daniel, in a black frame',[26] which belonged to a certain Pieter Croon, otherwise unknown, who was declared insolvent in 1650.

Probably in the same year Rembrandt executed a grisaille of *Joseph Telling his Dreams* (Genesis 37:10) [Fig. 117], which was painted in oil on paper stuck on card. It has recently been connected with several other grisailles, which were seemingly intended as preparatory designs for a series of large prints to be carried out by a professional printmaker. Here Rembrandt may have been emulating Rubens, who made a practice of commissioning reproductive engravings after his pictures to provide a valued additional source of income. When a print after the present work

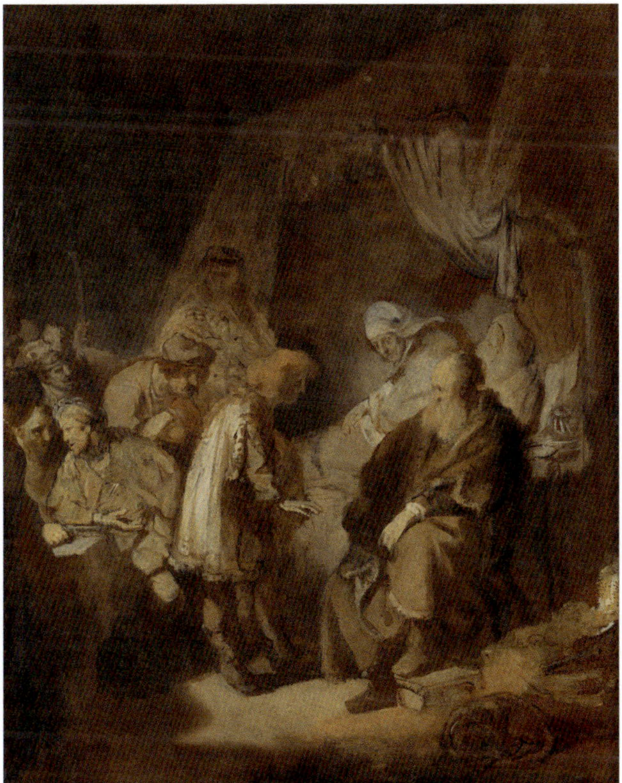

117. *Joseph Telling his Dreams*. *c.*1633. Grisaille on paper, stuck on card. 55.8 × 39.7 cm. Rijksmuseum, Amsterdam.

never materialised, Rembrandt, never an artist to waste a good design, used it five years later as the basis of a small etching of the same subject.

In a busy bedroom scene, Joseph stands before his father, Jacob, seated in front of a large four-poster bed, from which his mother, Rachel, peers out eagerly listening. In the lower right, a small dog is curled up in a basket before a glowing fire. The left hand side is given up to Joseph's numerous brothers, who were vexed over his position as the favourite son. Their reactions to what they are hearing, particularly those of the two brothers immediately behind Joseph, are highly expressive. Joseph, wearing 'the tunic of many colours' given him by his elderly father, which was the source of fraternal jealousy, is standing in a bowing position. This stance suggests that, much given as Joseph was to interpreting dreams. he is relating the one of 'the sun (his father), the moon (his mother) and eleven stars (his brothers) bowed down before me'. This claim to superiority caused his father's indignation and his brothers' envy.

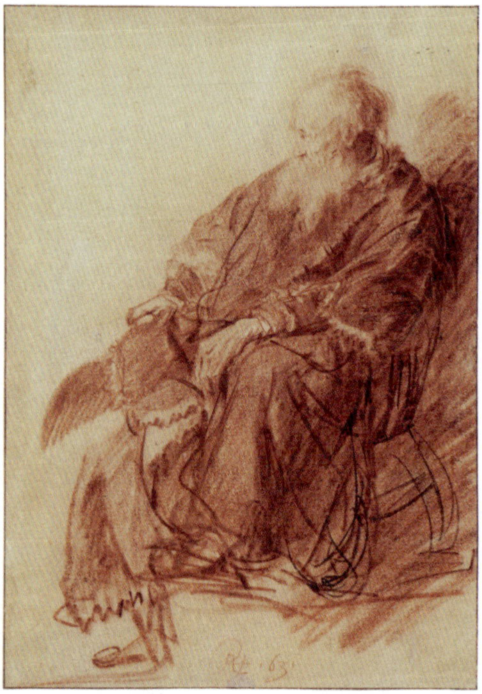

118. *A Seated Old Man in Profile*. 1631.
Red and black chalk on brown prepared paper.
22.9 × 25.9 cm. Private collection, New York.

The grisaille was executed in a wide shade of browns, including the eye-catching detail of Joseph's yellowish-brown hair. For such a freely-executed study, it was a carefully considered composition with numerous figures locked together, expressing a wide range of emotions. For the dominating figure of Jacob, Rembrandt relied on an earlier drawing of *A Seated Old Man in Profile* [Fig. 118], which is a masterly large study in red and some black chalk on prepared paper. Suggesting his satisfaction, he added his monogram and the date 1631, and kept it for reference.

In the etching of *Joseph and Potiphar's Wife* (Genesis 39:11–12) [Fig. 119], dated 1634, Rembrandt illustrated a later event in Joseph's life. Sold into slavery in Egypt by his brothers, he was employed in the household of Potiphar, captain of Pharoah's guard. There the latter's wife took a fancy to 'the handsome and well-favoured' young man. When finally 'she caught him by the garment, saying: 'Lie with me', Joseph reacted with a combination of horror at the idea of committing adultery and, as Rembrandt makes clear, disgust at the physical prospect before him; with her night-dress hitched up above her waist, she lies exposed as one of Rembrandt's least prepossessing nudes. In the struggle to escape from her embraces he lost his cloak which was then used as false evidence by the wife to assert, in revenge for her rejection, that Joseph tried to seduce her.

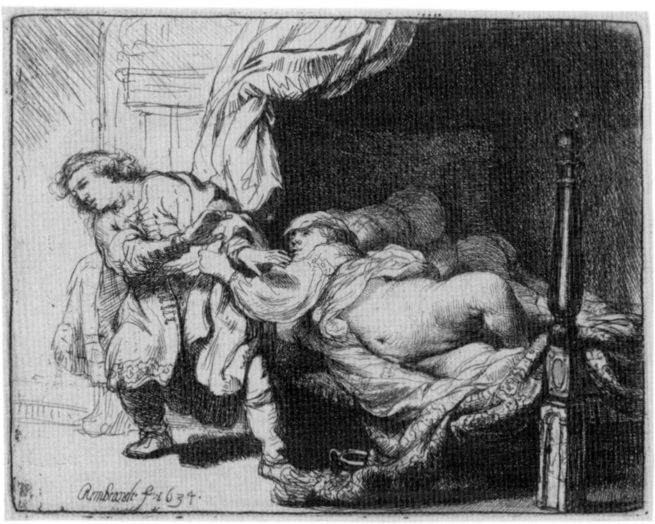

119. *Joseph and Potiphar's Wife*. 1634. Etching. 9.2 × 11.4 cm. Rijksmuseum, Amsterdam.

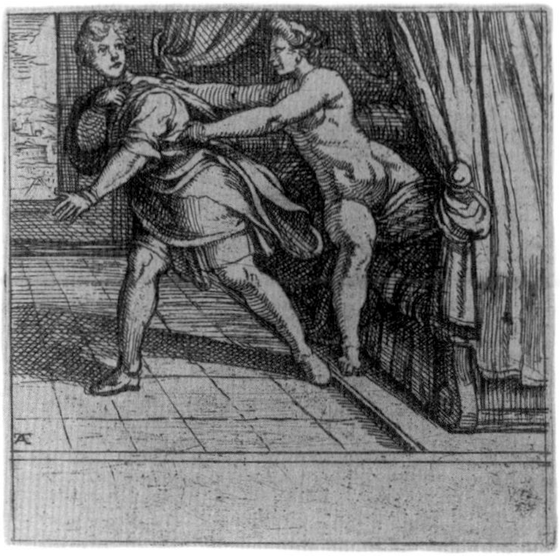

120. Antonio Tempesta, *Joseph and Potiphar's Wife*. 1590s. Etching. 5.8 × 6.7 cm. Museum of Fine Arts, Budapest.

Once again Rembrandt turned to Italian art as a source of inspiration. As a starting point for the composition he based it on an etching of the subject by Antonio Tempesta (1555–1630) [Fig. 120], examples of whose prints he certainly owned by 1656.[27] The placement of the four-poster bed and the arrangement of the two figures are roughly the same. But when it comes to the spirit of the piece the two works are worlds apart. Whereas Tempesta portrays two wooden figures lacking in emotion – they might as well be engaged in a lover's reluctant farewell – Rembrandt shows Jacob and Potiphar's wife in the grip of contrasting passions. The diagonal disposition of the various elements enhances the telling of the story. We follow it from the bedpost in the right foreground to the semi-naked woman stretched out with arms held out trying to seize Joseph, who defends himself with his hands from her lascivious grasp as he struggles to get out of the door. The psychological drama being played out between good and evil is underlined by the light background to the figure of Joseph on the left, etched mainly in outline, set beside the dark shaded areas of the inner recesses of the bed on the right, which form a backdrop to the figure of Potiphar's wife. During this period Rembrandt increasingly exhibits a taste for maximum expression, conveyed both in gesture and heightened chiaroscuro, a stylistic feature which continued to the early years of the next decade.

However dynamic the coming together of the Angel Gabriel and the Virgin in representations of the Annunciation may be – Rubens, for

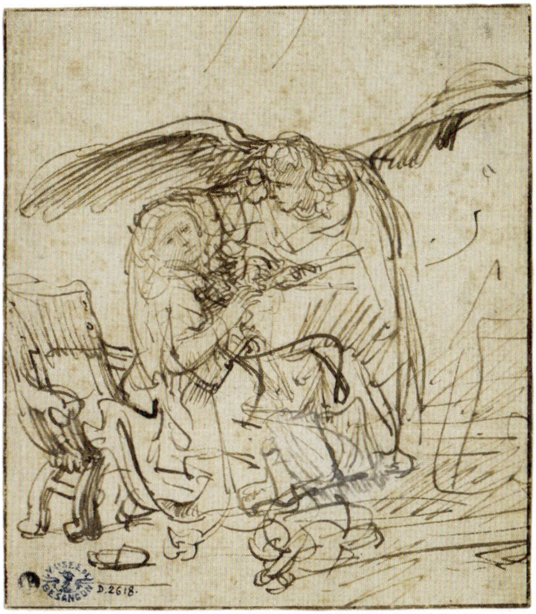

121. *Annunciation*. *c.*1635. Pen and brown ink. 14.4 × 12.4 cm. Musée des Beaux-Arts et d'Archéologie, Besançon.

example, depicts Gabriel arriving like a gust of wind – the two figures are kept apart from one another. But in a seemingly rapidly executed drawing in quill pen and brown ink [Fig. 121] Rembrandt brings the two figures into close physical proximity. The Angel Gabriel, with wings extended across the page, has just flown into the room to announce the good news; with an intent look on his face, he bends over to comfort the Virgin, seizing her hand as he does so. Although it is hard to decipher detail in the swirl of lines, the Virgin, in her emotion at what is happening, appears to have slid off the chair on to her knees, turning her face away from the Angel as she does so. A cast-off shoe lies on the floor beside her, and to the right, to suggest a homely touch, probably a cat. The drawing would seem to illustrate the moment when the Angel says, 'Do not be afraid, Mary'. There is a sense of drama and movement as the Virgin receives the news, but of an intimate kind.

In 1636 Rembrandt executed the first of two paintings of *Susanna and the Elders* [Fig. 122]. The subject, an iconic story of the helpless woman, whose chastity is threatened, was taken once again from the Apocrypha,

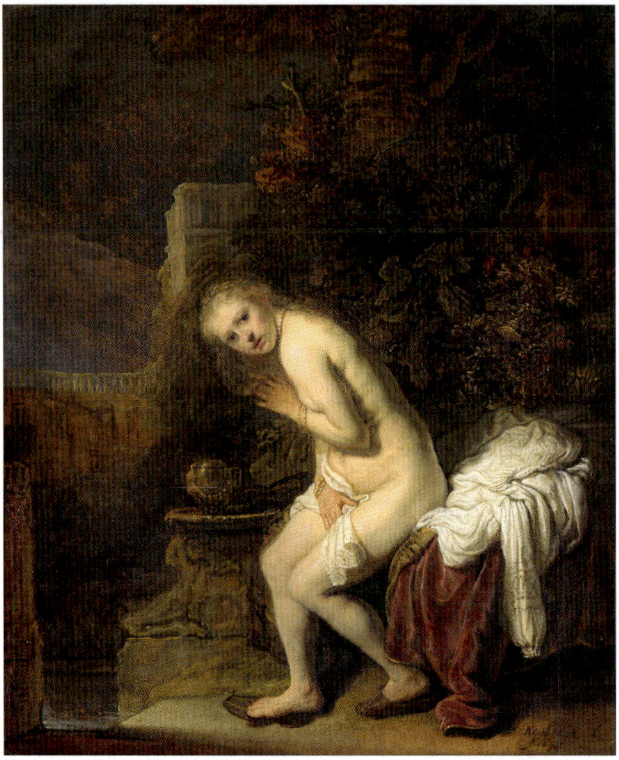

122. *Susanna and the Elders*. 1636. Panel. 47.4 × 38.6 cm.
Mauritshuis, The Hague.

on this occasion from the Book of Daniel (Susanna 11–19). Both in the sixteenth and seventeenth century it was extremely popular, offering the artist the representation of the female nude, heightened by the frisson of illicit spying on an unsuspecting victim. Susanna, the chaste wife of a rich Babylonian, was accustomed to take a bath in the seclusion of their garden. Two elders, recently appointed judges, who were friends of her husband, were consumed with desire for her and broke into her garden with the intention of seducing her. When she refused their advances, they spread false rumours about her morals, but she was saved from the consequent death penalty by the intervention of Daniel.

As a starting point Rembrandt turned once again to the example of his master, Pieter Lastman, by copying [Fig. 123] the latter's much earlier painting of *Susanna and the Elders* [Fig. 124]. Freely drawn in red chalk, Rembrandt largely takes Lastman's arrangement as he found it. But, in

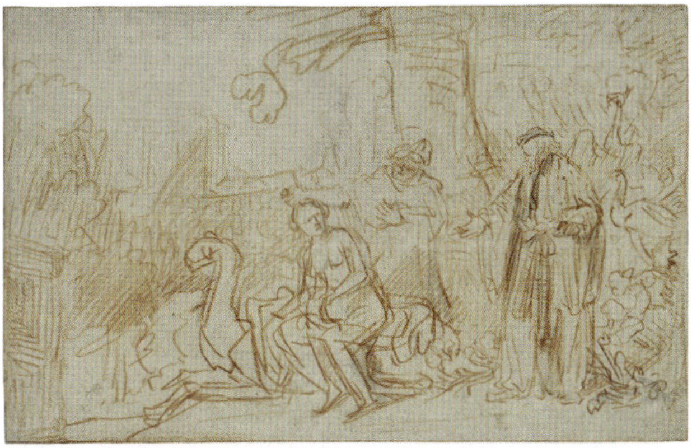

123. Copy after Lastman, *Susanna and the Elders*. *c.*1636. Red chalk, brush in grey wash by another hand. 23.5 × 36.3 cm. Kupferstichkabinett, Staatliche Museen zu Berlin.

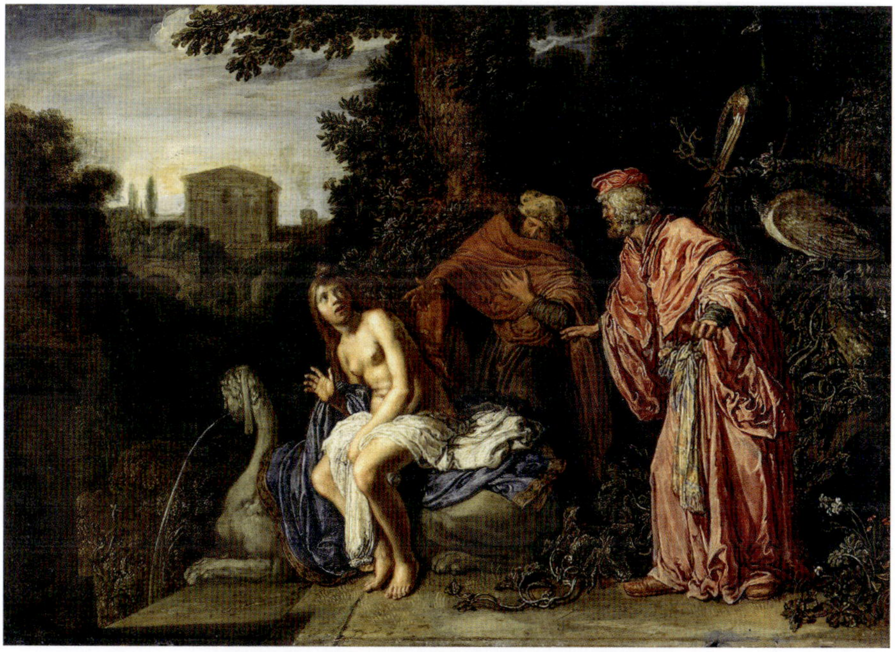

124. Pieter Lastman, *Susanna and the Elders*. 1614. Panel. 42 × 58 cm. Gemäldegalerie, Staatliche Museen zu Berlin.

his usual way, when making copies after other works of art, he did not hesitate to make some small but telling changes, the most meaningful of which is the position of Susanna's right hand; instead of being raised in a gesture of surprise, it is now placed on her lap protecting her modesty. At the same time he altered the angle of her head so that she no longer looks up at the elders.

If Rembrandt started with Lastman's picture at the back of his mind, he soon transformed what was a rectangular composition into an upright. (Originally arch shaped, the spandrels of the panel were subsequently filled in possibly by Rembrandt.) Losing much of the Lastman's background served to concentrate attention on the central figure of Susanna, now placed very prominently in the foreground so that her presence almost overwhelms us. In addition, he made two important changes to his construing of the story. Susanna, instead of turning to the elders, now looks out at the spectator. This unusual feature was first to be a found in a lost painting by Rubens, now only recorded in a reproductive engraving [Fig. 125], an impression of which was probably known to if not owned by Rembrandt. The second alteration was to banish the elders to near invisibility, hidden away in the bushes on the right. As a result the artist illustrates a slightly earlier moment in the story when Susanna,

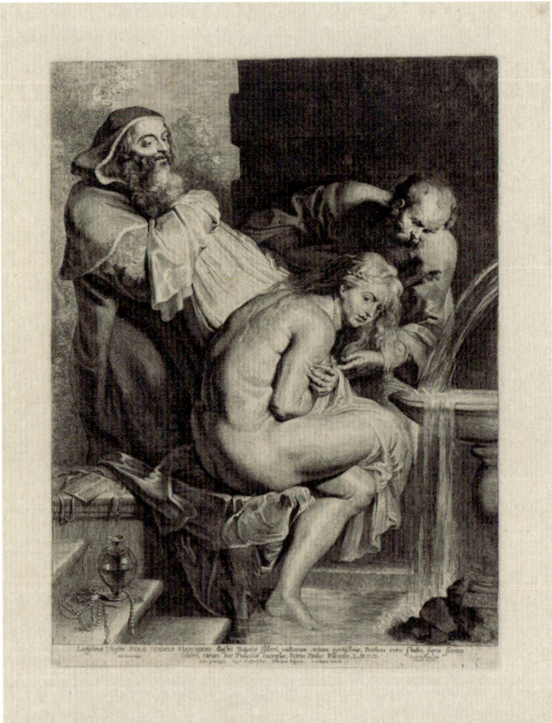

125. Lucas Vorsterman the Elder, after Rubens, *Susanna and the Elders*. 1620. Engraving. 38.5 × 28 cm. Rijksmuseum, Amsterdam.

her privacy disturbed by some unexplained noise, has yet to realise the presence of the elders. With her startled outward gaze and the elders all but unidentifiable, the viewer is encouraged to believe that he or she has become the voyeur, experiencing the pleasures of catching sight of a naked woman unawares.

In depicting Susanna seated on a pile of her clothes Rembrandt follows Lastman except for the positioning of her arms. The right hand, following the change already made in his copy after Lastman, is placed on her lap, while the left arm covers her breasts, leading to a pose, consciously or unconsciously, which echoes that found in the antique statue, known as the *Venus Pudica* (modest Venus) [Fig. 126]. Although trimmer of figure than some of Rembrandt's earlier nudes, Susanna is not in any way idealised or prettified; the folds of her soft flesh are plainly visible. Over the course of time, her life-like nude figure has elicited some very critical responses. Sir Joshua Reynolds, for example, although a great admirer and collector of Rembrandt, nevertheless accounted her 'a very

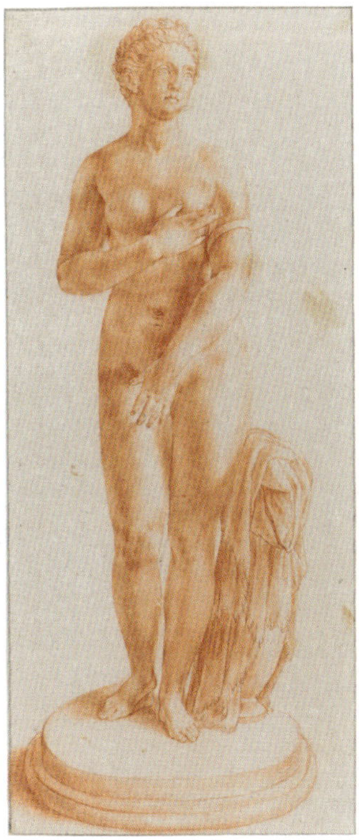

126. Attributed to Hendrick Goltzius, *Venus Pudica*. 1591. Red chalk. 36 × 15 cm. Teylers Museum, Haarlem.

ugly and ill-favoured figure'[28] when he saw the painting in The Hague. This seems harsh; comely might be a fairer description.

Whatever one's taste, the figure of Susanna stands out as beautifully modelled in smoothly-applied brushstrokes against the freer painting of the background. The brushwork is carefully varied in direction and thickness throughout the panel, according to the material that is being described; thick in the foliage, extended strokes on the drapery and, as said, smooth on the body. This use of varying brushwork to describe surfaces becomes a common feature in Rembrandt's paintings. The composition is carefully designed so that the highlight on the sidewall of the mansion in the background draws attention to the figure of Susanna, as does the diagonal outline of the trees behind her head. Apart from the wine red velvet cloak on which she is seated, the colour is muted. The contrast between the figure in highlight and very dark background so evident today may have increased over the course of time. When Rembrandt returned to the subject in a painting completed eleven years later (Gemäldegalerie, Berlin), he returned to the traditional representation of the story with Susanna actively engaged with the two elders.

In a small drawing executed in a few lines of the quill pen Rembrandt caught the essence of the story of *Lot and Daughters* (Genesis 19:33) [Fig.

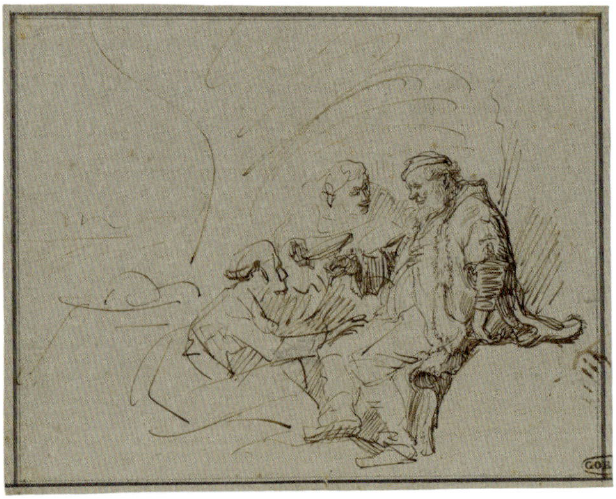

127. *Lot and Daughters*. *c.*1638.
Pen and brown ink. 15.2 × 19.1 cm.
Klassik Stiftung, Graphische Sammlung, Weimar.

127]. Having escaped from Sodom, father and daughters fled to a cave in the mountains. Living is isolation without a man in sight and no hope of being able to 'preserve seed of our father', the daughters decided to make their father drunk with wine and persuade him to 'lie' with them. The seated Lot is seen pressed to drink from a chalice eagerly proffered by one daughter leaning forward at his side, while the other, kneeling before him, beseeches him in an eloquent gesture with her arms held out before her. What completes the acuity of the artist's interpretation of the story is the relishing smile on Lot's face as he stretches out his right hand to reach for the chalice. One could describe the drawing as encompassing *multum in parvo*.

When Rembrandt came to etch the subject of *Adam and Eve* (Genesis 1:24–31) [Fig. 128] in 1638, he had two celebrated prototypes before him, impressions of both of which he may well have owned; Albrecht Dürer's engraving of *Adam and Eve* (B.4), in which the two figures stand full frontally side-by-side with Eve holding out an apple and, more

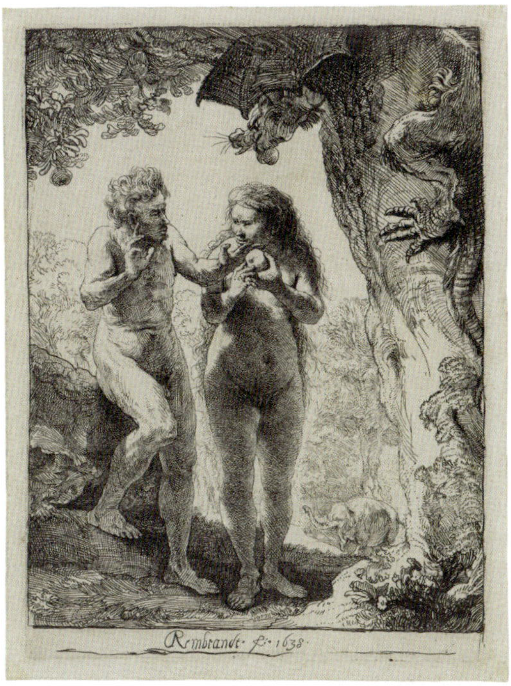

128. *Adam and Eve*. 1638. Etching.
16.3 × 11.7 cm. Rijksmuseum, Amsterdam.

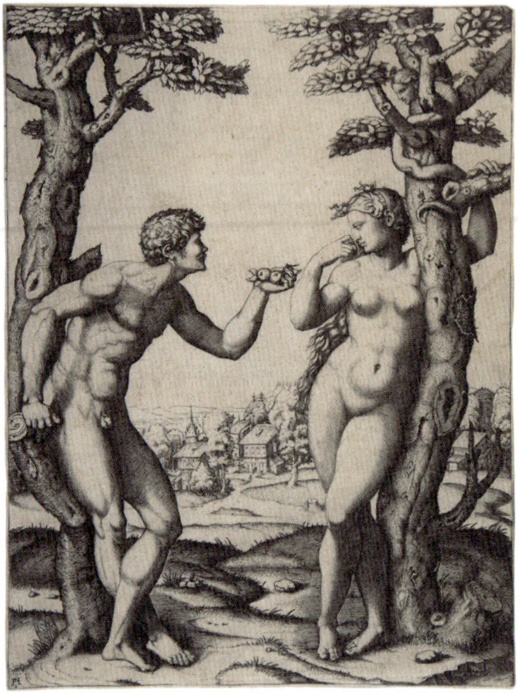

129. Marcantonio Raimondi, after Raphael, *The Fall of Man*. Engraving. 24.2 × 17.6 cm. Metropolitan Museum of Art, New York.

relevantly as will be seen, Marcantonio Raimondi's engraving after a design by Raphael of *The Fall of Man* [Fig. 129]. Both engravings were greatly influential well into the seventeenth century. If Rembrandt did not make much use of Dürer's *Adam and Eve*, he certainly took the lizard-like dragon, here assuming the role of the serpent, breathing threateningly down from the tree trunk from Dürer's engraving of *Christ in Limbo* [Fig. 130]. Since the beast, to which Rembrandt added large wings, appears in the same direction in both works, he must have worked in reverse on the plate. It is perhaps no coincidence that in the same year as the etching, Rembrandt bought a large group of prints by Dürer at an Amsterdam auction, including two from an unspecified Passion series.[29] In the case of Raimondi's design after Raphael, Adam and Eve, each backed by a tree trunk, stand either side of a balanced composition. Eve is concentrating on eating an apple, while Adam holds out several apples in his left hand, presumably remonstrating with his wife. The faces are

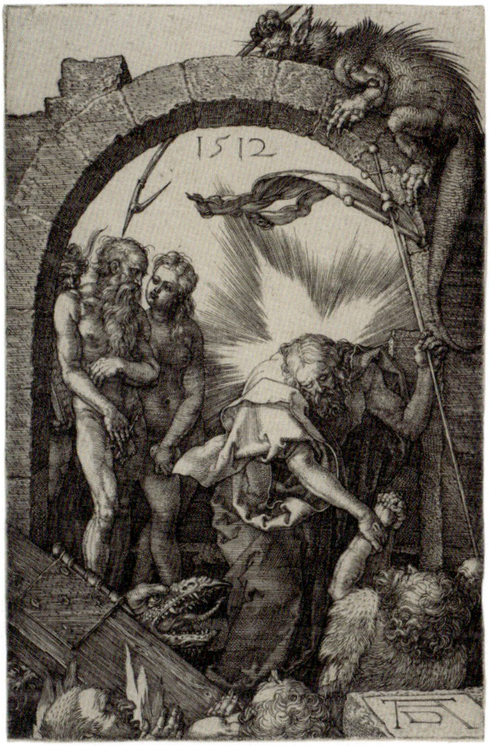

130. Albrecht Dürer, *Christ in Limbo. (Engraved Passion)*. 1512. Engraving. 11.6 × 7.4 cm. Metropolitan Museum of Art, New York.

without expression, so that the drama of Eve's persuading Adam to eat is downplayed.

What is immediately apparent is that whereas Dürer's and Raimondi's figures are youthful, attractive and well proportioned, Rembrandt, unlike his two predecessors, does not offer the traditional juxtaposition of the ideal male nude with the ideal female. His unidealised Adam and Eve are gnarled and middle-aged with ugly faces; they are real people. The way they stand in sinuous relationship to one another reflects the intimacy of their association. Eve, apple held out, tries to persuade Adam, who, with an upward gesture of his right hand pointing to heaven, extends his left hand to forewarn yet with a lingering wish to accept. The act of seduction with its fatal consequences is the focus of Rembrandt's print, and to work out a convincing psychological rendering, he relied on a preliminary

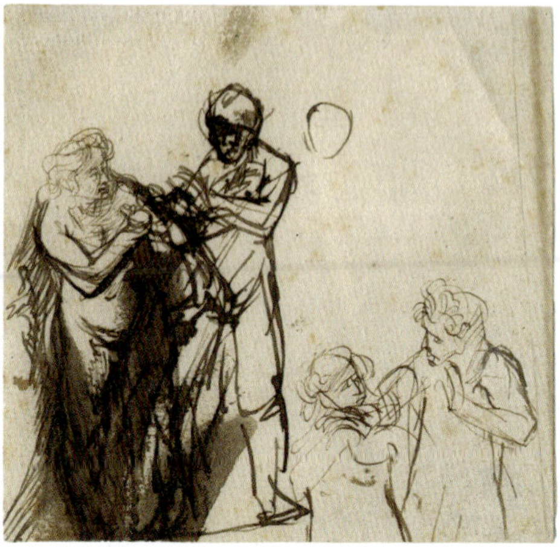

131. *Adam and Eve*. *c.*1638. Pen and brown ink with brown wash. 11.5 × 11.5 cm. Prentenkabinet der Universiteit, Leiden.

drawing [Fig. 131]; this is something which, as far as we know, he had never previously done in connexion with his prints. The sheet offers two solutions. In the more fully-worked-up version with the addition of wash on the left, Eve offers the apple, which is strongly rejected by Adam with his right arm thrust forward. Perhaps for the artist this offered too simple an account of what was going on in Adam's mind, and in the sketch on the right his raised right arm is now drawn back to his shoulder, suggesting that he is torn between accepting and rejecting This more nuanced interpretation was followed in reverse in the print.

The etching is pictorially rich, with the foreground darkened in contrast to the light background, producing a *contre-jour* effect of great subtlety. Much of the lighting comes from the side so that most of Adam and Eve's bodies, very clearly defined, are seen in shadow, with his silhouette reflected across her front. Her body, with its emphasis on the pubic area, which was possibly meant to allude to the couple's nakedness before *The Fall*, is beautifully modelled with delicate cross-hatching to suggest both light and form. Depth is given by the lightly-etched airy background, composed of, unlike Raimondi's anachronistic landscape with buildings, a glade with tall trees and inhabited by a wandering elephant with its trunk held high. The animal symbolises virtue and traditionally counterbalanced the evil serpent in the representations of *The*

Fall of Man. Its depiction here was freely based on the studies, such as the one drawn a year earlier (see Fig. 77).

2. The middle years

In the 1640s his attitude to his art changed, probably due more to an artistic reorientation than any effect of personal experiences. There were fewer pictures than in the previous decade and his work became simpler and more introspective. His paintings tended to more colourful than previously. His earlier strong chiaroscuro is now more muted to harmonise with his colour scheme. To achieve this, Rembrandt developed a much simpler style, eschewing theatrical gesture, and concentrating far more on describing inner emotion recalled in tranquillity. Figures usually in attendance, but not essential to the story, are omitted as the artist concentrates on the essential theme, sometimes, as already has been said, making it difficult to identify the subject.

This change of direction becomes apparent when Rembrandt returns to a subject, as, for example, happened in the case of the moving drawing of *The Return of the Prodigal Son* (Luke 15:11–32) [Fig. 132], which he

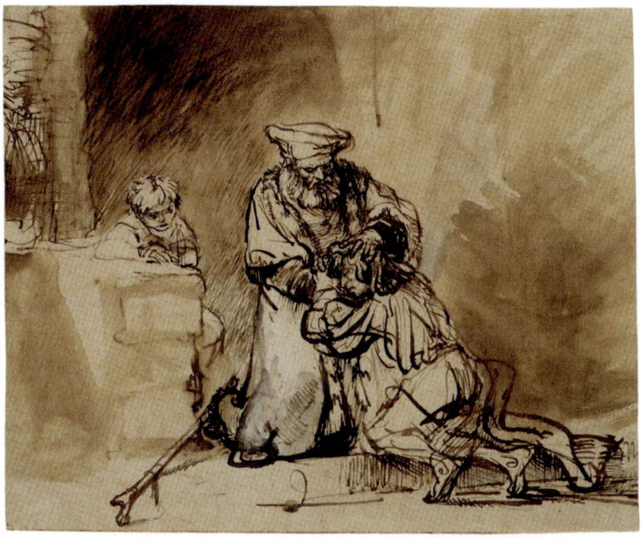

132. *The Return of the Prodigal Son*. *c.*1641. Pen and brown ink with brown wash, heightened with white. 19.1 × 22.7 cm. Teylers Museum, Haarlem.

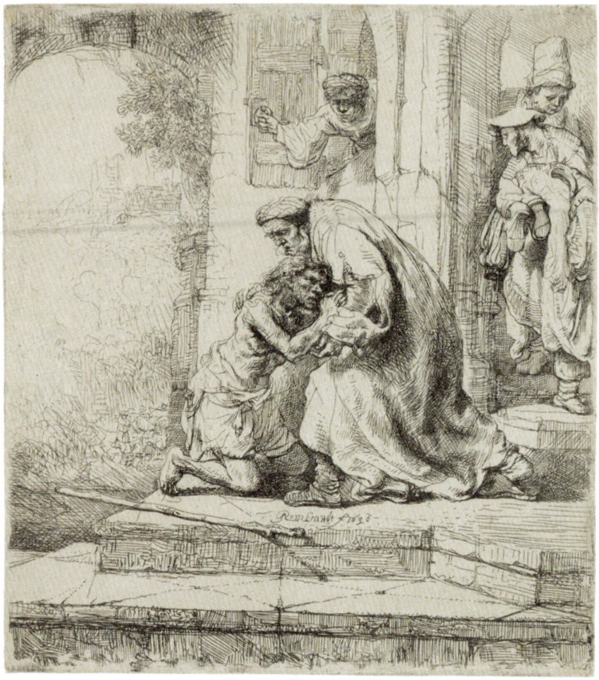

133. *The Return of the Prodigal Son.* 1636. Etching. 15.6 × 13.6 cm. Rijksmuseum, Amsterdam.

had already etched about five years earlier [Fig. 133]. With everyone reacting in their own way to the homecoming, the etching offers a lively scene characteristic of his work in the 1630s. Details related in the gospel are introduced. The robe and shoes called for by the father are carried down the steps by a servant, with presumably the jealous elder brother following him; the slaughter of the 'fatted calf' can just be made out in the background. In the foreground the father takes the final step to clasp his son in his arms; both men display intense emotions on their faces at their reunion.

In the drawing action is replaced by stillness. A bare setting of an arched space preceded by a rough wall jutting forward replaces the detailed architecture of the entrance to the house in the etching. Apart from a small boy, not mentioned in the gospel, looking curiously on and a man, presumably the jealous brother, just visible in the upper left, everything is concentrated on the dominant figures of father and younger son. Strong but calm expressions can be read on their faces, as they are clasped together, absorbed in their differing emotions of compassion and penitence. The drawing becomes less about telling the story of the return of the prodigal son than a meditation on the theme of forgiveness, which was in fact the *raison d'être* of St Luke's parable. Characteristic of his style in the 1640s, the figures of the father and son are forcefully outlined so that they stand out powerfully between the areas of wash, which establish a well-defined but limited space for the action. It is a drawing that stands very forcibly as a finished work of art.

Equally finished in its own way, the much smaller drawing of *Ruth and Boaz* (Ruth 3:15) [Fig. 134] is executed purely in line with no wash. With remarkable assurance the artist makes very few corrections as he sets down the elements of this rare subject, conveying a keen sense of the action taking place. Ruth, a Moabite widow, has travelled to Jerusalem with the intention of marrying Boaz, a relative of her deceased father-in-law. She takes on work as a labourer gleaning on his fields, where he finds her. He said to her: 'bring the veil that thou hast upon thee and hold it. And when she held it, he measured six measures of barley, and laid it on her'; with the outlines of three measures of grain visible on the ground, Boaz pours out the fourth measure from a wooden tub, rather than from her veil. Their marriage took place shortly afterwards.

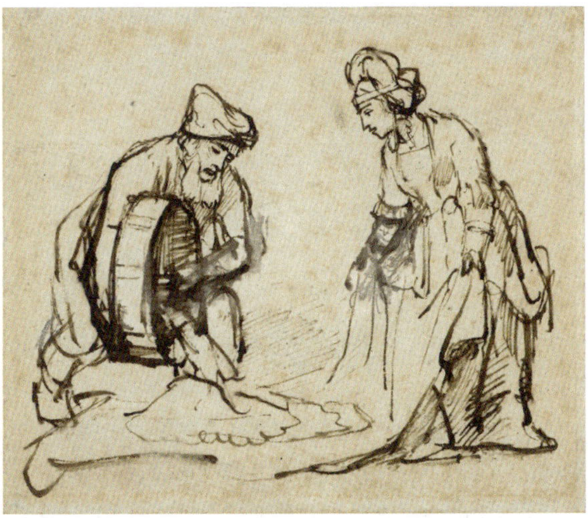

134. *Ruth and Boaz*. *c.*1641–5. Pen and brown ink, heightened with white. 12.6 × 14.3 cm. Rijksmuseum, Amsterdam.

A painting executed in the early 1640s – the last digit of the date is no longer visible – shows a young woman in a plain shift in bed, looking out from behind a curtain, which she has pushed aside with her left hand in a raised gesture [Fig. 135]. Her right shoulder and much of her left breast are exposed in a revealing manner. The setting has a sumptuous air; the bed is richly decorated, the pillow on which she is resting finely embroidered and the heavy red curtain with a patterned border fills the right hand side. She has character, but is not pretty and has large coarse hands. Over time, the painting has been thought to represent all three of the women in Rembrandt's life, but it matches neither the likeness of Saskia nor the supposed likenesses of Geertje Dircx and Hendrickje Stoffels.

The artist offers us no clear indication as to whether the subject is genre or a narrative, but there are several clues which strongly suggest the latter. On her head she wears an elaborate gold or gilt metal headdress,

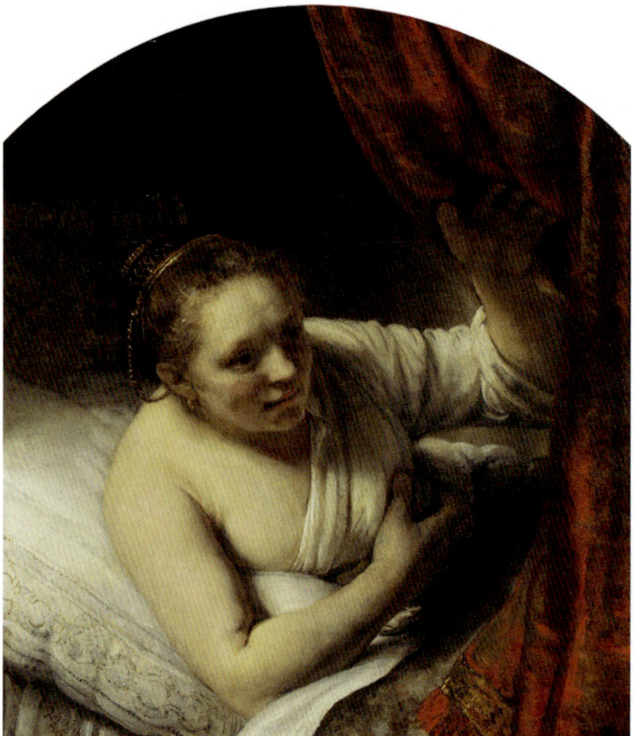

135. *Sarah Waiting for Tobias*. *c.*1643. Canvas on panel. 81.2 × 67.9 cm. National Gallery of Scotland, Edinburgh.

with an attached chain studded with precious stones, which is of a kind that no Dutch woman would have worn in bed or indeed elsewhere. It is to be noted that about the same time Rembrandt was giving *Danae* (Hermitage, St Petersburg) a very similar decorative metal headpiece. In addition the woman is not idly looking into space, as is the case in several drawings of women lying in bed. Her face displays an intent look of curiosity as to what is happening outside the picture. Even the curtain, usually no more than a decorative feature, is pushed aside in a way that underlines the woman's actions.

On the basis of a comparison with one part of a painting by Pieter Lastman [Fig. 136], it has been deduced that Rembrandt's picture in fact represents *Sarah Waiting for Tobias*, an event recorded in the Apocryphal Book of Tobit (6–8). As was his habit, Lastman retails the story in full. Sarah, who had already lost seven husbands on their wedding night slain by the devil Asmodeus, awaits to see whether Tobias can kill the evil spirit and survive to become her eighth husband. On the left Tobias can be seen burning the heart and liver of a fish together with incense, to produce smoke to drive away the devil, while overhead Tobias's guardian angel, Raphael, seizes the devil. Rembrandt appears to have taken over the

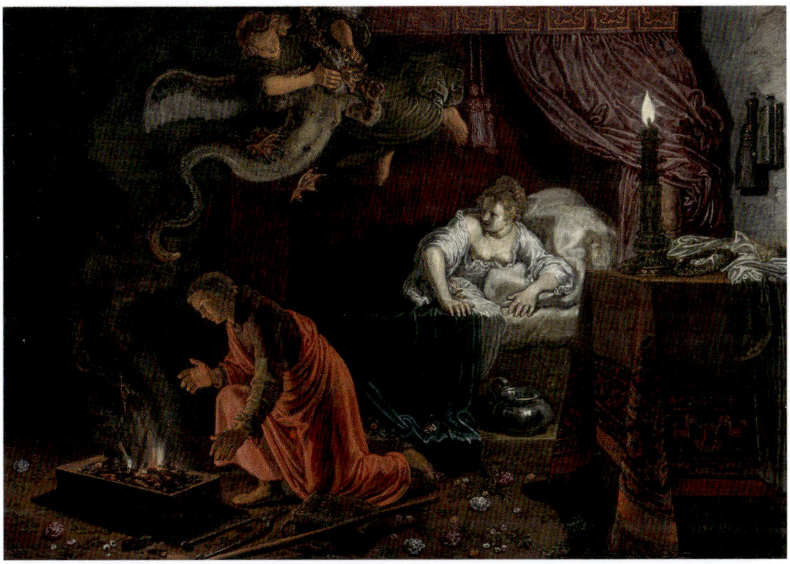

136. Pieter Lastman, *Sarah Waiting for Tobias*. 1611. Panel. 42 × 57 cm. Museum of Fine Arts, Boston.

figure of Sarah lying in a heavily-curtained bed, but omitted everything else in an extreme case of pruning of attendant detail to concentrate on the essential theme of Sarah's anticipation. The similarities between the two works are compelling, but if correctly identified one would have to assume that the recipient of the picture knew the story.

As to the painting's purpose, it has been suggested that it served as decoration to a box bed, an idea supported by the original attachment of the canvas to a panel, which would have been part of the bed. The *trompe l'œil* effect of the young woman leaning out into the spectator's space makes a very powerful impression. Executed very freely in the artist's rough manner, the beautifully painted white pillow with the rich red of the curtain provide a telling foil to the ivory colour of the young woman's skin and the auburn tints in her hair.

The subject of the Holy Family remained on Rembrandt's mind as he sought variations in the way he represented the theme, doubtless informed by his own recollections of nursery life. One of the most delightful is the drawing of *The Holy Family at Rest* [Fig. 137]. The baby (finally?) sleeps serenely, while Mary, seated beside the cot, rests her head on her hand in a gesture signalling infinite tiredness. In the foreground Joseph lies in

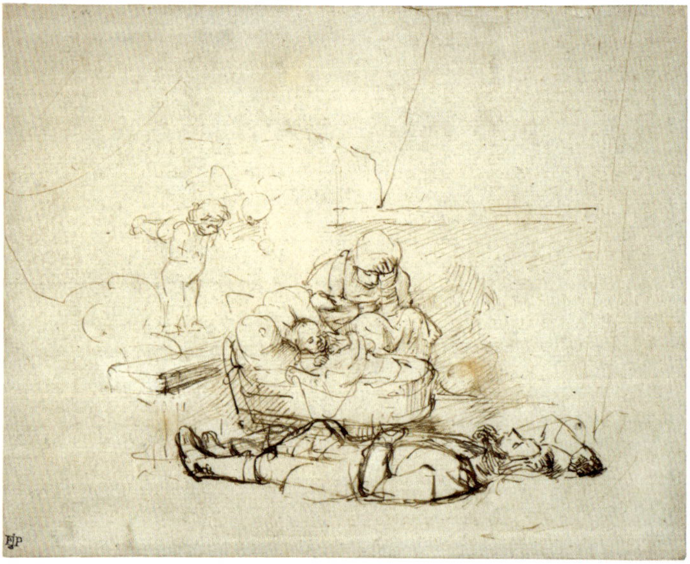

137. *The Holy Family at Rest*. *c.*1645. Pen and brown ink, heightened with white. 17.3 × 21.2 cm. Fitzwilliam Museum, Cambridge.

deep slumber flat out on the floor, with his right arm stretched out dramatically beside his head. In the left background a winged angel flies in to offer support, while in the centre what seems like a large fireplace can just be made out. The drawing offers a telling illustration of the common experience of parental exhaustion, but here linked to a particular narrative. The drawing is notable for its very clear sense of space established by the diagonal placing of the figures, one behind another, combined with the aerial perspective created by the variation in the pen strokes. The latter recede in thickness and colour from the dark bold lines defining St Joseph to the lighter lines describing mother and child, with the thinnest and palest introducing the figure of the angel and the background. Small areas of parallel shading enhance the effect of light and shadow. For such a seemingly spontaneously executed drawing, it is a remarkably calculated work of art, which, despite its perfunctory character, should be regarded as finished.

Unlike the previous drawing, with its prevailing atmosphere of somnolence, the scene in *The Holy Family in the Carpenter's Shop* [Fig. 138] is one of activity. St Joseph stands hard at work sawing at his workbench,

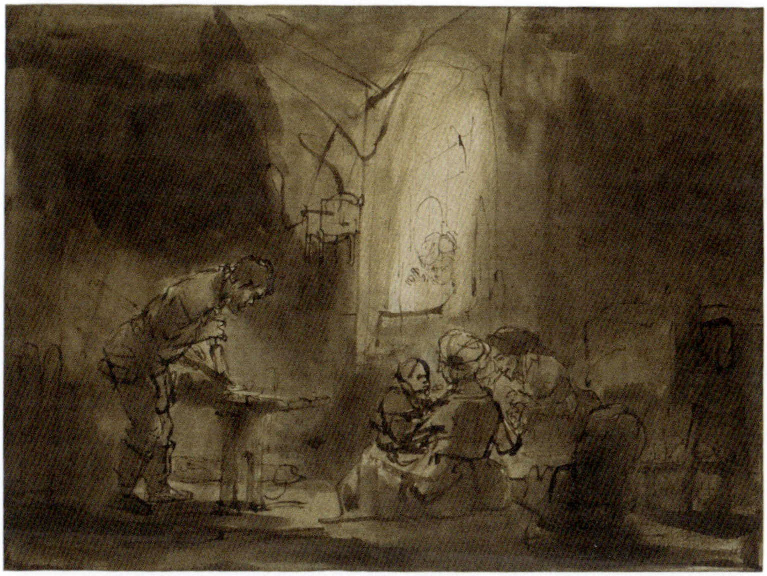

138. *The Holy Family in the Carpenter's Shop*. *c.*1645. Pen and brown ink with brown wash, heightened with white. 18.4 × 24.6 cm. British Museum, London.

while the Virgin, seated beside him, is actively engaged with a lively Infant Christ, with St Anne, a rare presence, joining in the conversation; a woman, perhaps St Elizabeth, taps on the window to gain attention. The drawing offers a snapshot of the kind of daily life led by not just the Holy Family. It could easily be classed as genre rather than narrative. Light flows in from the large window, picking out the heads of Joseph, Mary and Christ. The extensive use of varying shades of brush wash covering every inch of the whole sheet sets up a world of shadows in the otherwise dark high-vaulted room. One of the most pictorial of his drawings, the artist leaves us in no doubt that he considered it a finished work of art.

The *Nocturnal Landscape with the Holy Family* [Fig. 139], dated 1647, stands out in Rembrandt's *œuvre* as one of the most magical representations of figures in an all-embracing landscape on a dark night. So hidden in the murkiness are the participants in the story that for long the subject was not recognised, and the figures were reckoned to be no more than staffage. It was only when it was pointed out that the inspiration for the work clearly came from Adam Elsheimer's small painting on copper

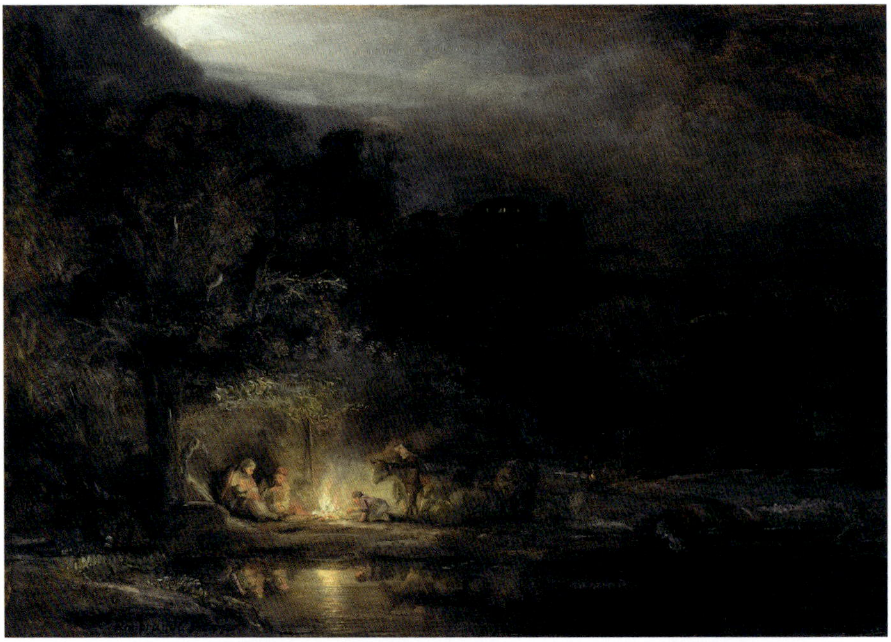

139. *Nocturnal Landscape with the Holy Family*. 1647. Panel. 33.8 × 47.8 cm. National Gallery of Ireland, Dublin.

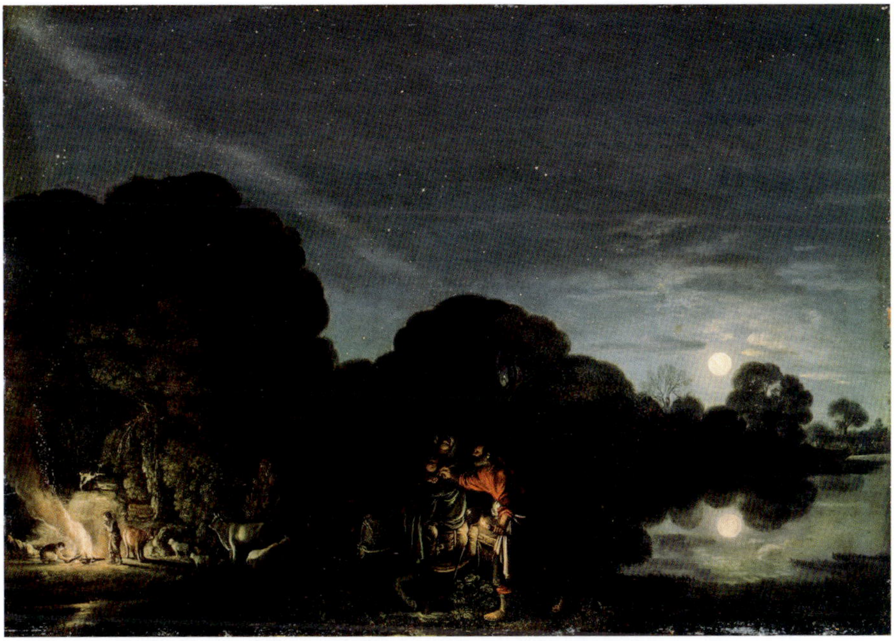

140. Adam Elsheimer, *The Flight into Egypt*. 1609. Copper. 31 × 41 cm.
Alte Pinakothek, Munich.

of *The Flight into Egypt* [Fig. 140] that the picture was recognised as having a specific theme. It was more likely that Rembrandt saw a copy of the German artist's painting, of which several existed, than the original, which, until 1628, was briefly in the Netherlands in the collection of the Utrecht artist, Hendrick Goudt, who made a fine engraving of it in reverse. If the latter was, however, Rembrandt's source, reversing the image would have posed no problem to such a well-versed printmaker, although one may wonder why he should have bothered to do so.

Rembrandt followed the basic composition of a diagonally placed landscape beside a stretch of water at night, but, apart from the kneeling shepherds in front of the fire, the details were changed. To begin with, a curved bank beside the river was introduced, establishing a greater area of water in the foreground. Merging Elsheimer's two small groups of figures, composed of shepherds on the left and the Holy Family in the centre, Rembrandt created a single group filling the left of the composition arranged around the figures of the Holy Family, now seen resting rather than on the move; the subject has been altered from the Flight into Egypt to the Rest on the Flight into Egypt. Beneath a thick cover of trees at the water's edge, the Virgin sits cradling the Infant Christ in her arms with Joseph seated beside her to the left of a fiercely burning fire. The latter feature is tended by a shepherd with another shepherd plus some cows and sheep behind him. Instead of being submerged in the prevailing gloom as in Elsheimer's work, Rembrandt's figures form a brightly-lit group glowing in the darkness, creating beautiful reflections in the water. The details of the hilly landscape, purely imaginary and bearing no resemblance to the Dutch countryside, can barely be made out, apart from the just-identifiable castle on the hill with light shining out from the windows.

But it is Rembrandt's treatment of the moon which changes the mood of Elsheimer's intimate painting. The *donnêe* in the latter was the brilliantly clear full moon, with its reflection in the water, in a star studded sky, which casts a silvery light over the serene landscape. This represented the first true moonlit landscape in European painting, a feature which inspired Rubens in his *Landscape with Moon and Stars* (Courtauld Gallery, London), which, before he painted them out, included the figures of the Holy Family. Seeking a different effect, Rembrandt hides the moon from sight, but we see its effects more dramatically rendered as it breaks through dark clouds and blue sky, creating overall a mysterious hazy atmosphere. In place of the overall pale tone in Elsheimer's painting, Rembrandt sets up a contrast between the warm yellow/orange area of the figure group with the cool light falling over the rest of the landscape. The paint surface varies between the impasted strokes defining the highlighted area, as well as the castle on the hill, with more thinly-applied strokes on the remainder of the picture. In no other representation of the story, which Rembrandt illustrated in a number of prints and drawings, does the landscape assume such a dominant role.

Two years earlier, Rembrandt produced the first of two etchings of the story of *Abraham and Isaac* (Genesis 21:9–21) [Fig. 141], which were to be very different in character from one another. In the earlier print, father and son have reached the appointed place for the latter's sacrifice, ordered by God to test Abraham's obedience, and are engaged in close discussion. To the the puzzled boy's question as to where is the sacrificial animal, Abraham points upwards with his left hand, saying God

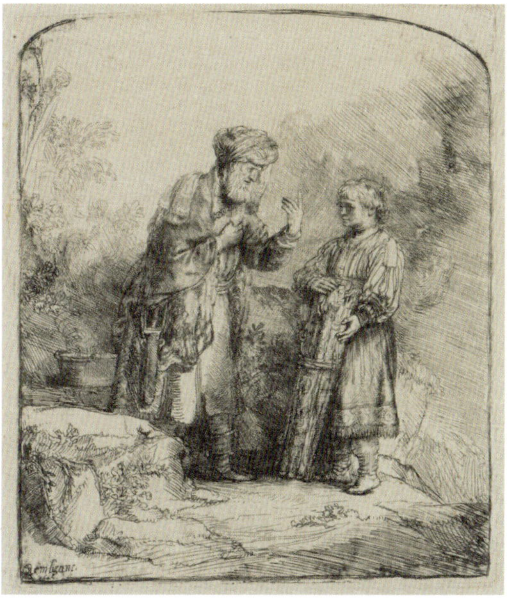

141. *Abraham and Isaac*. 1645. Etching.
15.7 × 13 cm. Rijksmuseum, Amsterdam.

will provide. With his right hand held to his chest to denote his anguish at the task ahead of him, Abraham's gaze is stern, while Isaac, clasping the bundle of wood for the fire, responds with an innocent trusting look. The conversation between the two was an unusual moment in the story to illustrate.

With some drypoint to darken the shading, the plate is very delicately etched. Previously shadows submerged the figures into the overall chiaroscuro, but now the figures are firmly outlined against their background, so that, even in the darkest shadow, Abraham's leg and foot are, for example, clearly visible. The hatching is devised to follow a definite pattern; small areas of finely drawn lines, varied in direction, model the figures, while longer parallel strokes drawn in a more regular form create a neutral setting from which Abraham and Isaac stand out like figures on a bas-relief.

On his return to the subject of Abraham and his much loved son eleven years later in *Abraham's Sacrifice* [Fig. 142], Rembrandt chose the more usually illustrated moment in the story; Abraham, knife in one hand the other held covering the boy's eyes, is about to carry out the

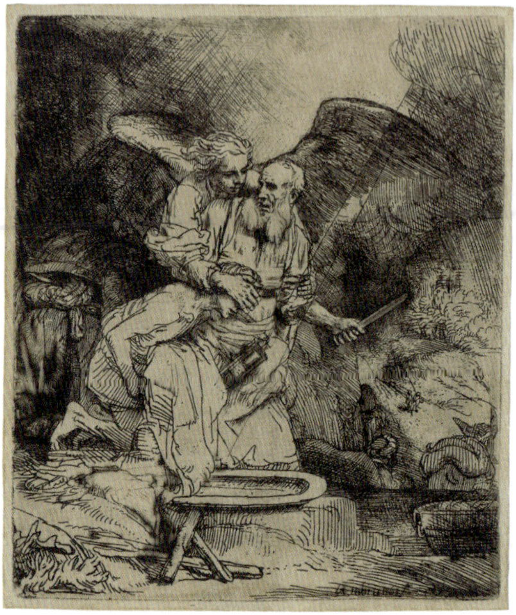

142. *Abraham's Sacrifice*. 1656. Etching and drypoint, on Japanese paper. 15.6 × 13.1 cm. Rijksmuseum, Amsterdam.

sacrifice, when the angel in a moment of high drama swoops down from above and seizes the old man's arm to stop him. It is a scene of sudden action rather than quiet conversation as in the earlier work.

The drawing of *Mercury and Argus* [Fig. 143] inimitably captures the spirit of Ovid's *Metamorphoses*. Io, one of Jupiter's many loves, was turned into a white heifer by the jealous Juno and consigned to the safeguarding of the hundred-eyed giant, Argus. Mercury was sent by Jupiter to rescue the 'girl'. The drawing depicts the moment when Mercury lulls Argus into sleep with the playing on his reed pipe before killing him. Seated side-by-side on a rock beside a tree – the wash is probably a later addition – Mercury momentarily breaks off from playing to cast a covert glance at his victim to assess his state of wakefulness. The latter, head fallen onto his right arm, and his staff in the other hand resting between his legs, enjoys that delicious moment of early slumber blissfully unaware of his impending fate. Lightly drawn, mainly in outline with only small areas of shading, it is remarkable how much expression Rembrandt, in only a few pen lines, is able to imbue his protagonists with. Their relationship,

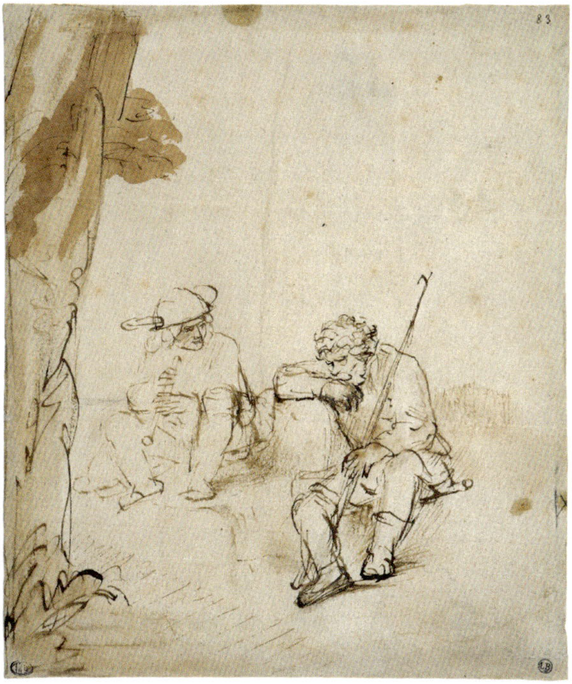

143. *Mercury and Argus*. *c.*1648. Pen and brown ink with brown wash. 17.8 × 14.6 cm. Musée du Louvre, Paris.

played out against a bare background, is perfectly encapsulated with the minimum of means.

The subject, if it has one, of the print now generally known as the *Jews in a Synagogue* [Fig. 144], dated 1648, has never been satisfactorily resolved. The setting is an ecclesiastical building, presumably intended as a synagogue, with the filtered light from the windows shining dimly

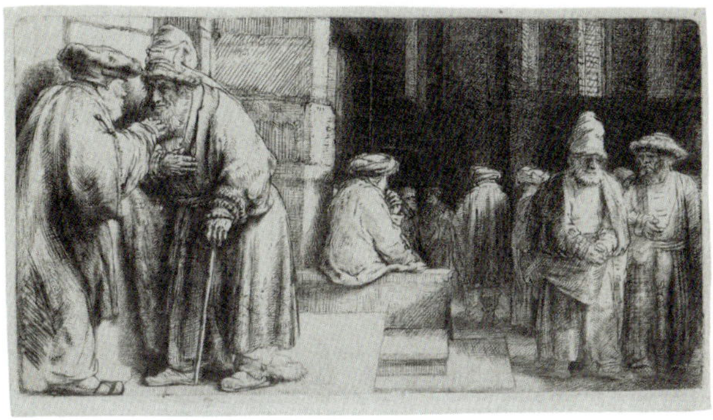

144. *Jews in a Synagogue*. 1648. Etching and drypoint. 7.1 × 12.9 cm. Rijksmuseum, Amsterdam.

on to the darkened nave on the right. The technique used is a mixture of tonal areas creating atmosphere and open drawing giving clear definition and weight to the figures. To encompass two groups and a single figure, all intentionally separated from one another, the plate, in relation to its height, is unusually wide. On the right, elderly Jews come and go, with the foremost pair in conversation. On the left, filling the height of the plate, two elderly Jews, so acutely observed, whisper conspiratorially to one another. In the centre sitting on a low wall with his back to us, another figure holds his hand to his face. There has been much discussion about the sect of Jew represented, but it has been argued that their clothing of long cloaks and tall fur hats belongs to the Ashkenazi. It may be that Rembrandt intended no more than a genre subject, portraying contemporary Jews in their place of worship.

But if there is more to the print than meets the eye, the key to the subject must be the seated figure on the wall. Not only is he in the centre of the composition, but he is framed by the vertical and horizontal line of the wall. His unshaded back creates a highlight which catches the eye. His action with his left hand suggests that he is gnawing his fingers in anguish. So distinctively set apart from the other figures, he would seem to be more than just another anonymous participant in the scene. Is he the subject of obloquy on the part of his fellow Jews? One attractive solution is that he represents the repentant Judas, but what we see does not match what Matthew (27:5) wrote; 'he cast down the (thirty) pieces of silver in the temple and departed'. One leaves the print with a nagging feeling that we are missing something, which the artist intended, and that on this occasion he has not offered us enough clues to read his mind.

3. The later years.

Despite the turmoil in Rembrandt's life the decade of the 1650s offers perhaps the most active and fruitful part of his career. Although the number of etchings produced in the 1640s and 1650s remained about the same, his activity as a painter increased from about fifty-four to seventy-eight, which included some of his best-known works; in view of the uncertainty over dating, the difference in the number of drawings is more difficult to quantify. In the 1660s he produced about fifty-five paintings, but the number of drawings was greatly reduced. Only one etching is dated after 1660, indicating that he virtually gave up printmaking when he moved to the Rosengracht, but one or two commissions, which came to nothing, suggest he had not given up the idea of making some more prints if the opportunity presented itself.

In style, there is greater simplicity in his work, with the tendency to illustrate subjects with fewer figures. With that went a new monumentality, to achieve which he turned increasingly to Italian art, either nurtured on his own collection or on what he could see around him. In painting his colours were limited to one or two in each canvas, but combined with a new feeling for light and atmosphere they acquired a greater richness of effect.

In 1652 Jan Six invited Rembrandt to contribute not one but two drawings to his *Album Amicorum*. Such books became popular from the later sixteenth century onwards, and were compiled by learned people commemorating their friends, their travels and their intellectual interests. Rembrandt's drawings were not on separate sheets of paper and inserted, but were drawn directly into the book, a procedure which, if Rembrandt did not borrow the album, must have taken place in Six's house. Possibly suggested by Six, their classical subject matter, *Homer Reciting his Verses* [Fig. 145], inscribed by the artist. *Rembrandt aen Johannes Six 1652* ('Rembrandt for Johannes Six 1652') and *Minerva in her Study* (see Fig. 147), signed *Rembrandt f. 1652*, paid tribute to Six's antiquarian interests; in the case of the former sheet, an implied compliment relating to his tragedy, *Medea*, which had been published in 1648 with an etched frontispiece by Rembrandt may have been intended. Whether by chance or design, the artist gave his patron two very different specimens of his draughtsmanship, one executed solely in pen and the other largely with wash, and both of exceptional quality.

In *Homer Reciting his Verses*, the poet, in full voice, is standing on a mound with his attentive audience arranged in a descending semi-circle on either side of him; two trees provide the rural setting. The composition shows knowledge of Raphael's fresco of *The Assembly of the Gods on Mount Parnassus*, in the Stanza della Segnatura in the Vatican, Rome, transmitted through Marcantonio Raimondi's engraving [Fig. 146], which may well have been known to Six as well as to the artist. Not only are Homer's

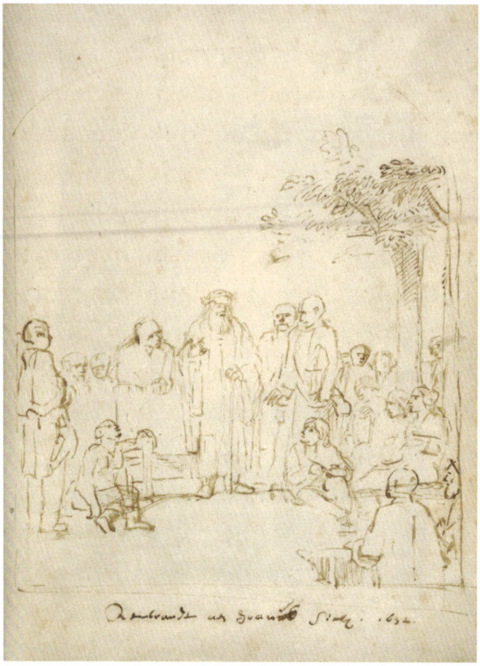

145. *Homer Reciting his Verses*. 1652.
Pen and brown ink. 19 × 16.5 cm.
Collection Six, Amsterdam.

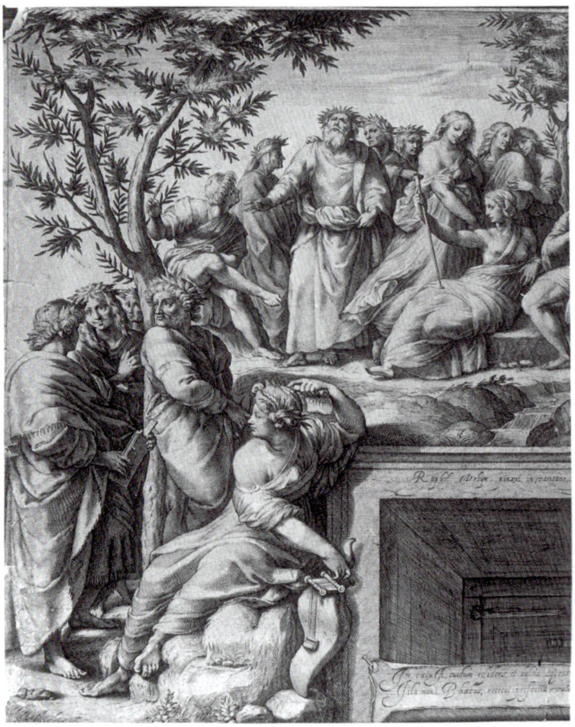

146. Marcantonio Raimondi, *The Assembly of the Gods on Mount Parnassus* (detail of left hand side). 1520. Engraving. 35.8 × 47 cm. British Museum, London.

hearers placed on raised ground descending on either side of the principal figure, but details such as the seated scribe, pen in hand, are repeated. The drawing offers a sophisticated exchange between a painter and a patron both knowledgeable in the history of art. The thick lines freely and assuredly defining the figures are complemented by the blobs of ink from the fully charged pen, which create a lively pattern across the page. With the minimum of strokes the artist gives an aura of listening to be observed in the facial expressions of the audience. As will be seen, it was a drawing which remained at the back of Rembrandt's mind.

The study of *Minerva in her Study* [Fig. 147] has given birth to the nice but unproven theory identifying, with flattering implications, the sitter as Six's mother, Anna Wijmer. It is certainly true that Minerva looks more like a old woman than a goddess, but it is difficult to discern any likeness with her supposed painted portrait (Six Foundation, Amsterdam) of eleven years earlier. Minerva, the goddess of wisdom, science and the arts, is seated at her desk in a high room draped with curtains; with her

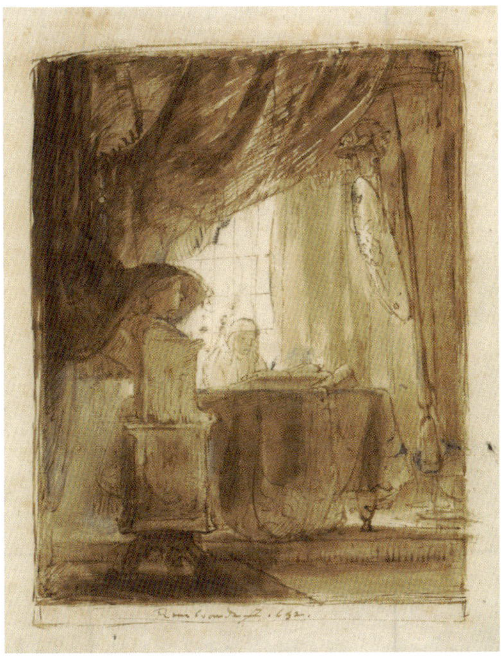

147. *Minerva in her Study*. 1652. Pen and brown ink with brown wash, heightened with white. 19 × 14 cm. Collection Six, Amsterdam.

back to a large bay window, she is writing in a large volume. On the right her shield decorated with Medusa's head hangs on the wall with her spear beside it. In the left foreground a cast-iron stove is surmounted by a bust, partly draped with a curtain, resting on a plinth. With the ample display of curtains hanging from above, it has the cosiness fit for the study of a learned figure. Apart from shield and spear, the room and its furnishing have the appearance of a house in Amsterdam in Rembrandt's time rather than that of an imagined classical interior. What gives the drawing its unusual character are the elaborate washes covering the whole sheet, leaving only a small amount of untouched paper to suggest the light flooding in from the window. To enhance this effect, touches of white paint have been added to one or two areas. The drawing is an exercise in the masterly depiction of bright light against the flickering shadows in a darkened interior, and in this respect it matches the contemporary study of the *Artist's Studio with a Model* (see Fig. 22).

In the beautifully atmospheric small etching of *The Agony in the Garden* [Fig. 148], the full moon, partly hidden by a bank of clouds, casts a nocturnal light over the landscape. In the left background, a fortress-like building, seen in silhouette, rises up to the top of the plate; at its foot soldiers

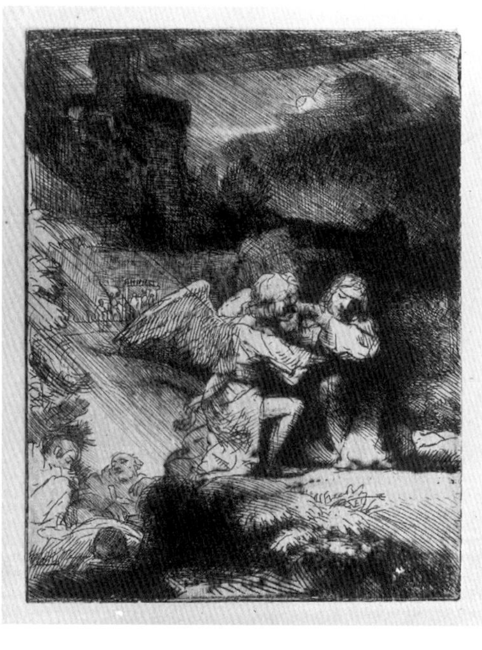

148. *The Agony in the Garden.* *c.*1652. Etching and drypoint, with surface tone. 11.1 × 8.4 cm. British Museum, London.

led by Judas Iscariot make their way to the garden of Cedron, where in the left foreground Peter and the two sons of Zebedee, despite Christ's exhortations to stay awake in company with him, are stretched out in slumber. On the Mount of Olives in the centre, Christ is kneeling succoured by an angel. Christ's face expresses the agony he is undergoing, as he turns his head way from looking at the angel. Rembrandt interprets the scene naturalistically, omitting the symbolic chalice, sometimes accompanied by a cross, often held by the angel in representations of the event. In a very compact composition, the artist has encompassed three different incidents in the story, an example of Rembrandt's skill in illustration.

The copper plate may be small, but he has worked at it with considerable endeavour to get the effects he wanted. Over an etched basis, with lines loosely drawn, he worked in drypoint, the burr producing dark accents on the two principal figures and the mound on which they are situated, as well as in the darkest recesses of the landscape. Beams of light follow the angel and illumine the foreground, which stands out from the largely darkened background. Intent on obtaining a mysterious light, Rembrandt varied the inking of the plate, so that one impression is hardly the same as the other. In the impression reproduced, the artist has left a thin film of ink over the plate, which produces a softer, more muted tone than in cleanly wiped impressions.

In the first half of the decade Rembrandt became preoccupied with the story of David, the shepherd boy who became the King of Israel; one drawing of *David Receiving the News of Uriah's Death*, two of *Nathan Admonishing David*, an etching of *David in Prayer*, dated 1652, and, with the king in *absentia*, the painting of *Bathsheba*, dated 1654. It should be noted that, with the exception of the print, Rembrandt's choice of incidents taken from the life of David is limited to examples of his sinfulness. In one drawing of *Nathan Admonishing David* [Fig. 149], the towering figure of Nathan looks down at the seated David and, with a forceful admonitory gesture, brings home God's message of displeasure; the expression on David's face reveals him deep in thought, coming to terms with his acts of adultery and virtual murder. The setting is bare with only a large table on the left, on which rests the king's crown; his harp is propped up at the side. It is strictly a drawing in outline only, but which conveys all that is necessary to describe the event.

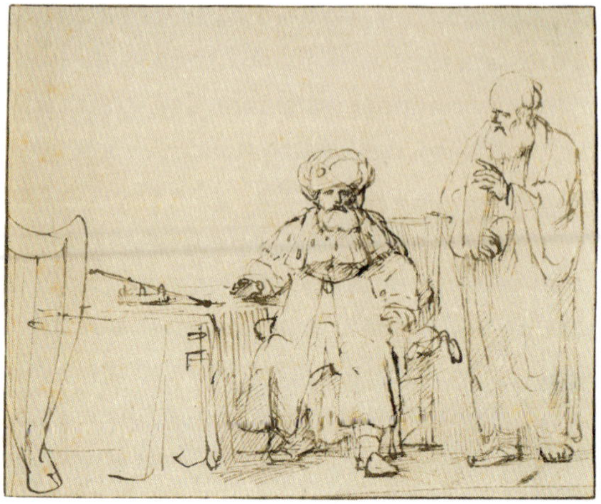

149. *Nathan Admonishing David. c.*1652. Pen and brown ink. 12.6 × 14.8 cm. Stirling and Francine Clark Art Institute, Williamstown.

In one of the most delectable and moving female nudes in his *œuvre*, Rembrandt painted *Bathsheba with King David's Letter* [Fig. 150]. The key to the story is described in a few words in the second Book of Samuel (2 Samuel 11:2): 'And it came to pass at eventide, that David arose from his bed, and walked upon the roof of the king's house. And from the roof he saw a woman washing herself, and the woman was very beautiful to look upon. And David sent and inquired about the woman'. From this chance espial arose David's infatuation. Although the Bible does not say so, pictorial tradition dictates that he sent a letter to her. Which is exactly what is happening in Rubens's brilliant painting, combining two moments in the story [Fig. 151]. The setting is exotic with curtains backing a flowing fountain, decorated with a dolphin supporting a cupid; David's classically-designed palace rises up in the background. A negro page, confronted by a yapping dog, delivers David's letter to Bathsheba, who is occupied in having her long tresses of blond hair combed by a handmaiden; David, a small figure on the roof, watches to see her reaction. Rubens tells it as a fast-moving event. There is nothing demure about Bathsheba as she looks enquiringly at the messenger. You could say she looks all too ready for a proposal.

When one turns to Rembrandt's version of the story one has to remember that the picture did not start out as we see it today. Almost certainly

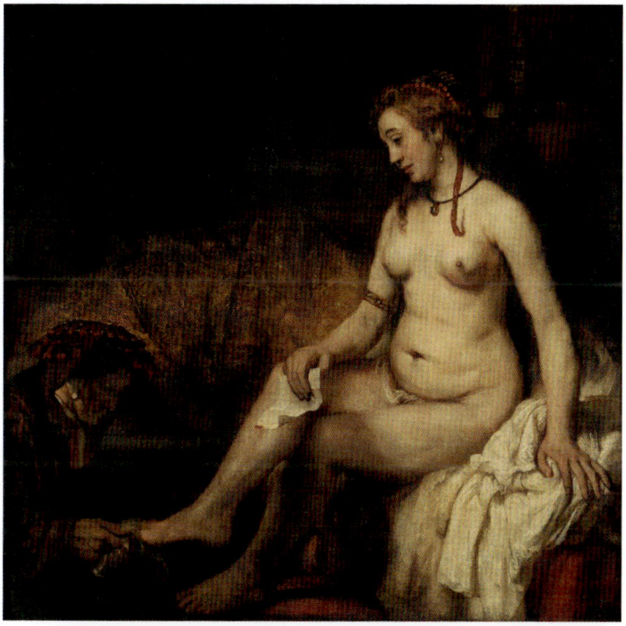

150. *Bathsheba with King David's Letter*. 1654. Canvas. 142 × 142 cm. Musée du Louvre, Paris.

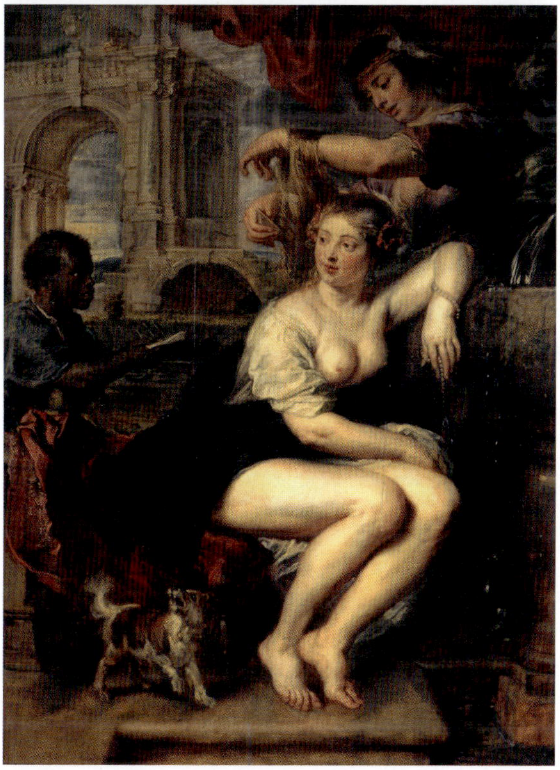

151. Peter Paul Rubens, *Bathsheba Receiving David's Letter*. *c.*1635. Panel. 175 × 126 cm. Gemäldegalerie, Dresden.

larger at the left and even more so at the top, the canvas was reduced in size very likely by Rembrandt himself. In addition X-rays reveal significant changes having taken place. The letter held in her hand appears to be an afterthought while originally the white drapery, now seen beside her, partly covered her legs and left arm, reducing the degree of nudity. But, most importantly, her head was originally depicted as looking up rather than down. One can speculate that the picture may have started off with the inclusion of David looking down at Bathsheba from above, but before the despatch of his letter. This has been altered to a later moment in the story, when Bathsheba has received and has read David's letter. Reflexion replaces action. The picture becomes essentially about depicting human emotion rather than relating narrative as was brilliantly done in Rubens's version.

Apart from representing Bathsheba's beauty, Rembrandt's final version does not correspond in detail with the Biblical text. A dark background of a curtain seals off the limited space with her richly-painted golden brocade robe laid out. Bathsheba, her life-size figure dominating the whole canvas, is seen seated, her crossed legs in profile but her body half turned to the front; her left hand rests on a mass of white drapery, while the inconspicuous figure of an old woman, cut at the shoulders, tends to Bathsheba's feet in the lower left corner. The design of the two figures set against a curtained background echoes that found on an ancient relief, which Rembrandt could have known from an engraving [Fig. 152] made shortly before. Seeing Bathsheba, now totally nude, her body beautifully modelled with fluent brushstrokes to suggest both the firmness and the softness of the flesh, increases the intimacy of the occasion. She may not be conventionally beautiful, but her appearance gives her an attractive cosiness. Lost in sad reverie after having just read David's letter, now clasped to her knee and a focal point in the picture, she displays an infinitely touching expression as she ponders its implications. One suspects Rubens's Bathsheba would have accepted the invitation without hesitation, but Rembrandt's is not nearly so sure. So bound up with the conflict taking place within her between the duty of marital fidelity against obedience to her king, she is hardly aware of the pedicure taking place in the shadows. As happened with the earlier painting of Susanna (see Fig. 122), the placing of the figure filling the picture surface

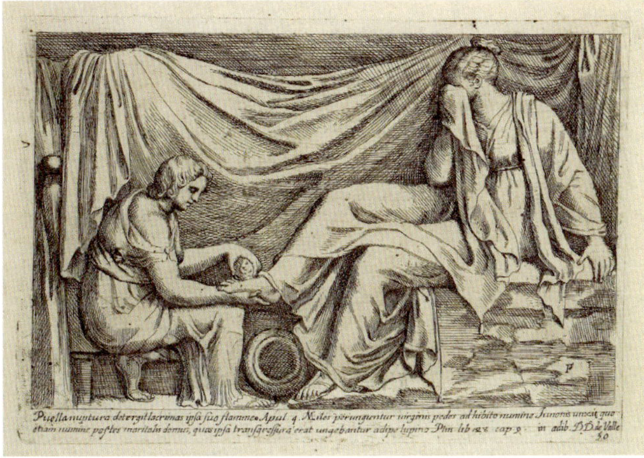

152. François Perrier, *Antique Relief* (from *Icones et Segmenta*). 1645. Engraving. 16.2 × 22.7 cm. Universitäts-Bibliothek, Heidelberg.

in the immediate foreground brings the spectator into overpowering contact with her naked form, an effect enhanced by the stillness of her pose. Without the presence of David, the spectator becomes the voyeur.

The drawing of *Jael Killing Sisera* [Fig. 153], executed about 1656, illustrates a brutal story taken from the Book of Judges (4:17), which Rembrandt tells with unredeemed relish. It accounts how Sisera, leader of the defeated Canaanite army, is offered refuge in her tent by a woman called Jael, who, though belonging to a tribe friendly with the Canaanites,

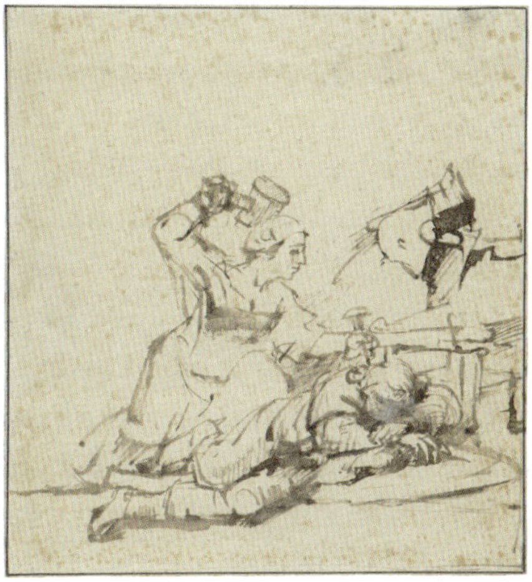

153. *Jael Killing Sisera*. *c.*1656. Pen and brown ink, heightened with white. 19.2 × 17.4 cm. Rijksmuseum, Amsterdam.

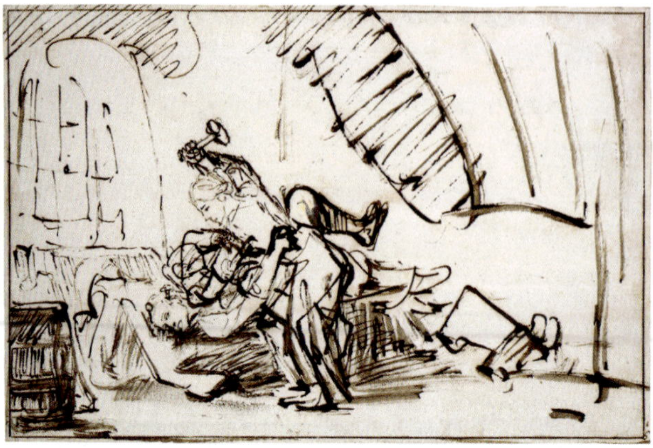

154. *Jael Killing Sisera*. *c.*1651. Pen and brown ink with white bodycolour, on paper. 17.3 × 25.5 cm. Ashmolean Museum, Oxford.

was personally a supporter of the cause of the victorious Israelites. Having fed Sisera and put him to bed, she 'took a nail of the tent, and took a hammer in her hand, and went softly unto him, and smote the nail into his temples. … So he died'. Sisera, resting his head on his hands on the mantle she had given him, lies in deep slumber on the floor; his armour is hung up on the side of the chair behind him. Jael, having placed the tent peg very precisely on the back of his head, is about to smite him with the hammer raised up high. The incident is vividly recorded by Rembrandt, and, such was its appeal to the artist, this sheet represents his second drawing of the subject. The latter [Fig. 154], carried out about five years earlier, offers a telling comparison between the different treatment of the subject and the different drawing techniques used in both studies.

In the earlier drawing Sisera is very much still alive as he furiously fights back after the first blow, kicking over a table with his foot. This is at variance with the Biblical account, which implies that he died immediately on being struck on the head. In his attempt to extract the maximum drama and action, Rembrandt has redrawn the arms and legs, so that it is now difficult to read which limb belongs to whom. The artist started with thin lines laying in the outline of the figures, and then, demonstrating the flexibility of the quill pen, developing his study of violence and pain with a flurry of broader lines. The melodrama of Sisera's murder is conveyed as much by the manner of execution as by the conception of the subject.

In the later version, Rembrandt, selects an earlier moment in the story, when the first blow of the hammer is about to be struck. There is a sense of action frozen in time, which imbues the drawing with a feeling of high tension, absent from the ongoing proceedings in the earlier drawing. With the unsuspecting Sisera deep in sleep, the drawing becomes a study of the inner drama involving Jael; yet from the expression on her face, she seems more concerned with taking accurate aim than by the murderous act she is about to perform. The angular strokes of the reed pen, different in character from those produced by the quill pen, vary in tone according to the amount of ink held by the pen; they sometimes widen into shadows, which, otherwise, are indicated by a few lines of hatching. Touches of white bodycolour were applied to lighten the colour on Sisera's face. Although seemingly so freely executed, the technical effects were carefully calculated.

In the later 1640s, Rembrandt spent considerable time working on his most famous etching of *Christ Preaching* [Fig. 155], popularly known as *'The Hundred Guilder Print'*, on account of the high price it fetched

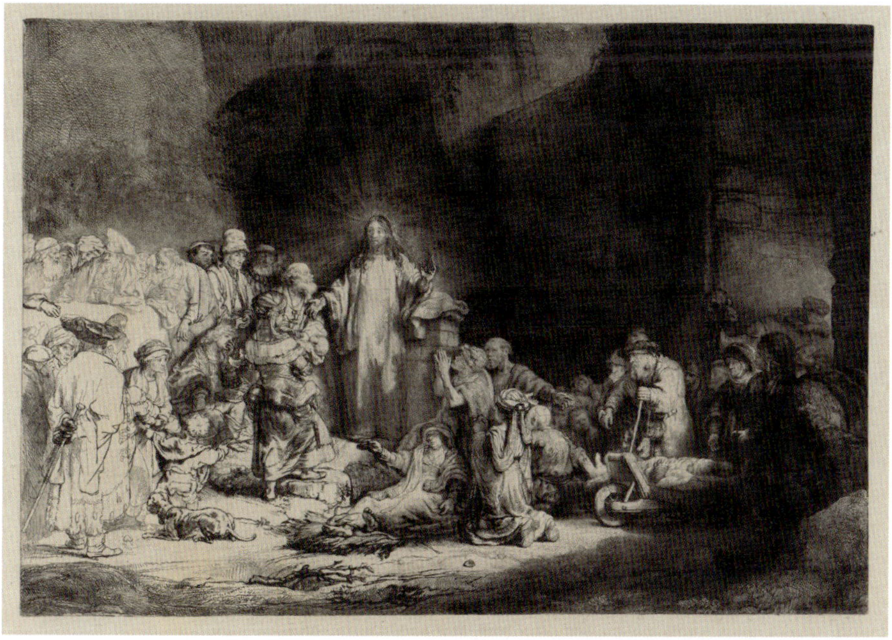

155. *Christ Preaching ('The Hundred Guilder Print')*. *c.*1648. Etching, engraving and drypoint, on Japanese paper. 28.2 × 39.5 cm. Rijksmuseum, Amsterdam.

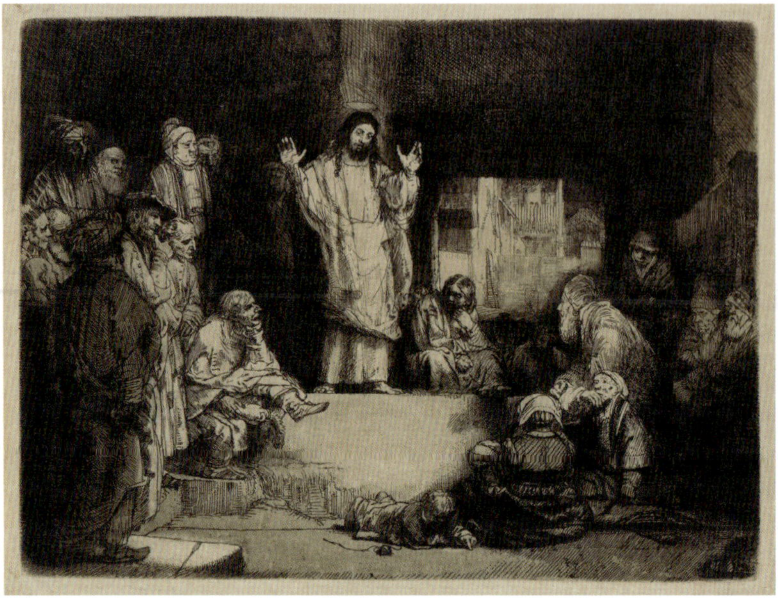

156. *Christ Preaching*. *c.*1657. Etching and drypoint, on Japanese paper. 15.5 × 20.2 cm. Rijksmuseum, Amsterdam.

shortly after its creation. It is a work of great technical and pictorial virtuosity, in which, Christ, like a conductor controlling a vast orchestra, stands at the centre of a vast throng, illustrating no less than three different themes. When in the next decade he turned again to the subject of Christ's ministry in another etching of *Christ Preaching* [Fig. 156], it was to portray a more intimate occasion rendered in a simpler technique. In a closed interior space opened up by a vista of buildings through the gateway in the right background, Christ addresses one audience instead of three, all totally bound up in his words. He stands on a raised platform, the horizontal line of which, combined with the vertical of the wall behind him, emphasising his central position. His audience is arranged on either side of him in a descending semi-circle on two levels, in a manner which recalls his drawing of *Homer Reciting his Verses* (see Fig. 145), and therefore ultimately acknowledging a debt to Raphael. Specific details, such as the seated old man seated on the platform below Christ, which shows a resonance with the similarly placed figure on the left of Homer. Unlike the complex technical build-up of the earlier *Christ Preaching*, the handling of the etching needle is straightforward. Open outlines, complemented with areas of hatching suggest the strong play of light and shadow within the enclosed space. Over an etched basis, Rembrandt worked the plate extensively with drypoint, so that patches of burr, varied according to the inking of the plate, impart great richness of tone throughout. He varied the papers he used, in a number of cases, as here, printing on Japanese paper, which because of its lesser absorbency compared with white paper, intensified the subtle chiaroscuro.

Rembrandt lavished great care in bringing out the individual responses of simple people to Christ's words. Each member of the audience, ranged between very old and very young, has their own character. There is an atmosphere of deep contemplation as each person silently reacts in their own way. The two seated figures on either side of Christ rest their chins on one hand, while lower left a seated old man, hand held to his face, looks thoughtfully upwards, as they all ponder the message. These figures in active thought are varied by the inclusion of a woman with a child in her arms, seen lower-right only from the back, her reaction to what she is hearing therefore unknown; at her side her elder child assuages its boredom by drawing in the earth. Although harmoniously composed in structural unity, it is a work which should be read detail by detail.

In the painting of *Venus and Cupid* [Fig. 157], the goddess, wearing a veil on her head and adorned with jewellery, caresses the boy with unexpected affection in a manner, which was rare but not unique in Northern art. (It has been pointed out that *Minnemoer* (loving mother or mother of love) was a synonym for Venus in the seventeenth century.) More often Cupid is shown as a pest, interrupting his mother's amatory activities. While she clasps his head, he presses his sorrowful face against her cheek, their crossed hands echoing the pattern of their heads. The half-length pose and format might be taken from a representation of a Madonna and Child. So realistic is the image of Venus, as well as the portrayal of Cupid as a child rather than the usual putto, that one might suspect that it was painted as a *portrait historié* (an individual represented as a figure from the Bible, mythology or ancient history). Suggestions that it shows Hendrickje with her daughter, Cornelia, are, however, not entirely convincing.

Although darkened by dirty varnish, the simple balance of the colours of their garments – gold for hers, and red for his – would glow if the

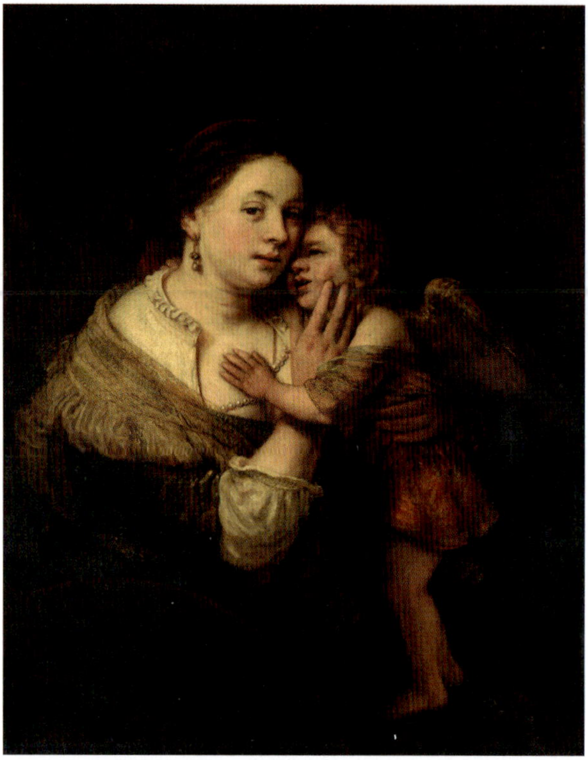

157. *Venus and Cupid*. *c.*1657. Canvas. 118 × 90 cm.
Musée du Louvre, Paris.

picture was cleaned. Demonstrating that Rembrandt did not invariably paint in the rough manner in his later work, the brushwork is more constrained than usual, dictated to by the texture of what is being described. In 1678 a certain Harman Becker, a dealer in jewels, textiles and further merchandise, who was a former creditor of the artist, owned, among twelve or fourteen paintings by Rembrandt, both an original and a copy of a *Venus and Cupid*.[30]

In the last but two works in his printed *œuvre*, dated 1659, Rembrandt returned to the subject of *Jupiter and Antiope*, taken from Ovid's *Metamorphoses* (6: 110–111) [Fig. 158], which he had etched nearly thirty years earlier [Fig. 159], thereby offering an *apercu* into his development as an etcher. From the loosely-scribbled etched lines in the earlier work, with outlines unstressed, Rembrandt progressed to a subtle combination of techniques; after a basic etched lay-in of the subject with firmly drawn

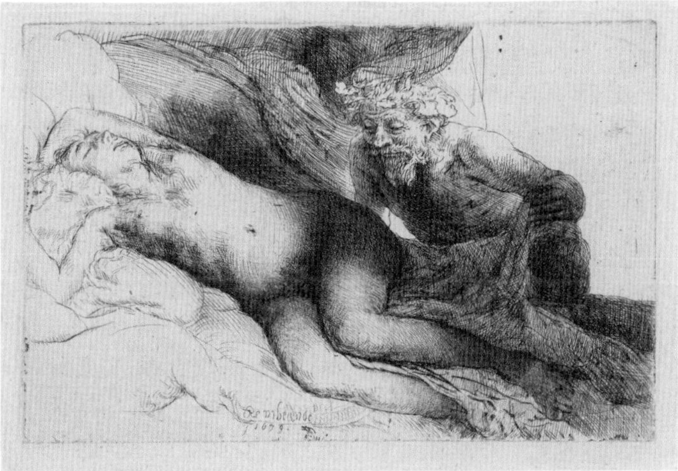

158. *Jupiter and Antiope*. 1659. Etching and drypoint. 13.9 × 20.5 cm. Rijksmuseum, Amsterdam.

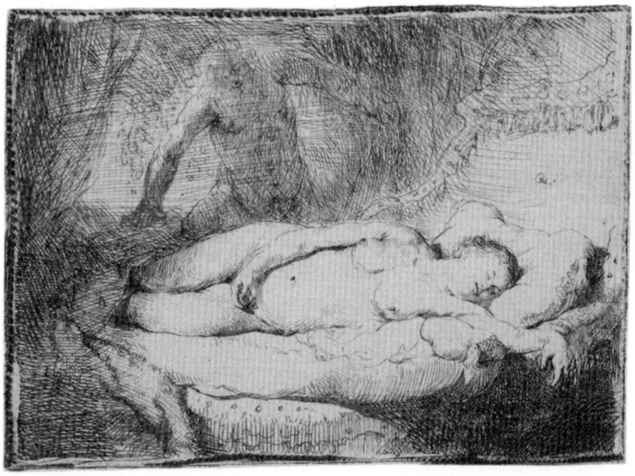

159. *Jupiter and Antiope*. 1631. Etching and engraving. 8.5 × 11.3 cm. Rijksmuseum, Amsterdam.

outlines, he added small areas of shading with the burin and dark accents with the drypoint needle, ending up with an all enveloping play of light and shadow. As was so often the case in his later prints, he varied both the inking of the plate and the papers on which he printed, here using a yellowish Japanese paper. Unlike other artists, his late works more often than not vary from impression to impression, so that one rarely finds a true duplicate amongst them. Leaning more in the direction of a monotype, they vary the repetitiveness inherent in the medium.

Turning to his interpretation of the subject, there is something light-hearted in the earlier print in the way Rembrandt treats this bawdy incident from the *Metamorphoses*, in which Jupiter, disguised as a satyr, ravishes a sleeping nymph. Here the elderly god, a heavily-whiskered figure with an unmistakable erection, clambers onto Antiope's bed, on which she, far away in her dreams, is stretched out like a corpse. By contrast, the later Jupiter, crowned with a wreath of leaves, stealthily pulls back the sheet as he earnestly inspects, like a seasoned connoisseur of the female form, the most private part of her body. With her arms stretched out behind her head, Antiope, her mouth open, lies on her pillow exposed in a seemingly natural position; but in fact in a pose probably derived from the antique, exemplified in the marble of the *Sleeping Ariadne* (Vatican, Rome), and already adapted by earlier artists such as Titian and Correggio. The subject may be imaginary, but it is serious story-telling.

Although one would not guess it, so personal is the language in which the story is presented, the design of the figures, diagonally disposed across the page, was clearly inspired by a print by Annibale Carracci [Fig. 160]; examples of his works, including erotica, were in Rembrandt's collection.[31] Apart from the omission of Cupid present in the Italian print, the similarity needs no stressing. Carracci offers a straightforward

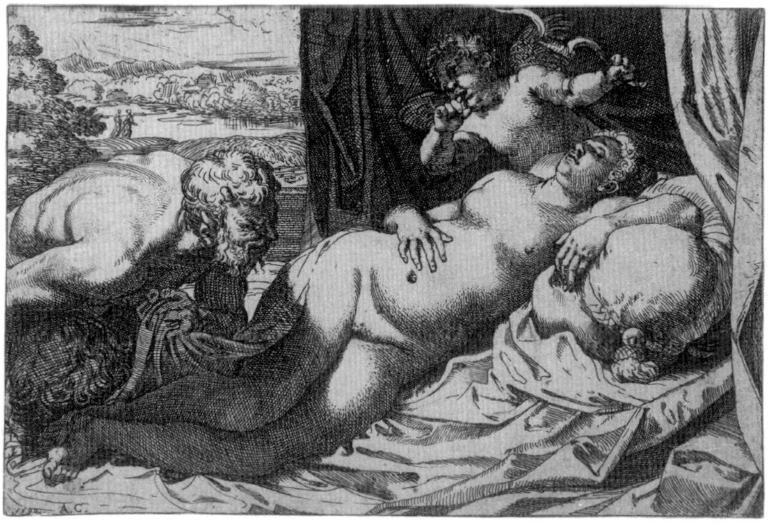

160. Annibale Carracci, *Jupiter and Antiope*. 1592. Etching and engraving. 15.6 × 22.7 cm. British Museum, London.

representation of a god viewing a nymph, an uncomplicated telling of a mythological tale. By contrast Rembrandt's Antiope and Jupiter, except for his horns and wreath, appear quite human. Rembrandt builds up the psychological aspects of the story by such means as introducing a diagonal area of shadow separating her body and his head, as well as covering her private parts, which intensifies the atmosphere of secrecy and furtiveness. By omitting Carracci's landscape, Rembrandt closes in the composition. It is a scene of erotic intimacy, which he artist invites the spectator to share with him.

The painting of *Isaac and Rebecca* (Genesis 24:67) [Fig. 161], painted only a few years before Rembrandt's death, has long been recognised as possibly the only *portrait historié* in his *œuvre*, in which a couple play a Biblical role. Although wearing fanciful fifteenth- or sixteenth-century costumes, the individuality of their appearance, and, as has been pointed out, their contemporary hairstyle and jewellery, support such a notion. Unfortunately no convincing identification of the sitters has ever been realised, so that one perhaps tends to regard the painting more as

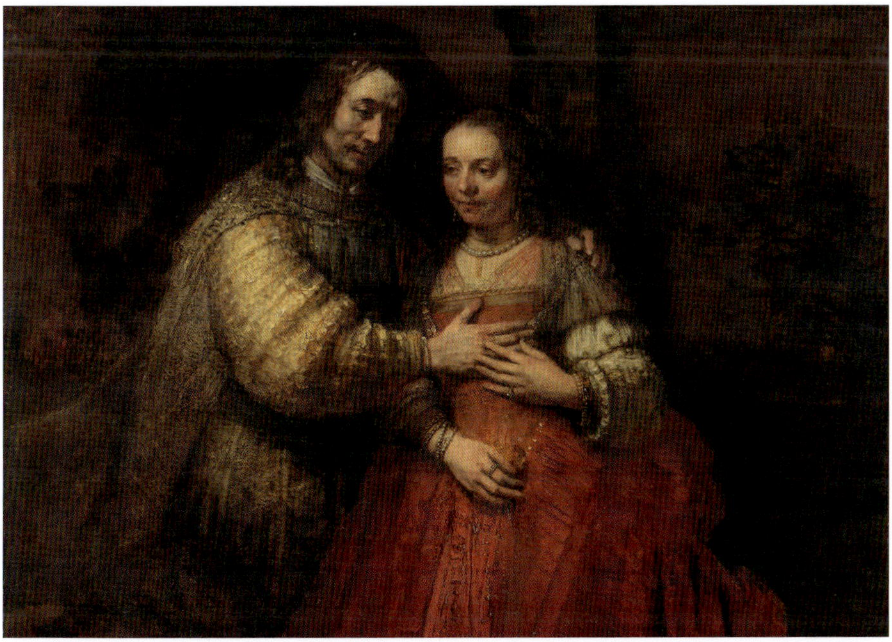

161. *Isaac and Rebecca ('The Jewish Bride')*. *c.*1665. Canvas. 121.5 × 166.5 cm. Rijksmuseum, Amsterdam.

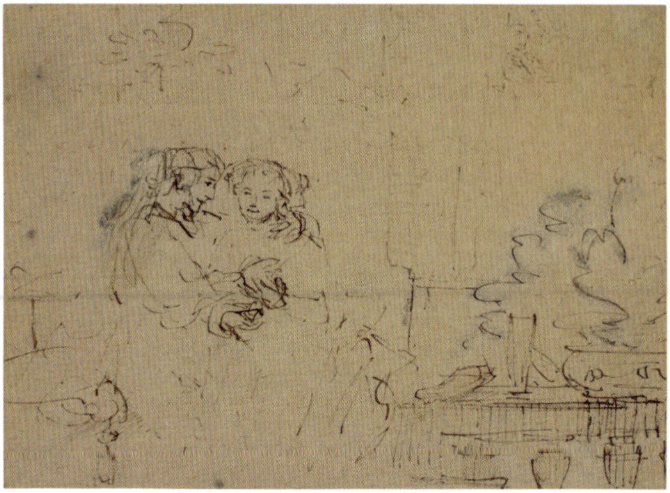

162. *Isaac and Rebecca Spied Upon by Abimelech. c.*1665.
Pen and brown ink, heightened with white. 14.5 × 18.5 cm.
Private Collection, New York.

a narrative scene than a portrait. As seen today, the picture consisting of a couple standing side-by-side, with the man placing his hand on the woman's breast, gives little away as to what its subject might be. Only through the study of its genesis can its story be identified with reasonable confidence.

The key to solving the problem is a drawing [Fig. 162], made about the same time, which unquestionably portrays *Isaac and Rebecca Spied Upon by Abimelech*. Once again the inspiration comes from an Italian work, since it can be seen to be freely-based on a design by Raphael, engraved by Sisto Badalocchio [Fig. 163]. On the left, the couple, seen three quarter-length, with Isaac in profile and Rebecca seated on his lap, have their hands clasped in a loving gesture, as they engage in amorous behaviour; on the right the figure of King Abimelech, seated looking out of the window, can barely be made out. The story, related in Genesis (26:8) and rarely found in art, tells of the devoted young couple, living incognito in Gerar in the land of the Philistines, who pretend to be brother and sister, lest her beauty attracts unwanted attention leading to his death. Spotted by the king behaving like lovers rather than siblings, their true relationship is revealed. When Rembrandt turned to his canvas with his drawing in mind, he cut the composition substantially

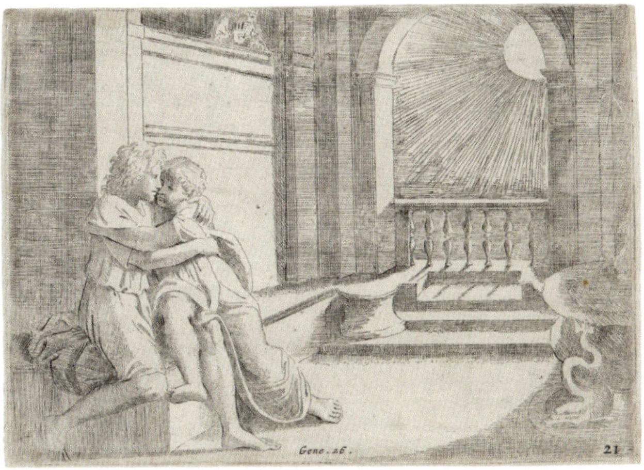

163. Sisto Badalocchio, after Raphael, *Isaac and Rebecca Spied Upon by Abimelech*. 1671. Etching. 13.5 × 18.2 cm. Philadelphia Museum of Art.

on the right to concentrate on the figures of Isaac and Rebecca. While omitting the figure of the king, who would have been *de trop* in a *portrait historié*, he kept the still life detail of the potted plant. But what he also retained from the drawing in the first stage of the picture, as X-rays show, was the figure of Rebecca seated on Isaac's lap; they were subsequently changed to two three-quarter length figures standing side-by-side, linked by the gestures of their hands. In contemporary pictorial language, the placing of the woman's leg over the man's was intended to refer to their sexual engagement, so that by omitting this detail, Rembrandt removes the erotic element inherent in the story.

Like the *Family Portrait* (see Fig. 49), the work is one of those marvels of painting, which would surely make even Titian look up in wonder, perhaps noting the influence he himself had exerted on the Dutch master. The picture is the *ne plus ultra* of his rough manner with its rich and varied brushwork. The paint is so thickly applied in places, such as his sleeve and her dress, that it rises in relief. The palette knife rather than the paintbrush is employed in certain areas of both their costumes, producing flat passages of thick paint. Continuing the trick already found in his earliest works, he makes an extensive use of the end of the brush to incise lines in the paint, a feature to be seen here, for example, in Isaac's costume. The colour is basically limited to grey-green on his costume and pink on her dress, over which light shimmers, projecting the figures from their dark background.

No less memorable is the way in which Rembrandt surpasses himself in the representation of human emotion, detached from the story it is supposed to be recounting. The touchingly reflective expressions on their faces reveal their love for one another. The spectator is keenly aware of her long fingers, which tenderly touch his in answer to his no less sensitive caress, two hands expressing a unified expression of love. The three hands, if you include her left hand resting on her abdomen, stand out as the emotional centre of the canvas, and, as much as the look on their faces, create the mood of the picture. Perhaps never before have spiritual and physical love been so movingly portrayed in a work of such overpowering simplicity.

NOTES

1. W. Strauss and M. Van der Meulen, *The Rembrandt Documents*, New York, 1979, p. 6.
2. Samuel van Hoogstraten, *Inleyding tot de hooge schoole der schilderkunst*, Rotterdam, 1678, pp. 237–8, writing about Jan Porcellis; quoted by Ernst van de Wetering, *Rembrandt. The Painter at Work*, Amsterdam, 1997, p. 84.
3. *Het Schilder-Boeck* (Haarlem, 1604, VI, 25 and 28.
4. Strauss and Van der Meulen, (op. cit, n.1), p. 223.
5. Strauss and Van der Meulen, (op. cit, n.1), p. 270–3.
6. Filippo Baldinucci, *Cominciamento, progresso dell'arte dell'intagiari in rame, colle vite di molti de più eccellenti Maestri della stessa Professione*, Florence, 1686, p. 79.
7. Arnold Houbraken, *De Groote Schouburgh der Nederlantsche Konstschilders en Schilderessen*, Amsterdam, 1718, I, p. 259.
8. Karel van Mander, *Het Schilder-Boeck ...*, Haarlem, 1604, Cap. 12. 22 and 23; cited by E. van der Wetering, *Rembrandt The Painter Thinking*, Amsterdam, 2016, p. 202.
9. Strauss and Van der Meulen, (op. cit, n.1), p. 318.
10. *Hollantsche Parnas (1660)*, quoted by S. Dickie, *Rembrandt Portraits in Print*, Amsterdam and Philadelphia, 2004, p. 117.
11. Houbraken (op. cit, n.7), p I, p. 271.
12. Strauss and Van der Meulen, (op. cit, n.1), p. 334.
13. Strauss and Van der Meulen, (op. cit, n.1), p. 322.
14. Edmé François Gersaint, *Catalogue raisonné de toutes les pièces qui forment l'œuvre de Rembrandt*. Paris, 1751.
15. *Relation de ce qui s'est passé à La Haye au mois de Fevrier l'an 1638 [Bɔ] à La Haye, de l'imprimerie, de Theodor Maire, 1638*. Quoted by M. Royalton-Kisch, *Drawings by Rembrandt in the British Museum* (London, 1991), p. 71.
16. Strauss and Van der Meulen, (op. cit, n.1), p. 375.
17. Strauss and Van der Meulen, (op. cit, n.1), p. 351.
18. Strauss and Van der Meulen, (op. cit, n.1), p. 379.
19. *The Diary of John Evelyn*, ed. R. Garnett, 1901, pp. 19–20.
20. *Teutsche Academie der edelen Bau- Bild und Mahlerey-Künste*, Nuremberg, 1675.
21. Strauss and Van der Meulen, (op. cit, n.1), p. 530.
22. Strauss and Van der Meulen, (op. cit, n.1), p. 375, nos. 256 and 259.
23. Strauss and Van der Meulen, (op. cit, n.1), p. 179, nos. 281–5.
24. *In praise of the Art of Painting*, Leiden, 1642, p. 211.
25. Strauss and Van der Meulen, (op. cit, n.1), p. 369, no. 209.
26. Strauss and Van der Meulen, (op. cit, n.1), p. 279.
27. Strauss and Van der Meulen, (op. cit, n.1), p. 369, no. 207.
28. *The Literary Works of Sir Joshua Reynolds*, ed. E. Malone, London, 1819, II, pp. 247–427.
29. Strauss and Van der Meulen, (op. cit, n.1), p. 150.
30. A. Bredius, 'Rembrandtiana', *Oud Holland*, 28, 2010, p. 195.
31. Strauss and Van der Meulen, (op. cit, n.1), p. 373, no. 232.

ILLUSTRATIONS

W. = Ernst van de Wetering, *Rembrandt's Paintings Revisited: A complete survey* (A reprint of *A Corpus of Rembrandt's Paintings VI*)), 2 vols., Dordrecht, 2017.

S. = Peter Schatborn and Erik Hinterding, *Rembrandt: The Complete Drawings and Etchings*, Cologne, 2019.

NKD = Erik Hinterding and Jako Rutgers, *The New Hollstein Dutch & Flemish Etchings Engravings and Woodcuts: Rembrandt*, 7 vols., Ouderkerk aan den Ijssel, 2013.

CHAPTER 1 The artist and his family

1. *Artist's Father*. *c.*1630. Red and black chalk, with brown wash. 19 × 24 cm. Ashmolean Museum, Oxford; inv. no.WA 1855.11. © Ashmolean Museum/Bridgeman Images. [S.D626]

2. *Old Woman in Prayer*. *c.*1630. Gilded copper. 15.5 × 12.2 cm. Residenzgalerie, Salzburg; inv. no. 549. Photo Lutz Braun. © 2022. Photo Scala, Florence/bpk, Bildagentur für Kunst, Kultur und Geschichte, Berlin. [W.34; T.311]

3. *Self-portrait Leaning Forward: Bust*. *c.*1629. Etching. 4.3 × 4 cm. Rijksmuseum, Amsterdam; inv. no. RP-P-OB-6. [NHD 13 III]

4. *Self-portrait Laughing*. *c.*1628. Copper. 22.2 × 17.1 cm. J.Paul Getty Museum, Los Angeles; inv. no. 2013.60. [W.18]

5. *Self-portrait in his Studio*. *c.*1628. Panel. 24.8 × 31.7 cm. Museum of Fine Arts, Boston; inv. no. 38.1838. Photograph © 2021 Museum of Fine Arts, Boston. All rights reserved./Zoe Oliver Sherman Collection/Bridgeman Images. [W.24]

6. *Self-portrait in a Heavy Fur Cap: Bust*. 1631. Etching, 6.3 × 5.7 cm. Rijksmuseum, Amsterdam ; inv. no. RP-P-OB-30. [NHD 80]

7. *Self-portrait with a Wide-brimmed Hat*. 1632. Panel. 64.4 × 47.6 cm. Burrell Collection, Glasgow; inv. no. 35.600. © CSG CIC Glasgow Museums Collection/Bridgeman Images. [W.66]

8. *Saskia*. 1633. Silverpoint on white prepared parchment. 18.5 × 10.6 cm. Kupferstichkabinett, Staatliche Museen zu Berlin; inv. no. KdZ 1152. [S.D629]

9. *Saskia Smiling*. 1633. Panel. 52.5 × 44.5 cm. Gemäldegalerie, Dresden; inv. no. 1556. Photo Hans-Peter Klut. © 2022. Photo Scala, Florence/bpk, Bildagentur für Kunst, Kultur und Geschichte, Berlin. [W.94]

10. *Self-portrait with Saskia*. 1636. Etching, 10.4 × 9.5 cm. Rijksmuseum, Amsterdam: inv. no. RP-P-1961-988. [NHD 158 I]

11. *Saskia Sitting Up in Bed*. *c.*1636. Pen and brown ink. 14.8 × 19.1 cm. Groninger Museum, loan from Municipality of Groningen, donation Hofstede de Groot, inv. no.1931.2055. Photo: Marten de Leeuw. [S.D266]

12. *Saskia Asleep in Bed. c.*1636. Pen and brown ink with brown wash. 13.7 × 20.3 cm. Ashmolean Museum, Oxford; inv. no. WA1954.141. © Ashmolean Museum/Bridgeman Images. [S.D267]

13. *Saskia Sitting Up in Bed with Rumbartus. c.*1636. Red chalk. 14 × 10.5 cm. Courtauld Gallery, London; inv. no. D.1978.PG.183. © Courtauld Gallery/The Samuel Courtauld Trust/Bridgeman Images. [S.D277]

14. *Saskia's Lying-in room. c.*1641. Pen and brown ink with brown and grey wash, some red and black chalk. 14.2 × 17.7 cm. Fondation Custodia, Collection Frits Lugt, Paris; inv. no. 266. [S.D364]

15. *Titia van Uylenburgh.* 1639. Pen and brown ink with brown wash. 14 × 14.6 cm. Nationalmuseum, Stockholm; inv. no. 2078/1863. Photo Cecilia Heisser/ Nationalmuseum, Stockholm (2078/1863). [S.D635]

16. *Sick Woman in a Large White Headdress. c.*1642. Etching and drypoint. 6.1 × 5.1 cm. Rijksmuseum, Amsterdam; inv. no. RP-P-OB-759. [NHD 228 II]

17. *Self-portrait in a Flat Cap and Embroidered Dress. c.*1642. Etching. 9.3 × 6.2 cm. Rijksmuseum, Amsterdam RP-P-OB-51. [NHD 210 I]

18. *A Woman in North Holland Costume (Geertje Dircx ?). c.*1641. Pen and brown ink with brown wash, 13 × 7.8 cm. British Museum, London; inv. no. 1895,0915.1270. © The Trustees of the British Museum. All rights reserved. [S.D295]

19. *A Woman in North Holland Costume, Seen from the Back (Geertje Dircx ?). c.*1641. Pen and brown ink with brown wash, 22.2 × 15.4 cm. Teylers Museum, Haarlem; inv. no. O+ 051. [S.D293]

20. *Self-portrait Etching at a Window.* 1648. Etching and drypoint, 16 × 13 cm. Rijksmuseum, Amsterdam; inv. no. RP-P-OB-39. [NHD 240 I]

21. *Self-portrait Standing. c.*1650. Pen and brown ink. 20.3 × 13.4 cm. The Rembrandt House Museum, Amsterdam; inv. no. 246.

22. *Artist's Studio with a Model. c.*1654. Pen and brown ink with brown wash, heightened with white, 20.5 × 19 cm. Ashmolean Museum, Oxford; inv. no. WA1855.8. © Ashmolean Museum/Bridgeman Images. [S.D438]

23. *Hendrickje Stoffels with a Fur Wrap. c.*1652. Canvas. 103.3 × 86.5 cm. National Gallery, London. Bought with a contribution from The Art Fund, 1976; inv. no. 6432. © 2022. Copyright The National Gallery, London/Scala, Florence. [W.223; T.324]

24. *Hendrickje Stoffels Wading in a Pool.* 1654. Panel. 61.8 × 47 cm. National Gallery, London. Holwell Carr Bequest, 1831; inv. no. 54. © 2022. Copyright The National Gallery, London/Scala, Florence. [W.229; T.325]

25. *Young Woman Sleeping. c.*1654. Brush in brown ink, heightened with white. 24.6 × 20.3 cm. British Museum, London; inv. no. 1895,0195.1279. © The Trustees of the British Museum. All rights reserved. [S.D441]

26. *Titus at a Desk.* 1655 (?). Canvas. 77 × 63 cm. Museum Boijmans Van Beuningen, Rotterdam; inv. no. St.2. Collection Museum Boijmans Van Beuningen, Rotterdam. Acquired with the support of Vereniging Rembrandt and 120 friends of the museum. Loan: Stichting Museum Boijmans Van Beuningen 1940/Photographer Studio Tromp. [W.242; T. 297]

27. *Titus Standing Holding a Flower. c.*1658. Pen and brown ink with brown wash. 17.5 × 11.8 cm. Musée du Louvre, Paris; inv. no. 22917. Photo © RMN-Grand Palais (Musée du Louvre)/Gérard Blot. [S.D648]

28. *Hendrickje Stoffels*. *c.*1660. Canvas. 78.4 × 68.9 cm. Metropolitan Museum of Art, New York. Gift of Archer M. Huntington, in memory of his father, Collis Potter Huntington, 1926; inv. no. 26.101.9. [W.278]

29. *Self-portrait*. 1658. Etching. 11.4 × 6.8 cm. Albertina, Vienna; inv. no. DG1930/562. [NHD 304]

30. *Self-portrait with Two Circles*. *c.*1665/9. Canvas. 114.3 × 94 cm. Iveagh Bequest, Kenwood House, London; inv. no. 57. © Historic England/Bridgeman Images. [W.319]

CHAPTER 2 Portraits *in situ*

31. *Jan Rijcksen, and his Wife, Griet Jans*. 1633. Canvas. 111 × 166 cm. H.M. The Queen, London; inv. no. RCIN 405533. © Royal Collection/Royal Collection Trust © Her Majesty Queen Elizabeth II, 2021/Bridgeman Images. [W.89]

32. Thomas de Keyser, *Constantijn Huygens and his (?) Clerk*. 1627. Panel. 92.4 × 69.3 cm. National Gallery, London. Bequeathed by Richard Simmons, 1847; inv. no. NG212. © 2022. Copyright The National Gallery, London/Scala, Florence

33. *The Remonstrant Preacher, Jan Uytenbogaert*. 1635. Etching. 24.9 × 18.5 cm. Rijksmuseum, Amsterdam; inv. no. RP-P-OB-560. [NHD 153 I]

34. *The Remonstrant Preacher, Jan Uytenbogaert*. 1635. Etching and black chalk. 25 × 18.7 cm. British Museum, London; inv. no. 1855,0414. [NHD 153 II]

35. *The Remonstrant Preacher, Jan Uytenbogaert*. 1635. Etching. 22.4 × 18.6 cm. Rijksmuseum, Amsterdam; inv. no. RP-P-OB-561. [NHD 153 IV]

36. *Jan Uytenbogaert (The Goldweigher)*. 1639. Etching and drypoint. 24.8 × 20.5 cm. Rijksmuseum, Amsterdam : inv. no. RP-P-OB-568. [NHD 172 II]

37. *Jan Uytenbogaert (The Goldweigher)*. 1639. Counterproof, etching and drypoint and black chalk. 25 × 20.4 cm. Rijksmuseum, Amsterdam inv. no. RP-P-OB-567. [NHD 172 I, counterproof]

38. *Andries de Graeff*. 1639. Canvas, 199 × 113.4 cm. Gemäldegalerie alter Meister, Museumlandschaft Hessen, Kassel; inv. No. GK 239. [W.168]

39. *Cornelis Claesz. Anslo and his Wife, Aeltje Schouten*. 1641. Canvas. 176 × 210 cm. Gemäldegalerie, Staatliche Museen zu Berlin; inv. no. 828. [W.183]

40. *Cornelis Claesz. Anslo*. 1640. Pen and brown ink with brown and grey wash, heightened with white, traces of red chalk. 20.6 × 20.1cm. Collection Edmund de Rothschild, Louvre, Paris; inv. no.192 D.R. Photo © RMN-Grand Palais (Musée du Louvre)/Gérard Blot. [S.D638]

41. *Ephraim Bonus*. 1647. Etching, engraving and drypoint. 24.1 × 17.7 cm. Rijksmuseum, Amsterdam; inv. no. RP-P-OB-558. [NHD 237 I]

42. *Ephraim Bonus*. *c.*1647. Panel. 19 × 15 cm. Rijksmuseum, Amsterdam; inv. no. SK-A-3982. [W.215; T.190]

43. *Jan Six*. 1647. Etching, engraving and drypoint, on Japanese paper. 24.4 × 19.1 cm. Rijksmuseum, Amsterdam; inv. no. RP-P-OB-578. [NHD 238 I]

44. *Jan Six*. *c.*1647. Pen and brown ink with brown wash, heightened with white. 22 × 17.7 cm. Collection Six, Amsterdam. [S.D643]

45. *Jan Six*. 1654. Canvas. 112 × 102 cm. Collection Six, Amsterdam; inv. no. 70. [W.233]

46. *Arnold Tholinx*. *c.*1656. Etching, engraving and drypoint, 19.8 × 14.9 cm. Rijksmuseum, Amsterdam ; inv. no. RP-P-OB-577. [NHD 294 I]

47. *Abraham Francen*. *c.*1657. Etching, engraving and drypoint, on Japanese paper, 15.8 × 20.8 cm. British Museum, London; inv. no. F,6.33. [NHD 301 I]

48. *Abraham Francen*. *c.*1657. Etching, engraving and drypoint, on Japanese paper, 15.8 × 20.8 cm. Rijksmuseum, Amsterdam; inv. no. RP-P-1962-98. [NHD 301 IV]

49. *Family Portrait*. *c.*1665. Canvas. 126 × 167 cm. Herzog Anton Ulrich-Museum, Braunschweig; inv. no. GG 238. [W.313]

CHAPTER 3 Everyday life in Amsterdam

50. *A Peasant Calling Out: 'Tis vinnich kout' (Damned Cold)*. 1634. Etching. 11.3 × 4.3 cm. Rijksmuseum, Amsterdam; inv. no. RP-P-OB-417. [NHD 131]

51. *A Peasant replying: 'Dats niet'*. 1634. Etching, 11.2 × 3.8 cm. Rijksmuseum, Amsterdam; inv. no. RP-P-OB-418. [NHD 132]

52. Hans Sebald Beham, *A Peasant Calling Out: 'Es ist kalt weter'*. 1542. Engraving. 4.5 × 2.9 cm. British Museum, London; inv. no. Gg,4C.55. [B.188]

53. Hans Sebald Beham, *A Peasant Replying: 'Das schadet nit'*. 1542. Engraving. 4.4 × 2.9 cm. British Museum, London; inv. no. Gg,4C.56. [B.189]

54. *Old Woman Seated in a Cottage*. *c.*1629. Etching, 12.8 × 8.5 cm. Rijksmuseum, Amsterdam; inv. no. RP-P-OB-223. [NHD 26 II]

55. *Beggar Seated Warming his Hands*. *c.*1630. Etching, 7.7 × 4.6 cm. Rijksmuseum, Amsterdam; inv. no. RP-P-OB-408. [NHD 44 II]

56. *The Blind Fiddler*. 1631. Etching, 7.8 × 5.3 cm. Rijksmuseum, Amsterdam; inv. no. RP-P-OB-357. [NHD 77 III]

57. *The Rat Catcher*. 1632. Etching. 14 × 12.5 cm. British Museum, London; inv. no. 1847,1120.5. [NHD 111 I]

58. *Mother & Child Frightened by a Dog*. *c.*1633/4. Pen and brown ink, 10.3 × 10.2 cm. Collection Frits Lugt, Fondation Custodia, Paris; inv. no. 5155. [S.D236]

59. *The Naughty Boy*. *c.*1635. Pen and brown ink with brown wash, heightened with white, 20.7 × 14.2 cm. Kupferstichkabinett, Staatliche Museen zu Berlin; inv. no. KDZ 3771. Photo Scala, Florence/bpk, Bildagentur für Kunst, Kultur und Geschichte, Berlin. [S.D238]

60. *Pancake Woman*. 1635. Etching, 10.9 × 7.7 cm. Rijksmuseum, Amsterdam; inv. no. RP-P-OB-212. [NHD 144 I]

61. *Pancake Woman*. 1635. Etching, 10.9 × 7.7 cm. Rijksmuseum, Amsterdam; inv. no. RP-P-OB-213. [NHD 144 II]

62. *Pancake Woman*. *c.*1635. Pen and brown ink, 10.8 × 14.4 cm. Rijksmuseum, Amsterdam; inv. no. RP-T-1891-A-2424. [S. D235]

63. *Woman and Child with Dog*. *c.*1635. Pen and brown ink, 18.2 × 14.5 cm. Szépmüvészeti Museum, Budapest; inv. no. 1589. Photo Jozsa Denes © 2022. The Museum of Fine Arts Budapest/Scala, Florence. [S.D237]

64. *Three Women and a Child Before a House*. *c.*1640. Pen and brown ink. 23.3 × 17.8 cm. Rijksmuseum, Amsterdam; inv. no. RP-T-1889-A-2056. [S.D362]

65. *Two Women Teaching a Child to Walk*. *c.*1636. Red chalk. 10.3 × 12.8 cm. British Museum, London; inv. no. 1910,0212.187. © The Trustees of the British Museum. All rights reserved. [S.D270]

66. *Male Nude Seated and Standing*. *c.*1646. Etching, 19.4 × 12.8 cm. Rijksmuseum, Amsterdam; inv. no. RP-P-OB-427. [NHD 233 I]

67. *Woman Teaching a Child to Walk*. *c.*1646. Pen and brown ink. 16 × 16.5 cm. Nationalmuseum, Stockholm; inv. no. 2074/1863. Photo Hans Thorwid / Nationalmuseum, Stockholm (2074/1863). [S.D234]

68. *Child Being Taught to Walk*. *c.*1656. Pen and brown ink on brownish paper, 9.3 × 15.4 cm. British Museum, London; inv. no. 1912,0416.2. © The Trustees of the British Museum. All rights reserved. [S.D446]

69. *Strolling Musicians*. *c.*1635. Etching, 13.8 × 11.5 cm. Rijksmuseum, Amsterdam; inv. no. RP-P-OB-207. [NHD 141 I]

70. *Two Butchers at Work*. *c.*1635. Pen and brown ink on light brown prepared paper. 14.9 × 19.9 cm. Städel Museum, Frankfurt am Main; inv. no. 3626. [S.D245]

71. *A Black Drummer and Commander Mounted on Mules*. *c.*1638. Pen and brown ink with brown and yellow wash, heightened with white, over red chalk. 23 × 17.1 cm. British Museum, London; inv. no. Oo, 10.122. © The Trustees of the British Museum. All rights reserved. [S.D302]

72. *The Skater*. *c.*1639. Etching and drypoint, 6.1 × 5.9 cm. Rijksmuseum, Amsterdam; inv. no. RP-P-OB-237. [NHD 179]

73. *Two Horses at a Resting Place*. *c.*1637. Red and black chalk, 17.3 × 27.1 cm. Rijksmuseum, Amsterdam; inv. no. RP-T-1961-77. [S.D460]

74. *Watchdog Sleeping in its Kennel*. *c.*1638/9. Pen and brown ink with brown wash. 14.3 × 16.8 cm. Museum of Fine Arts, Boston. John H. and Ernestine A. Payne Fund; inv. no. 56.519. Photograph © 2021 Museum of Fine Arts, Boston. All rights reserved./ Bridgeman Images. [S.D471]

75. *The Hog*. 1643. Etching and drypoint. 14.3 × 18.3 cm. Rijksmuseum, Amsterdam; inv. no. RP-P-OB-238. [NHD 215 II]

76. *Birds of Paradise*. *c.*1638. Pen and brown ink with brown wash, heightened with white. 18.1 × 15.5 cm. Musée du Louvre, Paris; inv. no. RF4687. Photo © RMN-Grand Palais (musée du Louvre)/Jean-Gilles Berizzi. [S.D468]

77. *Elephant*. 1637. Black chalk. 23.3 × 35.4 cm. Albertina, Vienna; inv. no. 17558. Bridgeman Images. [S.D464]

78. *Lioness Devouring a Bird*. *c.*1640. Charcoal, with grey wash, heightened with white, on brown prepared paper. 12.6 × 23.9 cm. British Museum, London; inv. no. Oo,9.71. © The Trustees of the British Museum. All rights reserved. [S.D473]

79. *Lion Resting*. 1650s. Pen and brown ink on brown paper. 12.2 × 21.2 cm. Rijksmuseum, Amsterdam; inv. no. RP-T-1901-A-4524. [S.D478]

80. *Star of the Kings*. *c.*1646. Pen and brown ink with brown wash, 20.4 × 32.3 cm. British Museum, London; inv. no. 1910,0212.189. © The Trustees of the British Museum. All rights reserved. [S.D384]

81. *A Blind Hurdy-gurdy Player and Family Receiving Alms*. 1648. Etching and drypoint. 16.5 × 12.8 cm. Rijksmuseum, Amsterdam; inv. no. RP-P-OB-413. [NHD 243 I]

82. *Old Town Hall after the Fire*. 1652. Pen and brown ink, some red chalk, 15 × 20.1 cm. The Rembrandt House Museum, Amsterdam; inv. no. 245. [S.D610]

83. *Man Drawing or Writing at a Desk*. *c.*1652. Pen and brown ink with brown and grey wash, heightened with white. 13.5 × 19.7 cm. Musée du Louvre, Paris; inv. no. RF11476. Photo © RMN-Grand Palais (musée du Louvre)/Tony Querrec. [S.D437]

84. *View from Diemerdijk*. *c.*1652. Pen and brown ink with brown wash, with later additions in grey wash. 7.8 × 13.8 cm. Museum Boijmans Van Beuningen, Rotterdam; inv. no. R 41 (PK). Collection Museum Boijmans Van Beuningen, Rotterdam. Loan: Stichting Museum Boijmans Van Beuningen 1940 (former collection Koenigs)/ Photographer. Studio Tromp. [S.D563]

85. *An old Woman Reading*. 1655. Canvas. 79 × 65 cm. Duke of Buccleuch, Drumlandrig Castle; inv. No. KBE 144. Reproduced with the kind permission of the Duke of Buccleuch & Queensberry, KT. The Buccleuch Collections/Bridgeman Images. [W.241]

86. *The Goldsmith*. 1655. Etching and drypoint. 7.7 × 5.6 cm. Rijksmuseum, Amsterdam; inv. no. RP-P-OB-210. [NHD 289 I]

87. *Woman Hanging on a Gibbet*. *c.*1664. Pen and brown ink with brown wash on light brown paper, 17.2 × 9 cm. Metropolitan Museum of Art, New York. H.O. Havermeyer Collection. Bequest of Mrs. H. O. Havemeyer, 1929; inv. no. 29.100.937. [S.D457]

CHAPTER 4 Landscape and the bucolic scene: life in the countryside

88. *Entrance to a Farm*. *c.*1638/9. Pen and brown ink with brown wash, heightened with white on light brown paper, 17.9 × 23.5 cm. Kunsthalle, Hamburg; inv. no. 22419. © 2022. Photo Scala, Florence/bpk, Bildagentur für Kunst, Kultur und Geschichte, Berlin [S.D485]

89. *Two Thatched Cottages*. *c.*1640. Pen and brown ink, heightened with white. 13.2 × 20.2 cm. J. Paul Getty Museum, Los Angeles; inv. no. 85.GA.93. [S.D484]

90. *Inner Courtyard of a Farmhouse*. *c.*1640. Pen and brown ink with brown wash. 15.4 × 22.3 cm. Szépmüvészeti Museum,Budapest; inv. no. 1577. Photo Jozsa Denes © 2022. The Museum of Fine Arts Budapest/Scala, Florence. [S.D492]

91. *Cow Standing in a Shed*. *c.*1638. Pen and brown ink with brown wash, heightened with white, on light-brown prepared paper. 15.3 × 18.2 cm. Rijksmuseum, Amsterdam; inv. no. RP-T-1930-59. [S.D472]

92. *Small Grey Landscape*. *c.*1640. Etching. 3.8 × 8.2 cm. Rijksmuseum, Amsterdam; inv. no. RP-P-OB-440. [NHD 181]

93. *Farmhouse with Artist Sketching*. *c.*1641. Etching. 13 × 20.8 cm. Rijksmuseum, Amsterdam; inv. no. RP-P-OB-278. [NHD 201]

94. *The Mill on the Bulwark 'Het Blauwhoofd'*. *c.*1645. Oiled charcoal on light-brown paper. 16.6 × 27.5 cm. Museum Boijmans Van Beuningen, Rotterdam, inv. no. R 26 (PK). Collection Museum Boijmans Van Beuningen, Rotterdam. Loan: Stichting Museum Boijmans Van Beuningen 1940 (former collection Koenigs)/Photographer Studio Tromp. [S.D528]

95. *Canal Between Bushes*. *c.*1645. Black chalk. 14.5 × 11.5 cm. Zakład Narodowy im. Ossolińskich, Wrocław; inv. no. 8728. The Museum of the Lubomirski Princes at the Ossoliński National Institute, Wroclaw. [S.D520]

96. *The Boat House*. 1645. Etching and drypoint. 12.5 × 13.2 cm. Rijksmuseum, Amsterdam; inv. no. RP-P-OB-469. [NHD 220 I]

97. *The Flute Player.* 1642. Etching and drypoint. 11.5 × 14.3 cm. Rijksmuseum, Amsterdam; inv. no. RP-P-OB-248. [NHD 211 IV]

98. *The Sleeping Herdsman. c.*1644. Etching and drypoint, 7.8 × 5.7 cm. Rijksmuseum, Amsterdam; inv. no. RP-P-OB-635. [NHD 217]

99. *The Omval.* 1645. Etching and drypoint, 18.4 × 22.5 cm. Rijksmuseum, Amsterdam; inv. no. RP-P-OB-270. [NHD 221 II]

100. *Winter Landscape.* 1646. Panel. 17 × 23 cm. Gemäldegalerie alter Meister, Museumlandschaft Hessen, Kassel; inv. No. GK 241. © Museumslandschaft Hessen Kassel/Ute Brunzel/Bridgeman Images. [W.207]

101. *The Swimmers.* 1651. Etching. 10.9 × 13.5 cm. Rijksmuseum, Amsterdam; inv. no. RP-P-OB-253. [NHD 258 I]

102. *View of Diemen with an Artist Drawing. c.*1649/50. Pen and brown ink with brown wash. 11.1 × 17.4 cm. Private collection, Netherlands. [S.D.549]

103. *The Amsteldijk at Meerhuizen. c.*1649/50. Pen and brown ink. 13.2 × 20.7 cm. The Duke of Devonshire and the Trustees of the Chatsworth Settlement, Chatsworth; inv. no. 1022. Reproduced by permission of Chatsworth Settlement Trustees/Bridgeman Images. [S.D531]

104. *The Amsteldijk at Meerhuizen. c.*1649/50. Pen and brown ink with brown wash on light-brown paper. 13 × 21.7 cm. The Duke of Devonshire and the Trustees of the Chatsworth Settlement, Chatsworth; inv. no. 1023. Reproduced by permission of Chatsworth Settlement Trustees/Bridgeman Images. [S.D532]

105. *Westpoort (Utrechtgate) at Rhenen. c.*1648–50. Pen and brown ink with brown wash, heightened with white. 16.3 × 22.6 cm. Teylers Museum, Haarlem; inv. no. O+ 054. [S.D603]

106. *The Amstel near Ouderkerk with a Man Rowing a Boat.* 1648–50. Pen and brown ink with brown wash, heightened with white. 13.2 × 19.8 cm. The Duke of Devonshire and the Trustees of the Chatsworth Settlement, Chatsworth; inv. no. 1033. Reproduced by permission of Chatsworth Settlement Trustees/Bridgeman Images. [S.D542]

107. *View of the Diemerdijk with a Milkman. c.*1650. Etching and drypoint, printed on Japanese paper. 6.4 × 17.5 cm. Rijksmuseum, Amsterdam; inv. no. RP-P-1962-81. [NHD 255 I]

108. *Clump of Trees.* 1652. Drypoint, with surface tone. 15.6 × 21.1 cm. Rijksmuseum, Amsterdam; inv. no. RP-P-OB-454. [NHD 272 I]

109. *Clump of Trees.* 1652. Drypoint. 12.4 × 21.1 cm. Rijksmuseum, Amsterdam: inv. no. RP-P-OB-455. [NHD 272 II]

110. River with Trees. c.1652/1656. Brush in brown wash. 13.6 × 18.6 cm. Musée du Louvre, Paris; inv. no. RF4709. Photo © RMN-Grand Palais (musée du Louvre)/Thierry Le Mage. [S.D624]

111. Claude Lorrain, *View of the Tiber, Rome. c.*1640. Brush drawing in brown. 18.5 × 26.8 cm. British Museum, London; inv. no. Oo,7.212. © The Trustees of the British Museum. All rights reserved

CHAPTER 5 Narrative subjects

112. *Tobit and Anna*. 1626. Panel. 40.1 × 29.9 cm. Rijksmuseum, Amsterdam; inv. no. SK-A-4717. [W.12; T.2]

113. Jan van der Velde II, after Willem Buytewech, *Tobit and Anna*. *c*.1620. Etching. 19.3 × 11.2 cm. Rijksmuseum, Amsterdam; inv. no. RP-P-OB-15.291

114. *Holy Family*. *c*.1632. Etching. 9.4 × 7.1 cm. Rijksmuseum, Amsterdam; inv. no. RP-P-OB-123. [NHD 114]

115. Annibale Carracci, *The Holy Family*. 1590. Etching and engraving. 16.2 × 21.7 cm. British Museum, London; inv. no. U.1.111. [B.17]

116. *The Prophet Daniel and King Cyrus before the Idol Bel*. 1633. Panel. 23.5 × 30.2 cm. J. Paul Getty Museum. Los Angeles; inv. no. 95.PB.15. [W.102]

117. *Joseph Telling his Dreams*. *c*.1633. Grisaille on paper, stuck on card. 55.8 × 39.7 cm. Rijksmuseum, Amsterdam; inv. no. SK-A-3477. [W. 108]

118. *A Seated Old Man in Profile*. 1631. Red and black chalk on brown prepared paper. 22.9 × 25.9 cm. Private collection, New York. [S.D11]

119. *Joseph and Potiphar's Wife*. 1634. Etching, 9.2 × 11.4 cm. Rijksmuseum, Amsterdam; inv. no. RP-P-OB-78. [NHD 128 I]

120. Antonio Tempesta, *Joseph and Potiphar's Wife*. 1590s. Etching, 5.8 × 6.7 cm. Museum of Fine Arts, Budapest; inv. no. 7897. [B.71]

121. *Annunciation*. *c*.1635. Pen and brown ink. 14.4 × 12.4 cm. Musée des Beaux-Arts et d'Archéologie, Besançon; inv. no D.2618. [S.D.36]

122. *Susanna and the Elders*. 1636. Panel. 47.4 × 38.6 cm. Mauritshuis, The Hague; inv. no. 147. [W.144]

123. Copy after Lastman, *Susanna and the Elders*. *c*.1636. Red chalk, brush in grey wash by another hand. 23.5 × 36.3 cm. Kupferstichkabinett, Staatliche Museen zu Berlin; inv. no. KdZ 5296. © 2022. Photo Scala, Florence/bpk, Bildagentur für Kunst, Kultur und Geschichte, Berlin. [S.D661]

124. Pieter Lastman, *Susanna and the Elders*. 1614. Panel. 42 × 58 cm. Gemäldegalerie, Staatliche Museen zu Berlin; inv. no. 1719. Photo Joerg P. Anders.© 2022. Photo Scala, Florence/bpk, Bildagentur für Kunst, Kultur und Geschichte, Berlin

125. Lucas Vorsterman the Elder, after Rubens, *Susanna and the Elders*. 1620. Engraving. 38.5 × 28 cm. Rijksmuseum, Amsterdam; RP-P-OB-33.003

126. Attributed to Hendrick Goltzius, *Venus Pudica*. 1591. Red chalk. 36 × 15 cm. Teylers Museum, Haarlem; inv. no. K III 027

127. *Lot and Daughters*. *c*.1638. Pen and brown ink. 15.2 × 19.1 cm. Klassik Stiftung, Graphische Sammlung, Weimar; inv. no. GHz/Sch.I.309,0874. Photo Mokansky Olaf. Weimar, Klassik Stiftung Weimar. © 2022. Photo Scala, Florence/bpk, Bildagentur für Kunst, Kultur und Geschichte, Berlin. [S.D57]

128. *Adam and Eve*. 1638. Etching. 16.3 × 11.7 cm. Rijksmuseum, Amsterdam; inv. no. RP-P-OB-53. [NHD 168 II]

129. Marcantonio Raimondi, after Raphael, *The Fall of Man*. Engraving. 24.2 × 17.6 cm. Metropolitan Museum of Art, New York. Purchase, Joseph Pulitzer Bequest, 1917; inv. no. 17.50.42

130. Albrecht Dürer, *Christ in Limbo. (Engraved Passion)*. 1512. Engraving, 11.6 × 7.4 cm. Metropolitan Museum of Art, New York. Fletcher Fund, 1919; inv. no. 19.73.16

131. *Adam and Eve*. *c.*1638. Pen and brown ink with brown wash. 11.5 × 11.5 cm. Prentenkabinet der Universiteit, Leiden; inv. no. PK-T-AW-1097. [S.D55]

132. *The Return of the Prodigal Son*. *c.*1641. Pen and brown ink with brown wash, heightened with white. 19.1 × 22.7 cm. Teylers Museum, Haarlem; inv. no. O+ 048. [S.D.76]

133. *The Return of the Prodigal Son*. 1636. Etching. 15.6 × 13.6 cm. Rijksmuseum, Amsterdam; inv. no. RP-P-OB-164. [NHD 159 I]

134. *Ruth and Boaz*. *c.*1641–5. Pen and brown ink, heightened with white. 12.6 × 14.3 cm. Rijksmuseum, Amsterdam; inv. no. RP-T-1930-9. [S.D.77]

135. *Sarah Waiting for Tobias*. *c.*1643. Canvas on panel. 81.2 × 67.9 cm. National Gallery of Scotland, Edinburgh; inv. no. NG 827. [W194]

136. Pieter Lastman, *Sarah Waiting for Tobias*. 1611. Panel. 42 × 57 cm. Museum of Fine Arts, Boston. Juliana Cheney Edwards Collection; inv. no. 62.985. © 2022. Museum of Fine Arts, Boston. All rights reserved/Scala, Florence

137. *The Holy Family at Rest*. *c.*1645. Pen and brown ink, heightened with white. 17.3 × 21.2 cm. Fitzwilliam Museum, Cambridge; inv. no. PD.42-1961. © Fitzwilliam Museum/ Bridgeman Images. [S.D72]

138. *The Holy Family in the Carpenter's Shop*. *c.*1645. Pen and brown ink with brown wash, heightened with white. 18.4 × 24.6 cm. British Museum, London, inv. no. 1900,0824.144. © The Trustees of the British Museum. All rights reserved. [S.D81]

139. *Nocturnal Landscape with the Holy Family*. 1647. Panel. 33.8 × 47.8 cm. National Gallery of Ireland, Dublin; inv. No. 215. [W.214]

140. Adam Elsheimer, *The Flight into Egypt*. 1609. Copper. 31 × 41 cm. Alte Pinakothek, Munich; inv. no. 216

141. *Abraham and Isaac*. 1645. Etching, 15.7 × 13 cm. Rijksmuseum, Amsterdam; inv. no. RP-P-OB-61. [NHD 224]

142. *Abraham's Sacrifice*. 1656. Etching and drypoint, on Japanese paper. 15.6 × 13.1 cm. Rijksmuseum, Amsterdam: inv. no. RP-P-OB-63. [NHD 287]

143. *Mercury and Argus*. *c.*1648. Pen and brown ink with brown wash. 17.8 × 14.6 cm. Musée du Louvre, Paris; inv. no. RF 4693, Recto. [S.D.94a]

144. *Jews in a Synagogue*. 1648. Etching and drypoint. 7.1 × 12.9 cm. Rijksmuseum, Amsterdam; inv. no. RP-P-1962-60. [NHD 242 I]

145. *Homer Reciting his Verses*. 1652. Pen and brown ink, 19 × 16.5 cm. Collection Six, Amsterdam. [S.D.114]

146. Marcantonio Raimondi, *The Assembly of the Gods on Mount Parnassus* (detail of left hand side). 1520. Engraving. 35.8 × 47 cm. British Museum, London; inv. no. H.2.27

147. *Minerva in her Study*. 1652. Pen and brown ink with brown wash, heightened with white. 19 × 14 cm. Collection Six, Amsterdam. [S.D113]

148. *The Agony in the Garden*. *c.*1652. Etching and drypoint, with surface tone. 11.1 × 8.4 cm. British Museum, London; inv. no. F,4.163. [NHD 269 I]

149. *Nathan Admonishing David*. *c.*1652. Pen and brown ink. 12.6 × 14.8 cm. Stirling and Francine Clark Art Institute, Williamstown; inv. no. 2003.9.29. [S.D.131]

150. *Bathsheba with King David's Letter*. 1654. Canvas. 142 × 142 cm. Musée du Louvre, Paris; inv. no. M.I. 957. Photo © Musée du Louvre, Dist. RMN-Grand Palais/Angèle Dequier. [W.231; T. 23]

151. Peter Paul Rubens, *Bathsheba Receiving David's Letter*. *c.*1635. Panel. 175 × 126 cm. Gemäldegalerie, Dresden; inv. no. 965. © Staatliche Kunstsammlungen Dresden/ Bridgeman Images

152. François Perrier, *Antique Relief* (from *Icones et Segementa*). 1645. Engraving. 16.2 × 22.7 cm. Universitäts-Bibliothek Heidelberg

153. *Jael Killing Sisera*. *c.*1656. Pen and brown ink, heightened with white. 19.2 × 17.4 cm. Rijksmuseum, Amsterdam; inv. no. RP-T-1930-8. [S.166]

154. *Jael Killing Sisera*. *c.*1651. Pen and brown ink, with white bodycolour, on paper. 17.3 × 25.5 cm. Ashmolean Museum, Oxford; inv. no. WA 1950.51. © Ashmolean Museum, University of Oxford/Bridgeman Images. [S.D100]

155. *Christ Preaching ('The Hundred Guilder Print')*. *c.*1648. Etching, engraving and drypoint, on Japanese paper. 28.2 × 39.5 cm. Rijksmuseum, Amsterdam; inv. no. RP-P-OB-601. [NHD 239 I]

156. *Christ Preaching*. *c.*1657. Etching and drypoint, on Japanese paper. 15.5 × 20.2 cm. Rijksmuseum, Amsterdam; inv. no. RP-P-OB-129. [NHD 298 I]

157. *Venus and Cupid*. *c.*1657. Canvas, 118 × 90 cm. Musée du Louvre, Paris; inv. no. 1743. Photo © RMN-Grand Palais (musée du Louvre)/Tony Querrec. [W.251]

158. *Jupiter and Antiope*. 1659. Etching and drypoint. 13.9 × 20.5 cm. Rijksmuseum, Amsterdam; inv. no. RP-P-OB-434. [NHD 311 I]

159. *Jupiter and Antiope*. 1631. Etching and engraving. 8.5 × 11.3 cm. Rijksmuseum, Amsterdam; inv. no. RP-P-OB-436. [NHD 78 I]

160. Annibale Carracci, *Jupiter and Antiope*. 1592. Etching and engraving, 15.6 × 22.7 cm. British Museum, London; inv. no. 1856,1213.36. [B.17]

161. *Isaac and Rebecca ('The Jewish Bride')*. *c.*1665. Canvas. 121.5 × 166.5 cm. Rijksmuseum, Amsterdam; inv. no. SK-C-216. [W.312; T.269]

162. *Isaac and Rebecca Spied Upon by Abimelech*. *c.*1665. Pen and brown ink, heightened with white. 14.5 × 18.5 cm. Private Collection, New York. [S.D180]

163. Sisto Badalocchio, after Raphael, *Isaac and Rebecca Spied Upon by Abimelech*. 1671. Etching. 13.5 × 18.2 cm. Philadelphia Museum of Art. The Muriel and Philip Berman Gift, acquired from the John S. Phillips bequest of 1876 to the Pennsylvania Academy of the Fine Arts, with funds contributed by Muriel and Philip Berman, gifts (by exchange) of Lisa Norris Elkins, Bryant W. Langston, Samuel S. White 3rd and Vera White, with additional funds contributed by John Howard McFadden, Jr., Thomas Skelton Harrison, and the Philip H. and A.S.W. Rosenbach Foundation, 1985; inv no. 1985-52-27463

SELECTED LITERATURE

General

W. Strauss and M. van der Meulen, *The Rembrandt Documents* (New York, 1979)

G. Schwartz, *Rembrandt's Universe His Art His Life His World* (London, 2006): comprehensive study of the artist's life and work

Paintings

J. Bruyn et al, *A Corpus of Rembrandt Paintings* (Rembrandt Research Project), 6 vols. (Various, 1982–2014): in depth catalogue of most of his paintings

Berlin, London and Amsterdam, *Rembrandt: the Master & his Workshop: Paintings*. Exhib. cat. By C. Brown et al, 1991–2)

C. Tümpel, *Rembrandt. All Paintings in Colour* (New York, 1993); good on iconography

C. Schneider, *Rembrandt's Landscapes* (New Haven and London, 1999)

E. van de Wetering, *Rembrandt's Paintings Revisited: A Complete Survey* (Dordrecht, 2017)

V. Manuth et al, *Rembrandt: The Complete Paintings* (Cologne, 2019): catalogue and large scale reproductions of all his paintings

Drawings

P. Schatborn, *Drawings by Rembrandt, his anonymous pupils and followwers* (Amsterdam, 1985): catalogue of drawings in the Rijksmuseum

M. Royalton-Kisch, *Drawings by Rembrandt in the British Museum* (London, 1991)

H.-M. Rotermund, *Rembrandt's Drawings and Etchings from the Bible* (Philadelphia and Boston, 1969)

Washington, *Rembrandt's Landscapes: Drawings and Prints*. Exhib cat. by C. Schneider et al.(1990)

Berlin, London and Amsterdam, *Rembrandt: the Master & his Workshop: Drawings & Etchings*. Exhib. cat. by H. Bevers et al, (1991–2)

B. Bakker et al, *Landscapes of Rembrandt: His favourite walks* (Bussum 1998)

S. Slive, *Rembrandt Drawings* (Los Angeles and London, 2009): a survey of his drawings

P. Schatborn and E. Hinterding, *Rembrandt: The Complete Drawings and Etchings* (Cologne, 2019): large scale reproductions of all his drawings and prints

M. Royalton-Kisch, *The Drawings of Rembrandt: A Revision of Otto Benesch's Catalogue raisonné, vols. I and II* (online catalogue, 2019)

A. Gnann, *Rembrandt Landschaftzeichnungen / Landscape Drawings* (Petersberg, 2021)

Etchings

L. Münz, *Rembrandt's Etchings*, 2 vols. (London, 1952): catalogue with long introductory essay

C. White, *Rembrandt as an Etcher: a study of the artist at work* (New Haven and London, 2nd. ed.,1999)

Amsterdam and London, *Rembrandt the Printmaker*. Exhib. cat., by E. Hinterding et al (2000)

S. Dickey, *Rembrandt: Portraits in Print* (Amsterdam and Philadelphia, 2004)

E. Hinterding, *Rembrandt's Etchings from the Frits Lugt Collection*, 2 vols. (Paris, 2008)

E. Hinterding and J. Rutgers, *The New Hollstein Dutch & Flemish Etchings, Engravings and Woodcuts: Rembrandt*, 7 vols. (Ouderkerk aan den Ijssel, 2013): catalogue raisonné

Special studies

K. Clark, *Rembrandt and the Italian Renaissance* (London, 1966)

E. van de Wetering, *The Painter at Work* (Amsterdam, 1997): examination of the artist's practice as a painter

Edinburgh, *Rembrandt's Women*, Exhib. cat. by J. Lloyd Williams et al (2001)

A. Golahny, *Rembrandt's reading: the artist's bookshelf of ancient poetry and history* (Amsterdam, 2003)

E. Sluijter, *Rembrandt and the Female Nude* (Amsterdam, 2006)

M. De Winkel, *Fashion and Fancy: Dress and Meanings in Rembrandt's Paintings* (Amsterdam, 2006)

London and Amsterdam, *Rembrandt the late works* (Exhib. cat. by J. Bikker et al (2014–5)

E. van de Wetering, *The Painter Thinking* (Amsterdam, 2016): examination of the artist's theory

Leiden and Oxford, *Young Rembrandt*. Exhib. cat. by C. Brown et al (2019–20): the artist's work from 1624 to 1634

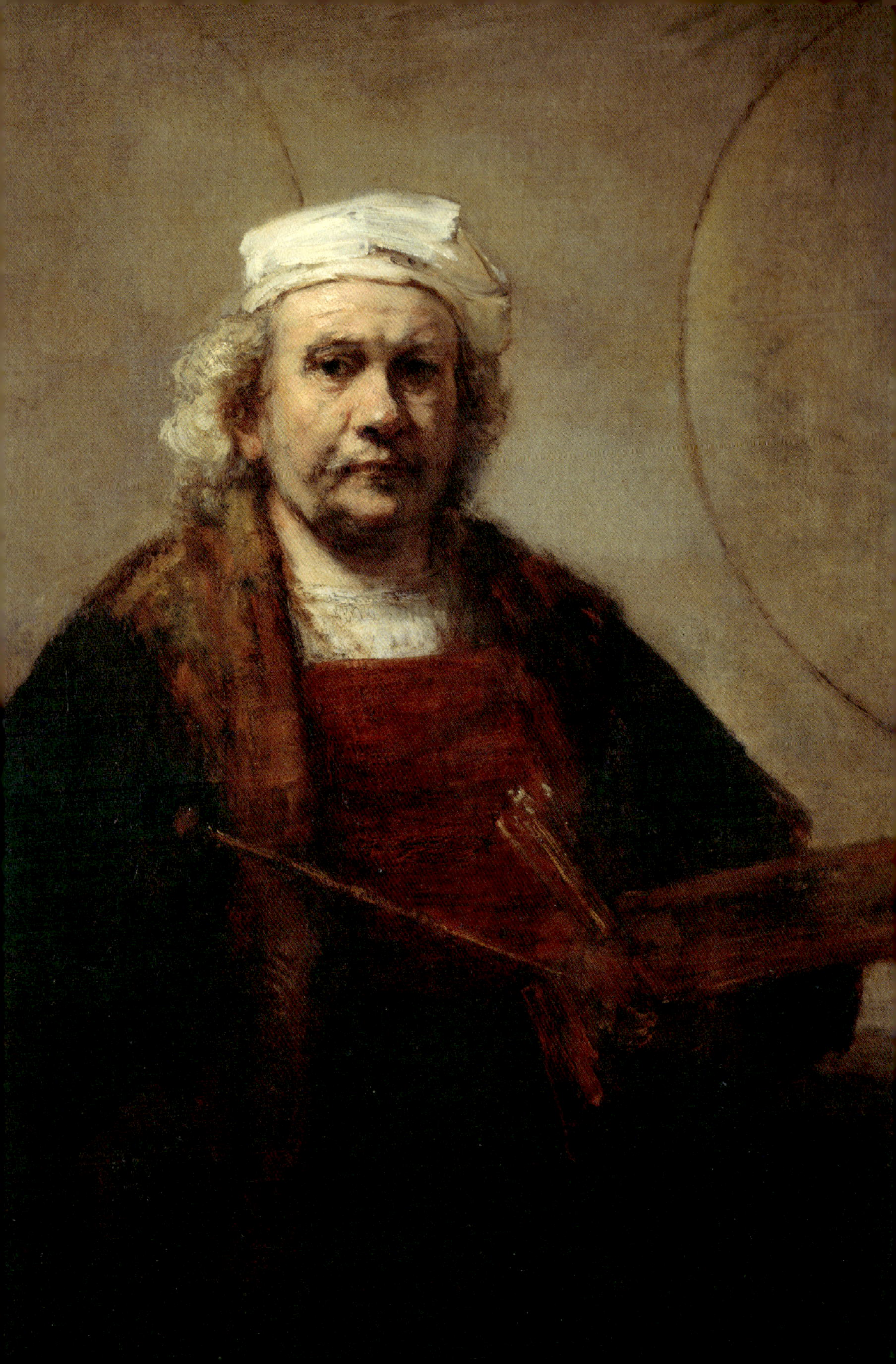

INDEX

Bold numerals in the Index refer to figure numbers.

GENERAL INDEX

Detail of *Self-portrait with Two Circles*. *c.*1665/9. (See Fig. 30)